Law, Pandemics and Ownership

Ius, Lex et Res Publica
Studies in Law, Philosophy and Political Cultures

Edited by Barbara Janusz-Pohl and Anna Jaroń

Volume 23

PETER LANG

Vladimír Sharp / Gabriela Blahoudková /
Jakub Handrlica (eds.)

Law, Pandemics and Ownership Restrictions

PETER LANG

Bibliographic Information published by the Deutsche Nationalbibliothek
The Deutsche Nationalbibliothek lists this publication
in the Deutsche Nationalbibliografie; detailed bibliographic
data is available online at http://dnb.d-nb.de.

Library of Congress Cataloging-in-Publication Data
A CIP catalog record for this book has been applied for at the
Library of Congress.

This publication was written under the umbrella of the project „Ownership
and its Limitation in the Mirror of Legal Dualism" (specific university research
scholarship SVV 260 496) researched at the Faculty of Law of Charles University
from 2020 to 2022.

Cover illustration: Courtesy of Benjamin Ben Chaim.

ISSN 2191-3250
ISBN 978-3-631-88202-3 (Print)
E-ISBN 978-3-631-89307-4 (E-Book)
E-ISBN 978-3-631-89407-1 (EPUB)
DOI 10.3726/b20422

© Peter Lang GmbH
International Academic Publishers
Berlin 2022
All rights reserved.

Peter Lang – Berlin· Lausanne · Bruxelles · New York ·
Oxford · Warszawa · Wien

All parts of this publication are protected by copyright.
Any utilisation outside the strict limits of the copyright law,
without the permission of the publisher, is forbidden and liable to prosecution.
This applies in particular to reproductions,
translations, microfilming, and storage and processing
in electronic retrieval systems.

www.peterlang.com

Table of Contents

About the Authors 7

Jakub Handrlica
Introductory Note on Law, Pandemics,
and Ownership Restrictions 11

*V. Dvorský, D. Macek, M. Novák, K. Stloukalová
and J. Ullmann*
Selected Aspects of Crises and Their Solutions in Roman Law and Politics ... 13

T. Blažková and J. Šouša
Selected Aspects of the Legal Regulations of Epidemics in the Czech
Lands
in the Period from the Nineteenth Century
to the Year 1948 71

J. Balounová and G. Prokopová
Administrative Measures in the Times
of Pandemics 119

V. Sharp
Ad Hoc Legislation: The Legal Dilemma behind the Customized
Approach Towards Crisis Management 141

G. Blahoudková
Compensation for Damage Caused by State Measures Adopted
to Combat a Pandemic 165

About the Authors

Jana Balounová holds a master's degree in law from the Faculty of Law of University of West Bohemia and a *juris doctor* degree from the Faculty of Law of Charles University. She also holds a Ph.D. in Administrative Law and defended her doctoral thesis entitled "Legal concepts of Administrative Law restricting the Right to property." Jana is a Senior Lecturer at the Faculty of Law of Charles University and at the Faculty of Law of University of West Bohemia.

Gabriela Blahoudková is a Junior Researcher at the Faculty of Law of Charles University. She is writing her doctoral thesis, titled "Liability of the State for Damages that Occured in Consequence of Extraordinary Pandemic Measures."

Tereza Blažková is a graduate of the Faculty of Law of Charles University and a Junior Researcher at the Faculty of Law of Charles University. He focuses on the legal history of Czechoslovakia after 1945. Tereza is currently completing her doctoral thesis entitled "An Ideal or a Mirror? The Principles and ideas of the Constitution of 9th May and of the Constitution of 1960 and their Reflection in Civil and Criminal Law".

Václav F. Dvorský is a Junior Researcher at the Faculty of Law of Charles University and at the Faculty of Law of KU Leuven. He is currently writing the doctoral thesis entitled "Depositum Irregulare and Similar Types of Deposite Contracts in Roman Law and in Later Historical Development." Václav completed his master's studies at Masaryk University in Brno while also spending two semesters at Georg-August University in Göttingen. His research interest are history and legal regulation of money and banking, Roman law of obligations and comparative law, especially in Central European context.

Jakub Handrlica is a Full Professor in Administrative Law at the Faculty of Law of Charles University, and also the head researcher of the project „Ownership and its Limitation in the Mirror of Legal Dualism". Jakub graduated from the Faculty of Law of Charles University (master's degree in law and *juris doctor*), where he later also received his Ph.D. in public law. Jakub also holds an LL.M. from Ruhr Universitat Bochum and a prestigious DSc. degree awarded by the Academy of Sciences of the Czech Republic as the highest national academic recognition. Jakub has authored and co-authored numerous books and other prominent publications indexed in WoS and Scopus databases.

Dominik Macek is a Junior Researcher at the Faculty of Law of Charles University. He is writing his doctoral thesis, entitled "Romanistic Roots of the Recent Heritage Law in Central Europe."

Marek Novák is an attorney-at-law based in Prague and a doctoral student at the Department of Legal History at the Faculty of Law of Charles University. In his legal practice, he mainly deals with civil, administrative, and religion law, and in his research and teaching activities he focuses on Roman law. His doctoral thesis concerns medieval reception of Roman law.

Gabriela Prokopová is a Lecturer at the Faculty of Law of Charles University. She is currently finishing her doctoral thesis entitled "Topical Issues of Legal Regulation of Audiovisual Media Services".

Vladimír Sharp graduated from the Faculty of Law of Charles University, where he later received a *juris doctor* degree and where he's currently pursuing a Ph.D. in the field of administrative law and administrative science. He's also finishing an LL.M. program at Nottingham Law School (England, UK). In his non-academic career, Vladimir currently serves as a senior executive at the Ministry of Justice of the Czech Republic. Before joining the civil service, Vladimir worked at several major international law firms, providing legal counsel mainly in the field of state regulations, commercial and labor law, financial and insolvency law, and law of new technologies. He has authored and co-authored a number of publications including several books. Vladimir lectures at several universities and at the Judicial Academy of the Czech Republic.

Kamila Stloukalová is a Researcher at the Faculty of Law of Charles University. She holds a Ph.D. in Roman Law and defended her doctoral thesis entitled "Statics and Dynamics of the Roman Family."

Jiří Šouša is graduate of the Faculty of Law of Charles University, where he subsequently passed a rigorous exam, completed his Ph.D. and after successful habilitation received the title of an Associate Professor. After graduation, in addition to the academic sphere, he also worked in legal practice (advocacy, Constitutional Court of the Czech Republic). He currently works at the Department of Legal History of the Faculty of Law of the University of Warsaw, and also teaches at the Faculty of Law of the University of Warsaw. From 2022, Jiří was appointed head of the Center for Legal Historical Studies of the Historical Institute of the Academy of Sciences of the Czech Republic and Charles University. Jiří participated in a number of grants and has authored a number of publications both nationally and abroad (Germany, Poland, Slovakia, Hungary, the Netherlands, etc.). His publication won the prize of The European Society for History of Law.

Jan Ullmann is a Researcher at the Faculty of Law of Charles University. He holds a Ph.D. in Roman Law and defended his doctoral thesis entitled "Development of Legal Framework of Religious Offenses and Offenses Against the State in Roman Law with Respect to the Procedural Law."

Jakub Handrlica

Introductory Note on Law, Pandemics, and Ownership Restrictions

At the end of the year 2019, a research project has been initiated by a group of scholars of the Faculty of Law of Charles University in order to conduct research addressing the issue of ownership limitations from various perspectives of private and public law. Not only academicians, devoting their research to aspects of recent law, but also legal historians and scholars dealing with Roman Law have been participating in this endeavor. The fact is, however, that the original scheme of the projects was gravelly amended by the events, which followed in the years 2020–2022, that means with the global pandemics of COVID-19. When writing this introduction in September of 2022, the academic community is still waiting for the definitive end of this pandemic, which will hopefully follow soon.

The project envisaged by our research group has faced a considerable challenge, represented by a pandemic, which appeared to be global, without respecting any boundaries of the States and at the same time, imprisoning the States into their own borders and consequently, into their own national legal frameworks. In this respect, our research group has faced a question, which we decided to decipher and answer: Are the extraordinary pandemic measures, which have established considerable restrictions in ownership rights in various jurisdictions, a newly appeared phenomenon? Or do they represent a classic reply of a State to pandemics of large scale and grave consequences?

Luckily enough, our research team has been composed of academicians from various background and being active in various fields of research. The team has been not only composed from scholars, researching public and private law (J. Handrlica, G. Blahoudková, G. Prokopová, J. Balounová and V. Sharp), but also from scholars of Roman Law (K. Stloukalová, V. Dvorský, D. Macek, M. Novák and J. Ullmann) and those, being active in the field of legal history (T. Blažková and J. Šouša). Consequently, each of the various members of the teams were able to tackle the main research question from a different perspective of their own expertise. Having said this, this publication now represents a final outcome of the project entitled "Restrictions of Ownership Rights in the Mirror of Legal Dualism."

The publication is divided into following chapters, each devoted to a specific aspect of ownership limitations from the perspective of pandemics.

In the first chapter, entitled "Selected Aspects of Crises and Their Solutions in Roman Law and Politics", a group of promising legal romanists is presenting an interesting study on historical parallels (not only) between the COVID-19 pandemics and the plague pandemics of the Roman period. Here, various sources of law are analyzed with the respect of ownership limitation, caused by extraordinary measures.

The second chapter, entitled "Selected Aspects of the Legal Regulations of Epidemics in the Czech Lands in the Period from the Nineteenth Century to the Year 1948" focuses on the topic from a purely national viewpoint of the Czech Lands, presenting historical parallels between COVID-19 measures and pandemic restrictions in the nineteenth and the first half of the twentieth century. Here, in particular the parallels between the pandemic of Spanish flu and the COVID-19 pandemics attracts attention and may be interesting for scholars beyond the field of law.

The third chapter, entitled "Administrative Measures in the Times of Pandemics" aims to address various forms of measures, that have appeared in order to cope with challenges arising from the COVID-19 pandemics. In several cases, such measures are of hybrid nature, which has been specially suited for particular aspect arising by appearance of the pandemic.

In the fourth chapter titled "Ad Hoc Legislation: The Legal Dilemma behind the Customized Approach Towards Crisis Management", the author exposes the highly relevant concept of so-called tailor-made laws and analyses their role in the process of crisis management. The chapter offers classification of these laws based on different factors and definitional criteria, identifies the risks of individualized legislation, and proposes solution for their mitigation.

While the previous chapters have addressed various types of measures, which may potentially limit ownership rights in the period of pandemics, the final chapter entitled "Compensation for damage caused by state measures adopted to combat a pandemic" addresses the other side of the same coin, that means compensations of damages occurred from such measures. Also here, various historical parallels with the historical developments can be identified.

I hope the readers of this book will find our interdisciplinary approach to the very current topic interesting and useful for their own research. The ambition of this book is not only to present analysis of the topic from various viewpoints, but also initiate a comparative discussion We will be also glad for any remarks, or critical comments, which can be send to the editors of this book.

Professor Jakub Handrlica
Faculty of Law, Charles University

V. Dvorský, D. Macek, M. Novák, K. Stloukalová
and J. Ullmann

Selected Aspects of Crises and Their Solutions in Roman Law and Politics

Today, we are going through the difficult period in which we must deal with various crises that, literally, following one after another, be it pandemics, wars, insufficiency of supplies and energies, inflation, and other monetary issues, and connected or unconnected political problems, as well. Each crisis influences all of us, explicitly or implicitly, nobody can avoid its impact. The solutions of crises are various, some of them "experimental", as we deal from our point of view with something, we never experienced before. However, this does not mean, that some similar situations were not present in the course of history and that the civilization did not face them before. Therefore, it is worth looking into the previous eras to inspire ourselves regarding the steps to overcome the crisis, or, as the case may be, to steer clear away from the solutions that were not successful or, at worse, harmful for the population, as the history can teach us.

The presented book shall be deeply dedicated to the topic of crisis and measures adopted to resolve it, with particular focus on ownership restrictions that are one of the typical accompanying phenomena of political and legal methods that are applied to handle with crisis. The pandemic of contagious disease is in the spotlight of the book, however, as the current course of global events shows us, our text shall not be restricted only to this particular problem, because there are many more questions, and say, crisis, arising concurrently.

It is a cliché, although still the truth, to state that Roman Empire successfully expanded its culture, the Roman law being probably one of the most important parts of it, and therefore influenced the cultural development not only of the continental Europe. Even today our civil codes draw the inspiration as well as concrete legal regulation from this ancient legal order.

However, this initial chapter will not repeat commonly known statements about Roman Empire, nor it will handle with individual institutions of Roman law. Rather it shall present a different look on the crises in broad manner, while its goals are manifold. In line with the focus of the entire book, the authors want to provide an analysis of how Romans were (or were not) able to deal with the crises of different nature – political and military crises, financial crises and last, but not least pandemic crises.

This chapter is divided into three subchapters. In the first one, the authors deal with selected moments of military and political crises during the times of the Roman Republic. The second subchapter relates to the previous text as of the period being mapped. It investigates the financial crises of Roman state during first century BC and first century AD, i.e., in the period of struggle between the declining republic and the emerging empire. Third part of this chapter is dedicated to the pandemics that from time to time attacked the Roman population. There are more waves during the whole time of existence of Roman state witnessed, however, we are most informed about the so-called Justinianic plague that emerged in the middle of the sixth century as regards the measures taken, if not to fight with it, as the contemporary state of medicine art was not sufficient to prevent the disease, to deal somehow with the consequences. It is worth saying, that the red line of the whole chapter is the focus on the ownership restrictions that were an inseparable companion of each solution of crisis then and even now.

The topics of described three subchapters reflect, as is not necessary to highlight, current issues of today – political crisis and war ongoing on European continent, problem of continuing inflation and still present COVID-19 pandemic that threatens to spread again. Naturally, the means to avoid, stop or slow down the crises varied now and then. As some of the solutions met in history can in no way be replicable in current era, they may at least serve as lessons learned or a to broaden horizons about the nation that gave Europe its legal foundations.

Military and Political Crises: Reactions of the Roman State

The objective of this part is to present some of the military and political crises that have struck the Roman state as well as means of resolution of such crises by the Roman public authorities, including evaluation of the success rate of the chosen solution and the impact on the lives of ordinary Roman citizens and their private rights. Due to the number of military and political crises during more than a thousand-year history of the Roman Empire, not all of them can be described in this part, therefore it will focus on the most important military and political crises that took place during the Roman Republic period and on the most important law institutes and changes in Roman law that had been adopted as a result of these crises.

The Establishment of the Roman Republic and *ius provocationis*

The first recorded political crisis of the Roman state relates to the very establishment of the Roman Republic. Last of the Roman kings, Lucius Tarquinius Superbus, is described quite negatively by historians, especially in the context of the abuse of his royal (absolutist) position and committing of illegal acts on Roman citizens.[1] It is, of course, likely that the Roman citizens who revolted against king Tarquinius Superbus and expelled him from Rome, as well as the historians from whose works we currently draw knowledge about the time (Titus Livius, Dionysius of Halicarnassus and others), described Tarquinius Superbus worse than would be the reality in order to justify the rebellion and the change of the state establishment, and also (especially in the case of historians who had described the events that happened several centuries ago) to highlight the advantages of the republican establishment over the kingdom. Nevertheless, we can deduce from the described events that the royal state was already obsolete due to the rapid development of the then Roman society. The absolutist state system no longer suited the citizens of Rome (represented especially by the social elites of Roman society, such as the rebel leaders Lucius Iunius Brutus and Publius Valerius). For this reason, there was a revolution and the expulsion of the last of the Roman kings, Tarquinius Superbus.[2]

However, the change of state establishment (with all related legal changes concerning the transfer from kingdom to republic) was not the only legal effect of this revolution. Very soon after this revolution, in 508 BC, consul Publius Valerius proposed the *lex Valeria de provocatione* which was the initial form of *ius provocationis*,[3] i.e., the right of provocation enjoyed by every Roman citizen which allowed them to appeal against a magistrate's decision imposing a capital or corporal punishment to the Centuriate Assembly. The *comitia centuriata* subsequently upheld or annulled the magistrate's decision. Therefore, this appeal cannot be understood in the sense of today's criminal law, as the magistrate's decision was not a court decision. From the point of view of today's law, *ius provocationis* is most similar to an appeal in administrative proceedings.

---

1 Livius I.58.
2 Livius I.59.
3 Smith, W. (1875). A Dictionary of Greek and Roman Antiquities, London, John Murray, p. 700.

As Cicero writes: "Legem ad populum tulit eam quae centuriatis comitiis prima lata est, ne quis magistratus civem Romanum adversus provocationem necaret neve verberaret."[4]

It can be reasonably assumed that such a strengthening of the legal position of Roman citizens was connected with one of the main reasons for the rebellion against the king, namely the violation of citizens' rights. Thanks to the emergence of *ius provocationis*, every Roman citizen became protected against the possible will of officials who wanted to abuse their position and deprive him of his life. This conclusion is also confirmed by the fact that the *ius provocationis* was gradually extended to the decisions of the magistrates, which imposed heavy fines (exceeding 3020 heavy assēs).

The Establishment of Tribunes of the Plebs

Another typical example of the political crisis was the so called first secession of the plebs (*secessio plebis*) in 494 BC, i.e., the legendary departure of the plebeians from Rome. It was a form of a political pressure on the ruling patrician class which aimed to strengthen the political status of the plebeians.

This political pressure proved to be successful, so the result of this political crisis in the Republic of Rome was the creation of a new magistracy, the tribunes of the people:

> Agi deinde de concordia coeptum, concessumque in condiciones ut plebi sui magistratus essent sacrosancti quibus auxilii latio adversus consules esset, neve cui patrum capere eum magistratum liceret. Ita tribuni plebei creati duo, C. Licinius et L. Albinus. Ii tres collegas sibi creaverunt. In his Sicinium fuisse, seditionis auctorem: de duobus, qui fuerint minus convenit. Sunt qui duos tantum in Sacro monte creatos tribunos esse dicant, ibique sacratam legem latam.[5]

---

4 "The first law passed by the Centuriate Assembly was that no magistrate can execute or physically punish a Roman citizen if he appeals [if he uses *ius provocationis* – author's note]." Cicero, De res publica II.3.53; author's translation.

5 "And then began the negotiations for peace between the people and the *patres*. They agreed on the terms that the people would have their own untouchable officials who would have the right to contribute to their help against the consuls, and that none of the patricians would be able to achieve this office. Two tribunes of the people were elected, Gaius Licinius and Lucius Albinus. They chose three more colleagues, including Sicinius, the originator of the eviction proposal. There is no agreement on who the other two were. Some writers say that only two tribunes were elected at Mons Sacra, and that an inviolability law was also promulgated there." Livius II.33; author's translation.

The tribunes of the people had *ius intercessionis*, i.e., the right to veto any decision of another magistrate. The law provided for their intangibility and the right to kill on the spot anyone who would prevent them from performing their duties or endanger them. Should anyone oppose to or interrupt the tribune while speaking to the people, or if someone did not pay the fine imposed on them by the tribune of the people for their transgression, their lives and property were forfeited.[6]

The legal impact of this political crisis was therefore the creation of a very important official function, which could only be held by members of a certain population group (plebeian) and which had very extensive powers and could even veto decisions of other magistrates.

Appointment of a Dictator

Roman law in the days of the Roman Republic knew a special office designed specifically to deal with military and political crises, namely the office of dictator. The first appointed dictator ever was Titus Larcius in 501 BC (or in 498 BC, it is not possible to determine which of these dates is correct[7]), and Spurius Cassius was appointed his cavalry commander. Livius states that this happened because of the war with the Latins and due to fears of a conspiracy of 30 tribes against Rome. Livius further states that both Titus Larcius and Spurius Cassius were former consuls, and only former consuls could be appointed to these offices, as provided by the law on the election of a dictator (*lex de dictatore creando*). Livius states greater obedience of the citizens of Rome as the main benefit of this appointment: "neque enim ut in consulibus qui pari potestate essent, alterius auxilium neque provocatio erat neque ullum usquam nisi in cura parendi auxilium."[8]

In view of the above, the appointment of a dictator can be considered one of the first (if not the first ever) examples of crisis legislation. On the contrary to today's approach to the modern dictatorships, Romans viewed appointment of a dictator as an element of rescue. From the very beginnings of the Roman Republic, more than 2,500 years ago, the Romans concluded that in certain situations it was necessary to temporarily suppress some fundamental rights

---

6   Dionysius VII.17.
7   Broughton, T. R. S. (1951). The Magistrates of the Roman Republic, vol. I. New York, The American Philological Association, p. 35.
8   "…under the dictator there was no call for help from anyone else or an appeal to the nation as under consuls, who both had the same authority. There was simply no means of protection but obedience." Livius II.18; author's translation.

of individuals so that the society as a whole would survive. Among the rights that could be suppressed Livius mentions the inability to exercise the right of "appeal to the nation", which means the impossibility of using *ius provocationis* against the dictator's decision. Thus, the dictator (during his dictatorship) could decide to impose a capital punishment and there was no possibility of appeal for a Roman citizen. Moreover, unlike other Roman authorities, the principle of collegiality did not apply to the office of dictator, only one dictator was appointed at a time, and the person appointed to this office ruled without any restrictions. The only limitation was the duration of the dictatorship, namely 6 months.

Due to the fact that the greatest threat to the continued existence of the Roman state was the possible defeat of Roman troops and the occupation of Rome, it was for this reason that dictators were most often appointed – only in 501–100 BC was the dictator *rei gerundae causa* (for resolution of a specific matter, by which Romans meant to solve a specific war issue) appointed in forty-nine cases.[9] It is likely that in fact there were even more dictators appointed for military purposes (in many cases we do not know the reason for the appointment of a dictator or there are several possible reasons).

There are even cases where a particular Roman proved himself so good as a dictator that he had been appointed dictator several times within a few years. An example is Marcus Furius Camillus, who was first appointed dictator in 396 BC to wage war against Falerii, Capena, and especially to conquer the city of Veii, with which the Romans had waged war for 10 years.[10] Although Marcus Furius Camillus successfully conquered Veii and defeated the troops of Falerii and Capena, he was soon accused of embezzling part of the loot from the conquest of Veii, went into exile and was sentenced to a fine of 15,000 heavy assēs.[11] However, the exile, which was under standard conditions for life and prevented the person concerned from ever returning to the city of Rome, did not last long in the case of Marcus Furius Camillus. After the Roman army was defeated by the Gauls at the Battle of the Allia who subsequently conquered not only the Capitol but the entire city of Rome, Camillus was summoned back from exile as soon as in 390 BC. The reason behind this was that even as an exile he achieved

---

9   Broughton, T. R. S. (1951). The Magistrates of the Roman Republic, vol. I. New York, The American Philological Association.
10 Ibid., p. 88.
11 Livius V.32.

the only military success against the Gauls when he organized a militia in the city of Ardea and killed their incoming troops.[12]

The Senate therefore appointed him dictator of the *rei gerundae causa* to help Rome defeat the invading Gallic troops.[13] Camillus fulfilled this task during his second dictatorship. The third dictatorship of Marcus Furius Camillus followed as early as 389 BC, when the Romans faced a threat from the Volsci, Etruscans, Latins and Hernici. After his appointment as dictator, Camillus suspended all courts, mobilized the army, and subsequently led a successful military campaign against the Volsci and Aequi.[14]

In addition to appointing dictators for military reasons, the Romans appointed dictators for other reasons, albeit much less often. These other reasons were, in particular, the *clavi figendi causa*, i.e. for religious reasons (to carry out a religious ceremony), the *comitiorum habendorum causa*, i.e., to hold elections, the *seditionis sedandae causa*, i.e., to resolve internal unrest, *feriarum constituendarum causa*, i.e., for the purpose of determining holidays due to religious signs, or *ludorum faciendorum causa*, i.e., for the purpose of organizing games.[15] From today's point of view, a dictatorship for the purpose of conducting elections or resolving internal unrest may seem to us to be a completely logical situation for the use of the dictator's crisis function, while other purposes we would probably not describe as a crisis today. Here, however, it is necessary to realize the importance that the Romans attached to the observance of religious customs, when achieving and maintaining *pax deorum*, i.e., peace with their deities, which the Romans considered absolutely essential for the continued existence of Rome and its well-being. From this point of view, the other reasons given, which are directly of religious nature or closely related to the religious customs of the Romans, also make sense in terms of using the dictator's crisis function.

In the first century BC, a new type of dictatorship emerged, namely a dictatorship lasting more than 6 months and adopted for a completely new purpose, *legibus faciendis et rei publicae constituendae causa*, i.e., for the purpose of drafting laws and organizing public affairs. In 82 BC, Lucius Cornelius Sulla was appointed dictator on the basis of the *lex Valeria de Sulla dictatore* for the purposes

---

12 To Gauls in Rome see, e.g., Polybios 2.18, to Marcus Furius Camillus see, e.g., Plutarchos, Camillus.
13 Livius V.45–46.
14 Livius VI.2.
15 Broughton, T. R. S. (1951). The Magistrates of the Roman Republic, vol. I. New York, The American Philological Association.

of drafting laws and the organization of public affairs, and the duration of this dictatorship was not determined.[16] This was also a crisis measure, as the Roman Republic had experienced a civil war in previous years (between the factions led by Gaius Marius and Lucius Cornelius Sulla) and the criminal and administrative system of the Roman Republic already needed a comprehensive reform to ensure its continued functioning, for which, in the standard way, elected consuls did not have (given the length of their term) enough time or sufficient political and factual power. Lucius Cornelius Sulla voluntarily resigned from the position of dictator in 79 BC after the necessary reforms (in the form of the so-called *leges Corneliae*, which, e.g., in the field of criminal law represented its complex regulation) and gave his dictatorship to review (whether he abused his powers).[17] A few decades later, in 44 BC, the last new type of dictatorship emerged, namely a dictatorship without a more precise purpose and for an indefinite period, when Gaius Iulius Caesar was appointed *dictator perpetuo*, a lifelong dictator (for completeness: Caesar had been appointed dictator of the *rei gerundae causa* several times in previous years).[18] In this case, however, it was no longer a crisis function and its proper use in accordance with the original intention, but rather the result of the previous civil war between Gaius Iulius Caesar and Gnaeus Pompeius Magnus, when Caesar, as the winner of this civil war *de facto* (and after his appointment as dictator *de iure*) concentrated almost absolute power within the Roman Republic in his hands.

Senatus Consultum Ultimum

Another example of Roman crisis legislation were the *senatus consulta ultima*. After the function of dictator ceased to be used after 202 BC (until Sulla's dictatorship in 82 BC) (as there was too much concern among the Romans about the possible abuse of such extensive powers of the dictator), another way to react to possible crises had to be developed. In 121 BC, the first *senatus consultum ultimum*, also called *senatus consultum de re publica defendenda*, appeared, i.e., a resolution of the senate adopted for the purpose of defending the republic. The aim of the *senatus consultum ultimum* was to eliminate the threat to the

---

16 Ibid., p. 66.
17 Ibid., p. 82.
18 Ibid., p. 317.

republican establishment,[19] and in clearly documented cases such a threat was posed by the persons against whom the *senatus consultum ultimum* was issued. This meant that the *senatus consultum ultimum* enabled the physical liquidation of those who had been declared enemies of the republic. The first documented *senatus consultum ultimum* was used in 121 BC against Gaius Sempronius Gracchus and Marcus Fulvius Flaccus, then in 63 BC during Catiline conspiracy, and finally in 49 BC against Gaius Julius Caesar.[20]

Although we can consider *senatus consultum ultimum* to be similar to the crisis law adopted to solve a specific situation, in this case it is a tool that is too easily misused for the purposes of power struggle – the liquidation of Gaius Sempronius Gracchus, i.e., the first demonstrable case of *senatus consultum ultimum*, could be considered as an example of such abuse. Thus, although it was a form of compensation for the function of a dictator, paradoxically the *senatus consultum ultimum* was a much less complex solution than dictatorship (since the dictator had unlimited powers and could therefore respond to the ongoing crisis in a number of different ways and possibly alter the measures applied). Above that it was more easily misused because, unlike a dictator, whose decisions could be reviewed after the end of the dictatorship, there was no such subsequent inspection in the case of *senatus consultum ultimum*. It is therefore not very surprising that the *senatus consultum ultimum* had only been used for several decades, and moreover not very frequently.

Proscription

The last of the Roman law measures to deal with political and military crises, which will be described, are the proscriptions. As in the case of *senatus consultum ultimum*, it is not a means of resolving military crises, but political (and to some extent economic) crises. The proscriptions were first used during the dictatorship of Lucius Cornelius Sulla in 82 BC, based on the *lex Cornelia de proscriptione et proscriptis* (this law is sometimes called the *lex Valeria de proscriptione et proscriptis*, as it is uncertain whether the *rogator* was Lucius Cornelius Sulla himself, or interrex Lucius Valerius Flaccus). However, no matter who was the *rogator* of the first proscription law, it is certain what was its content – it was

---

19 Shump, S. (2011). The Senatus Consultum Ultimum and its Relation to Late Republican History. Summer Research. Paper 99. p. 2. Available at: http://soundideas.pugetsound.edu/summer_research/99.
20 Ibid., p. 1.

a list of political opponents of Lucius Cornelius Sulla, who were declared outlaws under the proscription law, could be killed with impunity by anyone (there were even rewards paid to their killers) and all of their property was confiscated by the state and subsequently sold (especially to Sulla's followers).[21] Of course, it would be possible to see Sulla's proscription law only as a revenge on political opponents, but if we take into account the then situation of the Roman Republic, which was shaken by the just ended civil war and considerably financially exhausted in connection with it, we can also see crisis legislation elements in the proscription law, as through the liquidation of the political opposition Sulla at least temporarily stabilized the political situation in Rome (thus temporarily reducing the risk of renewed civil war) and at the same time improved the situation of the state treasury by confiscating the property of the enlisted Romans. Essentially the same situation occurred with the enactment of the second proscription act, which was passed by the Second Triumvirate (Marcus Antonius, Gaius Octavianus Caesar, and Aemilius Lepidus) in 43 BC, when the Triumvirs by means of proscription liquidated some of the adherents of the so-called *liberatores* (the second proscriptions should have been even more extensive than Sulla's proscriptions; based on proscription lists, up to 2,000 *equites* and 300 *senatorii* were to be assassinated and their property confiscated[22]), namely Marcus Junius Brutus and Gaius Cassius Longinus, while obtaining funds subsequently used for a military campaign against the liberators, which ended in 42 BC by the Battle of Philippi.

Evaluation of Roman Law Measures to Resolve Political and Military Crises

From the above-mentioned situations and measures, from the point of view of the author of this text, the appointment of a dictator seems to be a measure that is the most successful and at the same time the most similar to today's crisis laws. In Roman law and Roman society, this was a tried and tested concept which, in many cases, produced the desired results (as in the case of the dictatorships of Marcus Furius Camillus above) and actually saved the Roman Republic from demise. The similarity with today's crisis laws can be seen especially in the area of temporary centralization of executive power in the hands of one particular

---

21 Smith, W. (1875). A Dictionary of Greek and Roman Antiquities. London, John Murray, p. 963.
22 Ibid., p. 964.

person (in today's law rather in the hands of a collective body, especially the government), which may restrict some basic human rights (in Roman law *ius provocationis* against the decisions of the dictator, in today's law, which distinguishes far more fundamental human rights, we can talk, for example, about restrictions on freedom of movement, property rights, the right of assembly, etc.). Today's Czech legal system is certainly better in terms of supervising the crisis body, as unlike the Roman legal system, it allows the Chamber of Deputies to decide to lift the state of emergency on which the government bases its crisis powers, while in Roman law it was possible to review only retroactively, after the end of the dictatorship.

Paradoxically, the appointment of a dictator to deal with various crisis situations ceased to be used in the Roman Republic due to fears of excessive centralization of power in the hands of one citizen and possible abuse of such power, but the only alternatives which Roman law would come up with over the next 120 years, were *senatus consultum ultimum* and proscription laws that proved to be much more exploitable than the office of dictator. Moreover, by restricting the use of the dictator function, the republican establishment was not saved, but through several domestic political conflicts, civil wars, and the centralization of political power in the hands of several individuals (such as Gaius Marius Gracchus, Lucius Cornelius Sulla, Gnaeus Pompeius Magnus, or Gaius Iulius Caesar), the republic gradually transformed into a Principate.

Financial Crises and the Roman State's Reaction

In the second part of this chapter, the objective is to present financial crises that hit the Roman state and the way the authorities dealt with them while accessing to which degree these actions were successful and how they limited the property rights of private persons. However, before we commence the discussion on the merits, again, some confinements of the scope of this part are necessary. As already mentioned in previous section, due to the long span of the Roman history and the complexity of question, we shall limit the timespan and scope of our research. We shall concentrate on banking and are, therefore, only going to deal with the crises which to a higher involved the banking industry. At the same time, we are going to concentrate mostly on the turbulent end of the republic, which we already analyzed from the political crisis point of view. During this period the most crises to which we have the primary sources occurred. Due to its time and factual proximity with the previous crises as well as due to its impact the crisis of 33 AD shall also be subject of our deliberations.

Roman Money

The existence of money is a necessary prerequisite for the development of a banking industry. Let us therefore shortly review the development of Roman money.

First and foremost, we need to answer what might seem to be a rather trivial question: What is money? There is nearly a universal agreement among economists that money is a medium of exchange, a unit of account, and a store of value.[23] However, for our purposes it is important what could have been considered money in Roman setting. For that answer we must delve deep into Roman history.

As the classic in the field informs us, the money came into being as a medium of exchange.[24] These were the goods, that could serve not only their primary purpose, but could be also exchanged for other objects. They were easily divisible and durable. These properties are characteristic for precious metals, such as gold, silver and copper or their alloys such as bronze, which were used as commodity money throughout history. Romans were no exception to this and there is ample evidence that the use of money was widespread already in the fifth century BC. Let us shortly mention three proofs of this.[25]

Pliny the Elder expressly informs us that, according to Timaeus,[26] Romans first used nuggets of bronze as money which they called *aes rude* (rough bronze).[27] However, these nuggets were not standardized and their weight differed,[28] which

---

23 See, e.g., Mankiw, N. G. (2018). *Principles of Economics*. Boston, Cengage Learning, p. 609; Omlor, S. (2014). *Geldprivatrecht*. Tübingen, Mohr Siebeck, pp. 59–69, and the sources mentioned therein.
24 Menger, C. (2009). *On the Origins of Money*. Auburn, Ludwig von Mises institute (*On the Origins of Money* first appeared in the Economic Journal 2 (1892), pp. 239–55; translation is by C. A. Foley.), pp. 33–38.
25 Cf. work in Czech that shortly tackled the same problem. Dvorský, V. (2020). *Ochrana vkladatelů v právu římském*. In Tauchen, J. (ed.). VIII. česko-slovenské právněhistorické setkání doktorandů a postdoktorandů: sborník z conference. Brno: MUNI press, pp. 97–107, here pp. 98–101.
26 This Timaeus is not closely identified, but is most probably Timaeus of Tauromenium, one of the first Greek historians who dealt with Romans in their writing. For more information about him see Baron, C. (2012). *Timaeus of Tauromenium and Hellenistic Historiography*. Cambridge, Cambridge University Press, pp. 43–57.
27 Plinius Maior, *Naturalis Historia*, XXXIII.XIII.43.
28 Comparette, T. L. (1918). *Aes Signatum*, American Journal of Numismatics (1897–1924), 52, pp. 1–61, here: p. 10 and seqq.); Sear, D. R. (1988). Roman Coins and Their Values. London, Spink Books, pp. 53–54.

must have complicated their use as a medium of exchange. Therefore, again according to Pliny,[29] Roman king Servius Tullius introduced so called *aes signatum* (stamped bronze), which were bronze ingots of (somewhat) standardized weight[30] and quality embossed with a government stamp in form of a simple symbol such as sword, shield, wheat ear or a tripod.[31] Pliny mentions that the *ignots* introduced by Servius Tullius wore the image of cattle thus explaining the Roman word for money *pecunia*.[32] This legendary king supposedly reigned in the sixth century BC, but modern scholars put their appearance of *aes signatum* rather in the half of the fifth century BC with some insisting they only appeared in the third century BC.[33] Finally, at about 289 BC Romans started to cast bronze coins called *aes grave* and silver minted coinage was introduced during the time of the Pyrrhic war[34] with silver denarius appearing in ca. 211 BC.[35] It should be, however, noted that before minting their own coins, Romans made use of those provided by their Greek neighbors from *Magna Graecia* and the Hellenistic Mediterranean.[36]

The legal sources also shed a lot of light on the monetary conditions even before the introduction of coinage. One of the possibilities to transform property was

---

29 Plinius Maior, *Naturalis Historia*, XXXIII.XIII.43.
30 The level of standardization was not probably that high as there are ingots of different weights carrying the same symbols, see Comparette, T. L. (1918). *Aes Signatum*, American Journal of Numismatics (1897–1924), 52, pp. 1–61, here: p. 14. However, in our opinion too few examples of *aes sigantum* are available to draw far-reaching conclusions.
31 Evans, J. D. (1992). *The Art of Persuasion: Political Propaganda from Aeneas to Brutus*. Ann Arbor, University of Michigan Press, pp. 22–23.
32 Plinius Maior, *Naturalis Historia*, XXXIII.XIII.43; Varro I.5.92 and Festus 232 Peculatus.
33 See Crawford, M. H. (1985). *Coinage and Money Under the Roman Republic: Italy and the Mediterranean Economy*. Berkeley, Los Angeles, Univ. od California Press, p. 41; cf. Sear, D. R. (1988). Roman Coins and Their Values. London, Spink Books, pp. 53–54.
34 See Crawford, M. H. (1985). *Coinage and Money Under the Roman Republic: Italy and the Mediterranean Economy*. Berkeley, Los Angeles, Univ. od California Press, pp. 39–41.
35 See Crawford, M. H. (1985). *Coinage and Money Under the Roman Republic: Italy and the Mediterranean Economy*. Berkeley, Los Angeles, Univ. od California Press p. 35; Evans, J. D. (1992). *The Art of Persuasion: Political Propaganda from Aeneas to Brutus*. Ann Arbor, University of Michigan Press, p. 17. Kay, P. (2014). *Rome's economic revolution*. Oxford, Oxford University Press, p. 89, mentions 212 BC.
36 Reden, S. (2010). *Money in Classical Antiquity*. Cambridge: Cambridge University Press, p. 283.

mancipatio, a formal act during which parties to it used weights and a piece of metal to transfer the ownership.[37] This procedure originated well before the inception of the Law of the Twelve tables.[38] As only commodity money in form of nuggets of bronze existed, it was necessary to determine their quantity which was done by weighting. Later, as standardized money came to be used, weighting was no longer necessary and the act became only symbolical.[39]

Finally, it should be mentioned that not only Roman formulary procedure, but even its older counterpart the *legis actio* procedure which predates the Twelve Tables[40] were based on the principle of pecuniary condemnation, which means that if the defendant was sentenced, he was obliged to payment of a sum of money.[41] Such a rule automatically presupposes existence of money, albeit only commodity money.

Roman Money Supply

There has been much debate as to the state of development of Roman economy which led to the emergence of two basic views called the primitivism and the modernism.[42] Despite their schematism[43] and the fact that most researchers do not hold the very extreme positions, but rather some on the spectrum between them, they are quite useful for the sake of introduction. The members of the first group postulate that Roman economy did not reach much sophistication and its intrinsic limitations bared it from ever producing any kind of industrial revolution similar to that of the eighteenth and nineteenth century.[44] It means even the financial services and monetary system were necessarily primitive. As Finely asserts, the money supply consisted of coins and Romans financial operation did not extend further that to the provision

---

37 For the details see Gaius I.122; there were also two other similar acts called the *nexum* und *nexi liberatio*. About all see Kaser, M. (1971). *Das römische Privatrecht*. München, C. H. Beck, pp. 41–43.
38 Kaser, M. (1971). *Das römische Privatrecht*. München, C. H. Beck, pp. 45–48.
39 According to some researchers, it was the case already at the time of the Twelve Tables, see Kaser, M. (1971). *Das römische Privatrecht*. München, C. H. Beck, p. 46.
40 Kaser, M., Hackl, K. (1996). *Das römische Zivilprozessrecht*. München, C. H. Beck, p. 35.
41 Gaius IV.48.
42 Andreau, J. (1999). *Banking and business in the Roman world*. Cambridge, Cambridge University Press, p. 6; Collins, A., Walsh, J. (2015). *Debt Deflationary Crisis in the Late Roman Republic*. Ancient Society, 45, pp. 125–170, here: p. 139.
43 As mentioned by Andreau, J. (1999). *Banking and business in the Roman world*. Cambridge, Cambridge University Press, p. 6.
44 Andreau, J. (1999). *Banking and business in the Roman world*. Cambridge, Cambridge University Press, pp. 6–7.

of loans in cash.[45] Modernists, on the other hand, are of the opinion that Roman economy incorporated more sophisticated tools which enabled the credit money creation. As Harris put it, it was rather similar to Western European economy of sixteenth century.[46] This view has been recently embraced by the numerous authors.[47]

What was then used as a means of payment in the Republican and Imperial Rome? Surely, it was mainly the silver coins, but they were far from being exclusive means of payment. As Harris points out, using silver coins for larger transactions would be impractical as it would sometime involve moving literary tons of them.[48] This is so impractical to the point it is impossible. The obvious solution would be gold coins, but they were introduced only at the end of the republic, as we shall see later.[49] Then, transactions in bullion come into consideration.[50] However, there is limited evidence of them. They saw some use in border regions of the Empire,[51] but as Andreau has demonstrated, there were no bullions to be found in Vesuvian cities.[52]

---

45 Finley, M. I. (1985). *The Ancient Economy*. London: Hogarth Press, pp. 196–197.
46 Harris, W. V. (2006). *A Revisionist View of Roman Money*. The Journal of Roman Studies, 96, pp. 1–24. here: p. 8, and Harris, W. V. (2019). *Credit-Money in the Roman Economy*. Klio, 101 (1), pp. 158–189, here: p. 177.
47 See, e.g., Harris, W. V. (2006). *A Revisionist View of Roman Money*. The Journal of Roman Studies, 96, pp. 1–24 and Harris, W. V. (2019). *Credit-Money in the Roman Economy*. Klio, 101 (1), pp. 158–189, Collins, A., Walsh, J. (2014). *Fractional Reserve Banking in the Roman Republic and Empire*. Ancient Society, 44, pp. 179–212, Collins, A., Walsh, J. (2015). *Debt Deflationary Crisis in the Late Roman Republic*. Ancient Society, 45, pp. 125–170, Kay, P. (2014). *Rome's economic revolution*. Oxford, Oxford University Press.
48 Harris, W. V. (2006). *A Revisionist View of Roman Money*. The Journal of Roman Studies, 96, pp. 1–24, here: p. 3, and Harris, W. V. (2019). *Credit-Money in the Roman Economy*. Klio, 101 (1), pp. 158–189, here: p. 164.
49 Hollander, D. B. (2007). *Money in the Late Roman Republic*. Leiden, The Netherlands, Brill, p. 21.
50 This idea is defended by Verboven, K. (2009). *Currency, Bullion and Accounts Monetary Modes in the Roman World*. Belgisch Tijdschrift voor Numismatiek en Zegelkunde/ Revue Belge de Numismatique et de Sigillograph, 155, pp. 91–121, here: p. 110. See also Hollander, D. B. (2007). *Money in the Late Roman Republic*. Leiden, The Netherlands, Brill, pp. 31–33.
51 See Harris, W. V. (2019). *Credit-Money in the Roman Economy*. Klio, 101 (1), pp. 158–189, here: pp. 173–174.
52 Andreau, J. (2008). *The Use and Survival of Coins and of Gold and Silver in the Vesuvian Cities*. In Harris, W. V. (ed). *The monetary systems of the Greeks and Romans*, Oxford, Oxford University Press, pp. 208–225, here: pp. 222–225.

Finally, cashless transfers are an option. However, now we are not speaking primarily about the transfers made by the means of account balance to which we shall return later, but about transfers of debts. Taking or advancing credit seemed to be a normal part of the financial activities undertaken by the Roman elites for centuries as many examples testify. One might obviously object that there is a substantial difference between a loan (credit) and a payment, but against that it can be argued that a transferable loan can be used as a means of payment. In other words, not every loan could be considered money – medium of exchange, but a loan that circulates, which means it is being transferred, can.[53] The transfer of debt – mostly in the form of *delegatio* – seems to have been a common practice as Gaius informs as in his commentaries[54] and as multiple fragments of Digest attest.[55]

The above-described practice of credit transfer can be demonstrated on some examples. Already in the half of the second century BC *delegatio* is mentioned by Cato the Elder.[56] It should be also noted that the way he puts it does not seem to indicate it was something new, but rather a normal operation.[57] The works of Cicero contain numerous allusions to cashless transactions. One of them is a rather famous case of an equestrian Gaius Canius who bought a property on credit from the Sicilian banker Pythius. The account of Cicero contains a phrase *Nomina facit, negotium conficit*, which can be translated as *he wrote down the debt* [into the account books] *and completed the transaction*.[58] However, in this story, there are no mentions of further transfer of the debt. Some other works of Cicero,[59] on the other hand, testify to such procedures, namely *permutatio* which

---

53 For more details see Harris, W. V. (2019). *Credit-Money in the Roman Economy*. Klio, 101 (1), pp. 158–189, here: pp. 161–163.
54 Gaius III.130.
55 D. 46.2 *De novationibus et delegationibus*.
56 *De agri cultura* CXLVI: *Donicum pecuniam solverit aut satisfecerit aut delegarit, pecus et familia, quae illic erit, pigneri sunto*. Harris, W. V. (2019). *Credit-Money in the Roman Economy*. Klio, 101 (1), pp. 158–189, here: p. 167, mentions only this chapter of the *De agri cultura*, but it seems that the same procedure is alluded to in chapter CXLIV.
57 Harris, W. V. (2019). *Credit-Money in the Roman EconomyCredit-Money in the Roman EconomyCredit-Money in the Roman Economy*. Klio, 101 (1), pp. 158–189, here: pp. 167.
58 Cicero *De officiis* III.59.
59 Att. 16.2.1: *Sed cum uideas quantum de iure nostro decesserimus qui de res. CCCC milia HS CC milia praesentia soluerimus, reliqua rescribamus, loqui cum eo, si tibi uidebitur, poteris eum commodum nostrum exspectare debere, cum tanta sit a nobis iactura facta iuris.*

is a cashless payment the exact nature of which is unfortunately unclear.[60] Finally, there are some documents of provincial provenience which seem to signify that delegation was not uncommon even among the ranks of those who could hardly be described as the upper class.[61]

The practice of credit transfer is so important, because it enables the creation of new money through other means than by minting them coins or extracting precious metals. When a loan is granted, it does not yet constitute new money. However, in a moment it is transferred and used as a means of payment, it becomes money (or near-money) and leads to the increase of the money supply.[62] This is the way endogenous money is created. The process is typical for bank, but it can be really undertaken by any subject.

Banking

We shall now try to determine the importance and impact of banking on the Roman economy. First bankers known to us appeared in Rome between 318 and 310 BC.[63] It is questionable if they were Greeks or Romans. We know for sure that the deposit bankers existed in Greece already in the second half of the fifth century BC at the latest.[64] However, the first Roman banker whose name is historically preserved and who lived in the second century BC was called Lucius

---

60 Harris, W. V. (2006). *A Revisionist View of Roman Money*. The Journal of Roman Studies, 96, pp. 1–24, here: pp. 15–16, and Harris, W. V. (2019). *Credit-Money in the Roman EconomyCredit-Money in the Roman EconomyCredit-Money in the Roman Economy*. Klio, 101 (1), pp. 158–189, here: p. 164, and Hollander, D. B. (2007). *Money in the Late Roman Republic*. Leiden, The Netherlands, Brill, pp. 40–44.

61 P. Fouad I.45 = FIRA III no. 121 = Ch.L.A. XLII.1207; CIL III, pp. 934–5 (no. V) = FIRA no. 122 = IDR I.35. See also Harris, W. V. (2006). *A Revisionist View of Roman Money*. The Journal of Roman Studies, 96, pp. 1–24, here: p. 15, and Harris, W. V. (2019). *Credit-Money in the Roman EconomyCredit-Money in the Roman Economy*. Klio, 101 (1), pp. 158–189, here: p. 171.

62 For more on this see Collins, A., Walsh, J. (2014). *Fractional Reserve Banking in the Roman Republic and Empire*. Ancient Society, 44, pp. 179–212, here: p. 182, and Collins, A., Walsh, J. (2015). *Debt Deflationary Crisis in the Late Roman Republic*. Ancient Society, 45, pp. 125–170, here: pp. 141–145); Harris, W. V. (2006). *A Revisionist View of Roman Money*. The Journal of Roman Studies, 96, pp. 1–24, here: p. 7.

63 Andreau, J. (1999). *Banking and business in the Roman world*. Cambridge, Cambridge University Press, p. 30. See also Livius IX.40.16.

64 Andreau, J. (1999). *Banking and business in the Roman world*. Cambridge, Cambridge University Press, p. 30, and Isocrates, XVII. Trapeziticus.

Fulvius which is hardly Greek.[65] In any case, as Romans were in intensive contact with the Greeks, their influence on banking practice is probable, but their impact on legal regulation is somewhat less certain.[66]

Significant source of our knowledge about republican banking are the plays of Plautus and to a lesser degree Terence.[67] Plautus mentions bankers 34 times in plays![68] This seems to suggest that already in the second century BC, bankers must have played an important role in the financial life of Rome. To be sure, one might object that the plays of Plautus take place in Greece, so they do not reflect the realia of then-contemporary Rome. However, while these plays were set in Greece, which made them more exotic and therefore more attractive for the audience, and also shielded the author from possible consequences of his mockery of Romans, they rather represent the situation in Rome.[69] Otherwise, they would have not been understandable for the audience the vast majority of which had never been to Greece. Furthermore, numerous Roman realia serve as a proof of this statement. Kay, for example, mentions that "the character Epidicus, in the play that bears his name, parodies Roman augury (l. 182) and refers to such things as the senate (l. 188) and a Roman-style colony (l. 343)."[70] The same goes for Curculio where the connection to Rome is even more strongly articulated.[71]

As mentioned above, the plays of Plautus give us a substantial amount of information about bankers. Bankers represented there are money-changers, assayers and deposit bankers, all at once.[72] Normally, not much detail is given when

---

65 Andreau, J. (1999). *Banking and business in the Roman world*. Cambridge, Cambridge University Press, p. 30, and Plinius Maior, *Naturalis Historia*, XXI, 8.
66 This goes beyond the limits of this subchapter, but for the discussion and opinions see Andreau, J. (1999). *Banking and business in the Roman world*. Cambridge, Cambridge University Press, pp. 30–32.
67 Kay, P. (2014). *Rome's economic revolution*. Oxford: Oxford University Press, p. 116.
68 Harris, W. V. (2019). *Credit-Money in the Roman EconomyCredit-Money in the Roman Economy*. Klio, 101 (1), pp. 158–189, here: p. 167; Kay, P. (2014). *Rome's economic revolution*. Oxford: Oxford University Press, p. 120, mentions 39.
69 Kay, P. (2014). *Rome's economic revolution*. Oxford: Oxford University Press, p. 117; Moore, T. J. (1998). *The Theater of Plautus. Playing to the Audience*. Austin, University of Texas Press, p. 51.
70 Kay, P. (2014). *Rome's economic revolution*. Oxford: Oxford University Press, p. 117.
71 Ibid., p. 118.
72 Andreau, J. *Banking and business in the Roman world*. Cambridge, Cambridge University Press, p. 30. and Andreau, J. *La vie financière dans le monde romain. Les métiers de manieurs d'argent (IVe siècle av. J.-C. - IIIe siècle ap. J.-C.)*. Paris, Rome, École française de Rome, p. 333–56.

banking operations are mentioned in the text of the plays which seems to suggest that these were known to the audience, or at least to the part of it and no explanation was needed.[73] Still a lot of information can be found there. There are two passages which mention transfer made through a bank. The first of the comes from *Pseudolus*: "Sequere sis me ergo ad forum, ut solvam;[74] the second one from *Curculio*: "Ego quidem pro istac rem solvi ab trapezita meo."[75] Both passages describe quite clearly transfer of money done with the help of a banker. We incline to think that both these transfers might have been cashless, yet one cannot be certain. The next piece of evidence on the cashless transfers is the following text: "Nunc satagit: adducit [sc. trapezitam] domum etiam ultro et scribit nummos."[76] In this case, Exaerambus the wine-merchant as the buyer pays the price to Leonida the seller through his banker who did not pay any cash, but only made a record in his books.[77]

What is more important is the evidence of a deposit: "Mirum quin tibi ego crederem, ut idem mihi facere quod partim faciunt argentarii: ubi quid credideris, citius extemplo a foro fugiunt quam ex porta ludis cum emissust lepus."[78]

One might object that we cannot speak about deposit if the word *credere* and not *deponere* is used. However, such an argument would be superficial. First, one cannot expect a playwright to follow the legal terminology and second, at the

---

73 Kay, P. (2014). *Rome's economic revolution*. Oxford: Oxford University Press, p. 120. Harris, W. V. (2019). *Credit-Money in the Roman EconomyCredit-Money in the Roman Economy*. Klio, 101 (1), pp. 158–189, here: p. 167.
74 "Follow me to the forum [where the bankers operate – author's note], then, so that I can settle up." Plautus, Pseudolus 1229–30, as translated by Kay, P. (2014). *Rome's economic revolution*. Oxford: Oxford University Press, p. 120.
75 "I myself settled for that girl through my banker". Plautus, Curculio 618, as translated by Kay, P. (2014). *Rome's economic revolution*. Oxford: Oxford University Press, p. 120.
76 "Now he settles up: furthermore, he brings [his banker] to the house and 'writes money'." Plautus, Asinaria 440, as translated by Kay, P. (2014). *Rome's economic revolution*. Oxford: Oxford University Press, p. 121.
77 Cf. Barlow, C. T. (1978). *Bankers, Moneylenders, and Interest Rates in the Roman Republic* (diss., University of North Carolina), Chapel Hill, p. 77; Harris, W. V. (2006). *A Revisionist View of Roman Money*. The Journal of Roman Studies, 96, pp. 1–24, here: p. 16.
78 "Are you surprised that I wouldn't trust you to do the same to me as some bankers do? If you entrust them with anything, they are out of the forum faster than a hare from its cage door at the games." Plautus, Persa 433–6 as translated by Kay, P. (2014). *Rome's economic revolution*. Oxford: Oxford University Press, pp. 120–121.

time, deposit was not yet entirely established as a specific type of contract.[79] It is more important to note the situation which is described in the text. A client entrusts some money to the banker, while commenting on bankers in general or at least on some of them. Criticizing that they run with the funds they receive from their clients to the forum, where they can use them presumably to advance loans. This text then serves not only as evidence that bankers received deposits, but also of their practice of advancing loans.[80] There is also another passage which suggest that money could be withdrawn from the deposit account and paid out in cash.[81]

Let us, however, return to the question of granting loans from the deposits banker had at his disposal. This evidence is well documented in Greece already in the fourth century BC and there can be little doubt it was adopted by the bankers in Rome as well.[82] Plautus seem to confirm this assumption through mouth of one of his characters the treacherous banker Lyco:

> Beatus videor. Subduxi ratiunculam, quantum aeris mihi sit quantumque alieni siet. Dives sum, si non reddo eis quibus debeo. Si reddo illis quibus debeo, plus alieni est. Verum hercle vero cum belle recogito, si magis me instabunt, ad praetorem sufferam. Habent hunc morem plerique argentarii, ut alius alium poscant, reddant nemini, pugnis rem solvent, si quis poscat clarius.[83]

This passage refers to the situation where Lyco the banker is reviewing his balance sheet. He received the money from deposits and as Kay puts it: "the fact that Lyco claims not to have any money seems to indicate that he has lent out the

---

79 However, see rather critical deliberations of Watson, A. (1984). *The Evolution of Law: The Roman System of Contracts*. Law and History Review, 2(1), pp. 1–20, here: pp. 6–7.
80 Kay, P. (2014). *Rome's economic revolution*. Oxford: Oxford University Press, pp. 120–121.
81 Plautus, Captivi 449.
82 Isocrates, XVII. Trapeziticus.
83 "I seem to be blessed. I've drawn up a little account to work out how much money I have and how much I've borrowed. I'm rich, as long as I don't repay those whom I owe. If I do repay my creditors, there's more around to borrow. Truly though, by Hercules, when I think about it calmly, if they pressurize me anymore, I'll bring it up with the praetor. Most bankers have the habit of demanding their money back from everyone and repaying no one. They settle it with a fight, if anyone demands their money back too loudly." Plautus, Curculio 371–9, as translated by Kay, P. (2014). *Rome's economic revolution*. Oxford: Oxford University Press, p. 123.

funds he has received on deposit".[84] Now, he is unable to pay his creditors. What better illustration of a fractional reserve banking does one need?

The plays of Plautus are, however, not our only source of information on banking. Polybius provides us with the information on the financial dealings of Scipio family. According to him,[85] Scipio Aemilianus had 50 talents (more than 1.2 million HS[86]) deposited[87] with a banker, whom he ordered to make a transfer of 25 talents to each Tiberius Gracchus and Scipio Nasica. The use of word (διαγραφή, literally a "writing through"[88] strongly suggest that it was not a transaction in cash, but a balance transfer. Again, one can only hardly imagine transferring such a sum in physical money, especially silver coins.[89]

There is more evidence for cashless transactions and the bankers' activity in Republican times, but we do not need to go through every single example.[90] However, this strongly contrasts with the times of Cicero, whose works mention *argentarii* only a few times.[91] And their reappearance in the first century AD.[92] This suggest that something happened in the meantime. This something we dare to suggest were several liquidity crises, which are detrimental to fractional reserve banking.

---

84 Kay, P. (2014). *Rome's economic revolution*. Oxford: Oxford University Press, p. 123.
85 Polybios 31.27.6
86 Harris, W. V. (2006). *A Revisionist View of Roman Money*. The Journal of Roman Studies, 96, pp. 1–24, here: p. 12).
87 The authors of this article state that it was loaned to the banker. Collins, A., Walsh, J. (2014). *Fractional Reserve Banking in the Roman Republic and Empire*. Ancient Society, 44, pp. 179–212, here: p. 193.
88 Kay, P. (2014). *Rome's economic revolution*. Oxford: Oxford University Press, pp. 121 and 235.
89 Harris, W. V. (2006). *A Revisionist View of Roman Money*. The Journal of Roman Studies, 96, pp. 1–24, here: p. 3, and Harris, W. V. (2019). *Credit-Money in the Roman EconomyCredit-Money in the Roman Economy*. Klio, 101 (1), pp. 158–189, here: p. 164.
90 See e.g., Harris, W. V. (2006). *A Revisionist View of Roman Money*. The Journal of Roman Studies, 96, pp. 1–24, here: p. 16, and Harris, W. V. (2019). *Credit-Money in the Roman EconomyCredit-Money in the Roman Economy*. Klio, 101 (1), pp. 158–189, here: pp. 172–173, and Kay, P. (2014). *Rome's economic revolution*. Oxford: Oxford University Press, pp. 107, 128.
91 Kay, P. (2014). *Rome's economic revolution*. Oxford: Oxford University Press, p. 110.
92 Ibid., p. 242.

The Nature of a Crisis

To understand the crises, we are to talk about, one first needs to understand the nature of fractional reserve banking. Under this arrangement a bank acquires money of its clients and uses it for its own benefit (i.e., investing it), while the clients do the same which means they order their bank to transfer money to someone else or they withdraw it. In essence it is quite simple. A bank owes more money than it has liquidity, so it is never able to meet all its obligations when asked to return them at once. During this process, the bank hopes that the substantial number of clients would not withdraw their money, therefore it keeps only a part of the total sum at its disposal while using the most of it to generate profit. Both the client and the bank act as if they were the sole proprietor of the money, thus creating an illusion that there is more money in the existence than it corresponds to reality. This so-called fractional reserve banking enables monetary expansion which might be at first beneficial as it creates funds for new investments but is also detrimental to the bank and by the extension to the whole economy when the bank is unable to fulfil its obligations toward its clients as this leads to a chain effect of defaults and secondary insolvencies.[93]

The basic pattern of such crisis is rather simple. In the times of insecurity cash is usually preferred to credit which is uncertain and involves the counterparty risk. This phenomenon might be explained either by liquidity or time preference. The first one postulates the market actors demand to hold money of the highest and safest liquid form, i.e., cash.[94] According to the second one, the market actors undertake a relative valuation of goods available at earlier or on a later date and in case of crisis the smaller amount of cash is considered more valuable then debt which might bring more money, but in an uncertain future.[95] For our

---

[93] More on the fractional reserve banking and money multiplication can be found here: Mankiw, N. G. (2018). *Principles of Economics*. Boston: Cengage Learning, pp. 617–619; Huerta de Soto, J. (2020). *Money, Bank Credit, and Economic Cycles*. Auburn, Ludwig von Mises institute, pp. 167–264, and Hülsmann, J. G. (2008). *The ethics of money production*. Auburn: Ludwig von Mises institute, pp. 237–242.

[94] Collins, A., Walsh, J. (2015). *Debt Deflationary Crisis in the Late Roman Republic*. Ancient Society, 45, pp. 125–170, here: p. 144.

[95] Mises, L. von (1998). *Human Action*. Auburn, Ludwig von Mises institute, pp. 480–487. Among many others see also Huerta de Soto, J. (2020). *Money, Bank Credit, and Economic Cycles*. Auburn, Ludwig von Mises institute, p. 3. For more detailed work see, e.g., Frederick, S., Loewenstein, G., O'donoghue, T. (2002). *Time Discounting and Time Preference: A Critical Review*. Journal of Economic Literature, 40(2), pp. 351–401.

purposes, there is not much difference between the theories as they both lead to the same conclusion. As already mentioned above, in the times of uncertainty people generally prefer cash and that seems to have happened in Rome.

Some analyses of these crises have already been undertaken.[96] One has to mention insightful analysis of Collins and Walsh based on the neo-Keynesian theory of the theory of debt deflation[97] and also an analysis by Philip Kay which is part of his work on late republican economy.[98] As the first two authors have emphasized the analysis based on the heterodox economic currents might be useful, therefore an analysis incorporating the Austrian business cycle theory might be interesting, but that would require a lot more space than it has been allocated to us. Let us now concentrate on our topic, that is the reaction of the Roman state to crises and especially measures which led to the limitation of property rights.

The Crisis of 89–86 BC

Between 91 and 87 BC Italy was struck by social war during which Romans were fighting their Italian allies, which led to widespread devastation of the countryside.[99] These hardships of the war were further exacerbated by the invasion of

---

For the historical perspective see Decock, W. (2019). *Le marché du mérite: Penser le droit et l'économie avec Léonard Lessius*. Bruxelles: Zones sensibles, pp. 70–72.

96 Collins, A., Walsh, J. (2015). *Debt Deflationary Crisis in the Late Roman Republic*. Ancient Society, 45, pp. 125–170, here: p. 125. Give a rather lengthy list of literature. Let us just mention: Frederiksen M. W. (1966). *Cicero, Caesar and the Problem of Debt*. The Journal of Roman Studies, 56, pp. 128–141; Barlow, C. T. (1978). *Bankers, Moneylenders, and Interest Rates in the Roman Republic* (diss., University of North Carolina), Chapel Hill, pp. 179–191; Barlow, C. T. (1980). *The Roman Government and the Roman Economy, 92–80 B.C.*. The American Journal of Philology, 101(2), pp. 202–219; Verboven, K. (1997). *Caritas Nummorum. Deflation in the Late Roman Republic?*. Münstersche Beiträge Zur Antiken Handelsgeschichte, 16, pp. 40–78, and Andreau, J. (1999). *Banking and business in the Roman world*. Cambridge, Cambridge University Press, pp. 103–111.

97 Collins, A., Walsh, J. (2015). *Debt Deflationary Crisis in the Late Roman Republic*. Ancient Society, 45, pp. 125–170, here: pp. 127–148.

98 Kay, P. (2014). *Rome's economic revolution*. Oxford: Oxford University Press, pp. 235–265.

99 On the scale of the war see Salmon, E. T. (1958). *Notes on the Social War*. In Transactions and Proceedings of the American Philological Association, 89. Baltimore, Johns Hopkins University Press, pp. 159–184. On the political organization of rebels

the Roman province of Asia by Mithridates VI in 89–88 BC,[100] Sulla's first march on Rome (88 BC), and the *Bellum Octavianum* which in turn led to victory of Marian faction. As one can see this created a rather unstable environment.

It seems that debtors experienced trouble while settling their debts as their creditors demanded repayment.[101] A. Sempronius Asellio, the urban praetor of the year 89 BC, tried to alleviate the perilous position of debtors by allowing them to sue their creditors based on an old law forbidding usury. For this deed, he was lynched by the angry mob of creditors on the forum.[102]

Meanwhile the credit situation deteriorated even further as Roman credit system was hit hard by the Mithridates invasion of Asia. As Cicero states in his speech *Pro lege Manilia*:

> Deinde quod nos eadem Asia atque idem iste Mithridates initio belli Asiatici docuit, id quidem certe calamitate docti memoria retinere debemus. Nam tum, cum in Asia res magnas permulti amiserant, scimus Romae, solutione impedita, fidem concidisse. Non enim possunt una in civitate multi rem ac fortunas amittere, ut non plures secum in eandem trahant calamitatem. A quo periculo prohibete rem publicam, et mihi credite, id quod ipsi videtis: haec fides atque haec ratio pecuniarum, quae Romae, quae in foro versatur, implicata est cum illis pecuniis Asiaticis et cohaeret; ruere illa non possunt, ut haec non eodem labefacta motu concidant.[103]

---

see Dart, Ch. J. *The 'Italian Constitution' in the Social War: A Reassessment (91 to 88 BCE)*. Historia: Zeitschrift Für Alte Geschichte, 58(2), pp. 215–224.

100 Cicero, *Pro lege Manilia* 7.19.

101 Livius, Periochae 74: *Cum aere alieno pressa esset ciuitas, A. Sempronius Asellio praetor, quoniam secundum debitores ius dicebat, ab his qui faenerabant in foro occisus est.*

102 As Kay, P. (2014). *Rome's economic revolution*. Oxford: Oxford University Press, p. 246 points out. According to the epitomes of Livy (Livius Periochae 74) and Valerius Maximus 9.7.4 he was killed by the creditors. According to Appian it was the δανεισταί (moneylenders) who killed him (App. *B. Civ.*1.54).

103 "Secondly, we ought assuredly to remember the lesson which we learned from this same Mithridates at the beginning of the Asiatic war, since we were taught it through disaster. For then, when very many people lost large fortunes in Asia, we know that there was a collapse of trust (*fides*) at Rome, because repayments were interrupted (*solutione impedita*). It is indeed impossible for many individuals in a single state to lose their property and fortunes without involving still greater numbers in their ruin. Defend the Republic from this danger; and believe me when I tell you—what you see for yourselves—that this credit and this system of monies, which operates at Rome in the Forum, is bound up in, and is linked with, those Asian monies (*pecuniae Asiaticae*); the loss of the one inevitably undermines the other and causes its collapse." Cicero, *Pro lege Manilia* 19. As translated by Kay, P. (2014). *Rome's economic revolution*. Oxford: Oxford University Press, p. 245, based on Loeb IX 31, slightly revised. Kay

From this passage, we learn that Roman capital invested in Asia was wiped out by the invasion of Mithridates. Indeed, the Pontian king made the financiers special targets.[104] One can imagine that their debtors were not entirely against this idea. Many Romans who invested in Asia were presumably themselves debtors in Rome and since they lost their funds there, they were now unable to repay their debts at home. It is impossible to determine which of these debts were repayable on demand (like most bank deposits today are) and which at a fixed date. However, one can be reasonably certain that both groups were involved and those whose debts could be called in immediately were hit especially hard. To repay their debts, they had to sell their assets, but this distress selling led to fall in prices which made the repayment of debts in nominal terms difficult.[105] Some debts were repaid which meant that they could no longer be transferred and thus used as transferable instruments, a.k.a. means of payment. Given the environment those who still had money were reluctant to engage in lending, which is exactly when the liquidity or time preference mentioned above comes in. This not only meant debtors were denied a possibility of bridge loans, but also limited the number of transferable instruments as new debt were not being created. The hoarding of money also increased further limiting the available liquidity.[106] This was a perfect storm – a deflationary spiral.

Naturally, Roman officials tried to remedy the situation, but their actions had sometimes rather negative effects. So was the case of *plebiscitum* originally proposed in 88 BC by the tribune of the plebs Sulpicius Rufus, which limited the amount of money each senator could owe to 2,000 drachmas, a particularly low sum.[107] We have no information as to the motives of this law. Maybe it was meant to limit the indebtedness of senators many of whom must have been hit by the present crisis thus preventing a future one. It is also possible it was just a personal vengeance of Sulpicius who as Plutarch informs us did not get on well

---

translates *fides* in this place as "credit" which we believe goes too far. We are inclined to think that Cicero meant that trust in general collapsed which of course led to collapse of the credit market as credit relations are based on trust. Cf. Collins, A., Walsh, J. (2015). *Debt Deflationary Crisis in the Late Roman Republic*. Ancient Society, 45, pp. 125–170, here: p. 149.
104 App. *Mith.* 22.
105 Collins, A., Walsh, J. (2015). *Debt Deflationary Crisis in the Late Roman Republic*. Ancient Society, 45, pp. 125–170, here: p. 150.
106 Ibid.
107 Plutarchos, Sulla 8.2. It was quite hypocritical of Sulpicius, because as Plutarch informs us, that when he died, he left behind a debt of three million drachmas.

with the senate. In any case, it certainly limited the possibility of the senators to freely dispose with their property. However, the law was declared invalid soon after the death of Sulpicius who died the same year. Thus, its consequences were probably limited.

However, the problem of debt remained pressing and so in the same year consuls Sulla and Pompeius proposed a new legislation *lex Cornelia Pompeia unicaria*. It is mentioned only in one fragment by Sextus Pompeius Festus:

> Unciaria lex appellari coepta est, quam L. Sulla et Q. Pom (peius Rufus) tulerunt, qua sanctum est ut debitores <duo>decimam partem...[108]

By this law, the interest rate was capped at 1/12 of the principal a year.[109] This should have probably improved the position of the debtors. Collins and Walsh also add that amount of principal owed was reduced by 10%, but we do not see any hint of that in the fragment.[110]

However, even the *lex Cornelia Pompeia unicaria* failed to bring the relief to beleaguered debtors. Meanwhile, Sulla departed to the east to fight Mithridates and Marian faction returned to power. Now, it was their time to try to solve the crisis. In 86 BC *consul suffectus* L. Valerius Flaccus proposed and carried out much more radical solution so called *lex Valeria de aere alieno*. In this case, we have more sources. Some like C. Velleius Paterculus[111] criticize the law, some like Sallust[112] uphold

---

108 "The law, passed by L. Sulla and Q. Pompeius Rufus, began to be called 'the unciarial law', by which it was permitted that debtors...<twelfth> part...)." Fest. 516L, as translated by Kay, P. (2014). *Rome's economic revolution*. Oxford: Oxford University Press, p. 246.
109 Collins, A., Walsh, J. (2015). *Debt Deflationary Crisis in the Late Roman Republic*. Ancient Society, 45, pp. 125–170, here: p. 149, agree on the interest rate.
110 Collins, A., Walsh, J. (2015). *Debt Deflationary Crisis in the Late Roman Republic*. Ancient Society, 45, pp. 125–170, here: p. 149.
111 Velleius Paterculus 2.23.2: *...suffectus Valerius Flaccus, turpissimae legis auctor, qua creditoribus quadrantem solvi iusserat...* "...the suffect consul Valerius Flaccus, the author of a very shameful law, in which he had decreed that one quarter of a debt should be paid to creditors...", as translated by Kay, P. (2014). *Rome's economic revolution*. Oxford: Oxford University Press, p. 246.
112 Sallustius, Catilina 33. 2: *ac novissume memoria nostra propter magnitudinem aeris alieni volentibus omnibus bonis argentum aere solutum est.* – "and not long ago, within our memory, because of the scale of outstanding debt, silver was paid in bronze, with the consent of all good men." As translated by Kay (2014: 246). Silver was paid in bronze means that one silver sestertius of debt could be repaid with a copper as. See

it.[113] Even Cicero seemed to make some allusions to it.[114] So, why was the law so controversial? Because it cut the debts by 75%! We possess no information to which debts the law applied, but it is reasonable to supposed, as Royer does, and Collins and Walsh agree, that it only applied to debts contracted before year 88 BC.[115] The amount of the cancelled debt probably corresponded to the general fall in asset prices in general as well as land prices in particular.[116]

Lex Valeria de aere alieno must have brought some relief to the debtors as the nominal debts were more or less aligned with new asset prices. This probably helped to restore fides and credit market and thus the crisis was basically overcome.[117] Some suggest the law was revoked by Sulla,[118] but there is hardly any evidence for that.[119] Furthermore, it is difficult to imagine how this revocation would work in reality with some debt meanwhile repaid under the conditions set by the *Lex Valeria*. This would be simply unpractical and therefore improbable.

Let us shortly return to the banks. How did their fortunes evolve during the crisis? The deflationary environment is especially difficult for banks operation on fractional reserves as debts are set in nominal terms, but the prices of the pledged

---

Collins, A., Walsh, J. (2015). *Debt Deflationary Crisis in the Late Roman Republic.* Ancient Society, 45, pp. 125–170, here: p. 152.

113 For other ancient sources see also Cicero, Pro Fonteio 1–2. and Cicero, Pro Quinctio 17.
114 Cicero, Pro Quinctio 17, see Kay, P. (2014). *Rome's economic revolution.* Oxford: Oxford University Press, p. 247 and his comments on it.
115 Royer, J.-P. (1967). Le problème des dettes a la fin de la République romaine. Revue historique de droit français et étranger. 45, pp. 191–240 and pp. 407–450, here: p. 439, Collins, A., Walsh, J. (2015). *Debt Deflationary Crisis in the Late Roman Republic.* Ancient Society, 45, pp. 125–170, here: p. 152.
116 Barlow, C. T. (1980). *The Roman Government and the Roman Economy, 92–80 B.C..* The American Journal of Philology. 101(2), pp. 202–219, here: p. 216. Collins, A., Walsh, J. (2015). *Debt Deflationary Crisis in the Late Roman Republic.* Ancient Society, 45, pp. 125–170, here: p. 152 agree.
117 Barlow, C. T. (1980). *The Roman Government and the Roman Economy, 92–80 B.C..* The American Journal of Philology. 101(2), pp. 202–219, here: p. 216. Collins, A., Walsh, J. (2015). *Debt Deflationary Crisis in the Late Roman Republic.* Ancient Society, 45, pp. 125–170, here: p. 152.
118 Frank, T. (1935). 'The Financial Crisis of 33 A. D'. The American Journal of Philology. 56(4), pp. 336–341, here: p. 57; and Royer, J.-P. (1967). Le problème des dettes a la fin de la République romaine. Revue historique de droit français et étranger. 45, pp. 191–240 and pp. 407–450, here: p. 439.
119 Collins, A., Walsh, J. (2015). *Debt Deflationary Crisis in the Late Roman Republic.* Ancient Society, 45, pp. 125–170, here: p. 152.

assets fall which makes it very difficult for a bank to recover what is owed to it. The debts being set in nominal values also means that no matter the deflation, the bank as a debtor must pay them to its creditors in their original amount. One hardly needs to emphasize how perilous situation it is. Still, Barlow[120] and Collins and Walsh[121] suggest they suffered only little because they only received ¼ of the money originally lent, but it had now as much purchasing power as the original sum. Kay[122] disagrees and believes many bankers were bankrupt pointing the adverse conditions mentioned above as well as some sources[123] we have at our disposal. We are inclined to side with him. It is true that bankers might have benefited from the *lex Valeria de aere alieno* as described above, but one should remember that it only went into effect after more than two years of a deflationary crisis. In that time, bankers were supposed to pay the money to their creditors on nominal terms while many of their own debtors were in default and the prices of assets pledged as securities were falling, thus limiting their capacity to repay debts. It is reasonable to infer that by 86 BC many bankers were themselves bankrupt.

Apart from the measures listed above, it also seems that Roman government increased the minting of money, which certainly helped to increase liquidity.[124] However, it is difficult to establish to what degree as the hoarding of money continued throughout the 80s.[125]

---

120 Barlow, C. T. (1980). *The Roman Government and the Roman Economy, 92–80 B.C.*. The American Journal of Philology. 101(2), pp. 202–219, here: p. 216.
121 Collins, A., Walsh, J. (2015). *Debt Deflationary Crisis in the Late Roman Republic.* Ancient Society, 45, pp. 125–170, here: p. 152–153.
122 Kay, P. (2014). *Rome's economic revolution.* Oxford: Oxford University Press, pp. 252–257.
123 Cicero, *Pro Caecina* 10–11.
124 Kay, P. (2014). *Rome's economic revolution.* Oxford: Oxford University Press, p. 249.
125 Verboven, K. (1997). *Caritas Nummorum. Deflation in the Late Roman Republic?.* Münstersche Beiträge Zur Antiken Handelsgeschichte. 16, pp. 40–78, here: p. 53, and Verboven, K. (2003). *54–44 BCE: Financial or Monetary Crisis?.* In: Lo Caseio, E. (ed). Credito e moneta nel mondo romano. Atti degli Incontri capresi di storia dell'economia antica (Capri, 12–14 ottobre 2000). Bari: Edipuglia, pp. 49–68, here: p. 55.

Crisis of 49–46 BC

As the previously discussed crisis this is also connected to war more specifically to the Caesar's civil war.[126] On the 6th of January 49 BC *senatus consultum ultimum* aimed against Caesar was passed by the senate.[127] Caesar himself crossed Rubicon on the 11th of January.[128] The Optimates did not have an army in the Italy to stop him, so many of them swiftly fled Rome to avoid probable repressions.[129] This exile of the large part of Roman nobility together with the fears of some,[130] which were hopes of the others,[131] that Caesar might cancel debts, had profound effects on the economy. Creditors now demanded repayment in cash which implies negotiable instruments were not being accepted.[132] Cicero calls it *nummorum caritas* and indeed those who could were trying to get cash and hold it.[133] Hoarding increased and cash was thus being withdrawn from the circulation.[134] In order to get the money, debtors started selling their property, but this only reinforced the trend as at least some of those fleeing Rome probably did the same thing. Furthermore, the fear of confiscation,[135] which was well-founded and soon materialized further helped to bring the asset prices, including those of the land, down.[136]

---

126 There might have been some economic problems already before the start of the war. See Kay, P. (2014). *Rome's economic revolution*. Oxford: Oxford University Press, p. 260, Collins, A., Walsh, J. (2015). *Debt Deflationary Crisis in the Late Roman Republic*. Ancient Society, 45, pp. 125–170, here: p. 153.
127 App. *B. Civ*.2.33; Caesar, *De Bello Civili* 1.5.3–5; Dio Cassius 45.27.2.; Plutarchos, *Caesar* 31.2; Suetonius, *Iulius* 31.1.
128 App. *B. Civ*.2.35; Dio Cassius 41.4.1; Plutarchos, *Caesar* 32.4–8; Suetonius, *Iulius* 32.
129 Caesar, *De Bello Civili* 1.14.1–3; Dio Cassius 41.6.1; Plutarchos, *Caesar* 33.4–6, 34.1.
130 Cicero, *Ad Atticum* 7.11.1; 10.8.2.
131 Cicero, *Ad Atticum* 7.3.5.
132 App. *B. Civ*.2.198; Caesar, *De Bello Civili* 3.1, and 20; Dio Cassius 41.37–8; Plutarchos, *Caesar* 37.1; Suetonius, *Iulius* 42.2.
133 Cicero, *Ad Atticum* 9.9.4: *sed nunc omnia ista iacere puto propter nummorum caritate*.
134 Dio Cassius 41.38.1; Crawford, M.H. (1985). *Coinage and Money Under the Roman Republic: Italy and the Mediterranean Economy*. Berkeley, Los Angeles: Univ. od California Press, p. 192, Frederiksen M. W. (1966). *Cicero, Caesar and the Problem of Debt*. The Journal of Roman Studies, 56, pp. 128–141, here: pp. 132–133, Kay, P. (2014). *Rome's economic revolution*. Oxford: Oxford University Press, p. 260.
135 Cicero, *Ad Atticum* 10.14.1; Dio Cassius 42.51.2.
136 Cicero, *Ad Atticum* 7.18.4; 9.9.4.

Seeing the situation, even Caesar complained that credit in the Italy was tighter as loans were not being repaid.[137] What he did not mention thought was that he himself was partly responsible for the situation. Not only he invaded Italy which sparked the crisis, but his subsequent steps like the seizure of the state treasury (*aerarium*) only increased the feeling of insecurity.[138] Nevertheless, it was now up to him to salvage the situation.

During much of the 49 BC Caesar campaigned in Spain returning to Rome only in December.[139] Upon his arrival, he implemented first measures to solve the crisis.[140] As the creditors only accepted cash, the debtors very trying to obtain it by selling or at least pledging their property, but as mentioned above this flooded the market and let to price decrease. Therefore, Caesar ordered creditors to accept property at the pre-crisis valuation in lieu of money, thus trying to deal with the problem of insufficient liquidity.[141] One cannot help but to see there the same model which later became known as *datio in solutum*.[142] Moreover, seeing the hoarding was a problem, by revoking some older law, Caesar forbid anyone from holding more than HS 60.000 in cash.[143] These measures seem not to have been enough because some other followed. According to Dio Cassius, Caesar ordered all the interest paid since the beginning of the war to be cancelled, thus the sum already paid was deducted from the principal.[144] This is supported by Suetonius who informs us that in happened in 48 BC and since the maximum interest rate at the time was 12% p.a.

---

137 *Cum fides tota Italia esset angustior neque creditae pecuniae solverentur.* Translated by Kay, P. (2014). *Rome's economic revolution.* Oxford: Oxford University Press, p. 260 as follows: "Since credit in the whole of Italy was tighter and loans were not being repaid."
138 App. *B. Civ.*2. 41; Cicero, *Ad Atticum* 7. 21. 2, 10. 4. 8, 10. 8. 6; Dio Cassius 41. 17. 1–2; Orosius 6. 15. 5; Plinius Maior, *Naturalis Historia* XXXIII.56; Plutarchos, *Caesar* 35. However, as Kay, P. (2014). *Rome's economic revolution.* Oxford: Oxford University Press, p. 260 points out, Caesar did not mention this deed. See Caesar, *De Bello Civili* 1.33.3.
139 Caesar, *De Bello Civili* 3.2.1; Plutarchos, *Caesar* 37.1–2.
140 All the measures as mentioned by the ancient authors are listed by Frederiksen M. W. (1966). *Cicero, Caesar and the Problem of Debt.* The Journal of Roman Studies, 56, pp. 128–141, here: pp. 133–134.
141 App. *B. Civ.*2.48; Cicero, *Ad Atticum* 7.17.1; Caesar, *De Bello Civili* 3.1.1; Suetonius, *Iulius* 42.3; See also Frederiksen M. W. (1966). *Cicero, Caesar and the Problem of Debt.* The Journal of Roman Studies, 56, pp. 128–141, here: pp. 133–134.
142 See, e.g., Zimmermann, R. (1990). *The Law of Obligations: Roman Foundations of the Civilian Tradition.* Cape Town, Juta, pp. 753–754.
143 Dio Cassius 41.38.1.
144 Dio Cassius 41.51.1.

this effectively meant decreasing of the sum owed by ¼.[145] This applied not only to interest paid in cash, but apparently also to hat paid in negotiable instruments such as *nomina*. It is possible this measure should have also helped to restore faith in the credit market.[146] Finally, one year's rent up to a maximum of HS 2,000 were cancelled as well.[147]

It is likely the crisis continued because Cicero informs us that in 45 BC the credit was still tight.[148] It is therefore not surprising that some new measures were undertaken. One of them was *lex Caesaris dictatoris de modo credendi possidendique intra Italiam* about which we have some knowledge thanks to Tacitus.[149] Some suggest this law was already passed in 49 BC and it was only amended in 45 BC.[150] However, this does not sound likely as previous measures were rather introduced by the decrees of the magistrates and not by a statue.[151] As the very name of the law suggest, persons of wealth had to invest portion of their property into Italian land. It is unclear how much it originally was, but as it was reviewed in the times of Tiberius, nothing seems to suggest there were any changes introduced.[152] In that case, the amount of wealth invested in the Italian land would amount to 2/3 of the overall property.[153] There were also clauses setting limits to the amount of money which could be advanced as interest bearing loans.[154] The intention of this law might have been to prop up the low prices of the land in Italy.[155]

---

145 Suetonius, *Iulius* 42.2.
146 Collins, A., Walsh, J. (2015). *Debt Deflationary Crisis in the Late Roman Republic.* Ancient Society, 45, pp. 125–170, here: pp. 157–158.
147 Dio Cassius 41.51.1.
148 Cicero, *Ad Atticum* 12, 21, 4; 22, 3; 28, 3 and 51, 3.
149 Tacitus, Annales 6.16–17.
150 Mommsen, T. (1922). *Römische Geschichte. Band 3, Von Sullas Tode bis zur Schlacht von Thapsus.* Berlin, Deutsche Buch-Gemeinschaft, p. 537; Collins, A., Walsh, J. (2015). *Debt Deflationary Crisis in the Late Roman Republic.* Ancient Society, 45, pp. 125–170, here: p. 158.
151 Frederiksen, M. W. (1966). *Cicero, Caesar and the Problem of Debt.* The Journal of Roman Studies, 56, pp. 128–141, here: pp. 133–134.
152 Suetonius, Tiberius 48.
153 Tacitus, Annales 6.16–17. See Frederiksen, M. W. (1966). *Cicero, Caesar and the Problem of Debt.* The Journal of Roman Studies, 56, pp. 128–141, here: pp. 134 and 140. Collins, A., Walsh, J. (2015). *Debt Deflationary Crisis in the Late Roman Republic.* Ancient Society, 45, pp. 125–170, here: pp. 158–159, agree with the 2/3 proportion, while discussing other possibilities.
154 Tacitus, Annales 6.16.
155 Collins, A., Walsh, J. (2015). *Debt Deflationary Crisis in the Late Roman Republic.* Ancient Society, 45, pp. 125–170, here: p. 159.

Another piece of legislation introduced in connection with the crisis was *lex Julia de bonis cedendis*. It was meant to alleviate the position of overindebted debtors. If they pleaded bankrupt and ceded almost all of their property to the creditors, they were left with some modest resources to sustain themselves and were not stricken by the infamy[156] which was quite beneficial for their further functioning in Roman society.[157] We do not know any more details about the law and all our knowledge about *cessio bonorum* comes from the later stages of development of the Roman law,[158] so we are unable to say what were the conditions under which it was granted, but it can be hardly assumed that everyone would meet them.[159]

Finally, an important measure was minting of new gold coins. Romans used mostly silver money and since silver was scarce, Caesar introduced gold as the additional source of coinage. First emissions of 48–47 BC were followed by a bigger one in 46 BC.[160] It should also be remembered that he used the funds of *aerarium* to pay his soldiers, thus increasing the liquidity in circulation.

When did the crisis end? Difficult to say. While the worst may have been over in 46 BC thanks to the increased liquidity, one can only hardly argue that Roman economy prospered in the next year. The assassination of Caesar plunged the Republic into another civil war which ended after the Philippi in 42 BC. However, we would doubt that this would be the end to the crisis.[161] The economic difficulties have in some form probably continued due to the blockade of Italy by Pompey the Younger and subsequent civil war between Octavianus and Marc Anthony until the defeat of the latter.

---

156 Cod. Iust. 2.11.11. Note, however, that this is a later source.
157 Collins, A., Walsh, J. (2015). *Debt Deflationary Crisis in the Late Roman Republic*. Ancient Society, 45, pp. 125–170, here: p. 159; Frederiksen M. W. (1966). *Cicero, Caesar and the Problem of Debt*. The Journal of Roman Studies, 56, pp. 128–141, here: p. 135, and Kay, P. (2014). *Rome's economic revolution*. Oxford: Oxford University Press, pp. 261–262).
158 See especially D. 42.3 *De cessione bonorum*; Kaser, M., Hackl, K. (1996). Das römische Zivilprozessrecht. München: C.H. Beck, pp. 405–407.
159 For the discussion about this topic see Frederiksen M. W. (1966). *Cicero, Caesar and the Problem of Debt*. The Journal of Roman Studies, 56, pp. 128–141, here: p. 135.
160 With huge complexity Woytek, B. (2003). *Arma et Nummi, Forschungen zur römischen Finanzgeschichte und Münzprägung der Jahre 49 bis 42 v. Chr.* Vienna: Verlag der österreichischen Akademie der Wissenschaften, pp. 218–310.
161 Collins, A., Walsh, J. (2015). *Debt Deflationary Crisis in the Late Roman Republic*. Ancient Society, 45, pp. 125–170, here: p. 160.

Crisis of 33 AD

Finally, there is the crisis of 33 AD which is described in some detail in the Histories of Tacitus:

> 6.16. Interea magna vis accusatorum in eos inrupit qui pecunias faenore auctitabant adversum legem dictatoris Caesaris qua de modo credendi possidendique intra Italiam cavetur, omissam olim, quia privato usui bonum publicum postponitur. sane vetus urbi faenebre malum et seditionum discordiarumque creberrima causa eoque cohibebatur antiquis quoque et minus corruptis moribus. nam primo duodecim tabulis sanctum ne quis unciario faenore amplius exerceret, cum antea ex libidine locupletium agitaretur; dein rogatione tribunicia ad semuncias redactum, postremo vetita versura. multisque plebi scitis obviam itum fraudibus quae toties repressae miras per artes rursum oriebantur. sed tum Gracchus praetor, cui ea quaestio evenerat, multitudine periclitantium subactus rettulit ad senatum, trepidique patres (neque enim quisquam tali culpa vacuus) veniam a principe petivere; et concedente annus in posterum sexque menses dati quis secundum iussa legis rationes familiaris quisque componerent.
>
> 17. Hinc inopia rei nummariae, commoto simul omnium aere alieno, et quia tot damnatis bonisque eorum divenditis signatum argentum fisco vel aerario attinebatur. ad hoc senatus praescripserat, duas quisque faenoris partis in agris per Italiam conlocaret. sed creditores in solidum appellabant nec decorum appellatis minuere fidem. ita primo concursatio et preces, dein strepere praetoris tribunal, eaque quae remedio quaesita, venditio et emptio, in contrarium mutari quia faeneratores omnem pecuniam mercandis agris considerant. copiam vendendi secuta vilitate, quanto quis obaeratior, aegrius distrahebant, multique fortunis provolvebantur; eversio rei familiaris dignitatem ac famam praeceps dabat, donec tulit opem Caesar disposito per mensas milies sestertio factaque mutuandi copia sine usuris per triennium, si debitor populo in duplum praediis cavisset. sic refecta fides et paulatim privati quoque creditores reperti. neque emptio agrorum exercita ad formam senatus consulti, acribus, ut ferme talia, initiis, incurioso fine.[162]

---

162 Tacitus, Annales 6.16–17: "16. Meanwhile a great force of accusers fell on those who were increasing their money by lending at interest in defiance of a law passed by Caesar, the dictator, about the procedure for lending money and for holding land in Italy, a law long obsolete because the public good takes second place to private interest…But then, Gracchus, the praetor, who had responsibility for the inquiry, was compelled by the number of people at risk to refer the matter to the senate. The nervous senators, not one of whom was free from similar guilt, sought indulgence from the emperor. He yielded and a year and six months were granted, within which everyone had to arrange their private finances in accordance with the law.
17. Hence there was a scarcity of money, since, at the same time, a great shock had been given to the whole credit market, and minted coin was ending up in the imperial treasury or the state treasury, because so many people had been convicted and their property sold piecemeal. To address this, the senate had directed that every creditor should invest two-thirds of their capital in Italian land. But creditors were demanding

As some authors rightfully mention the description entails *extensive and surprisingly sophisticated reporting*.[163] Roman authors were not especially interested in economic history, so the fact that not only Tacitus, but also Suetonius (Tiberius 48) and Cassius Dio (58.21) mention it is a testament to the severity of the crisis. The cause of the crisis was apparently the renewed application of the abovementioned *lex Caesaris dictatoris de modo credendi possidendique intra Italiam* which limited how much money could be loaned and prescribed the proportion of property which had to be invested in Italian land. Especially the senators many of whom[164] were in breach of the law were terrified by it and asked the emperor to grant them some time to comply with the law. He granted them a year and a half, during which they started to sell their land property. Many of them then started calling in their loans, thus the credit declined and many debtors had to sell their property to repay the debts. However, by doing so, they flooded the market with real estates which led to decline in their prices. The property of debtors was thus losing value and they were unable to sell it at prices which would allow them to meet their obligations. Senate then unsuccessfully tried to prop up the land prices by decreeing every senator should invest 2/3 of his property into Italian land, but this also failed. Finally, the emperor came to the rescue and distributed a huge sum of HS 100 million through the banks which secured enough liquidity in the market that was used by the debtors to stabilize their situation and stopped the fall of the property prices thus ending the crisis.

> payment in full and it was not seemly to break faith if one faced such a demand. So, at first, there were disorderly meetings and entreaties; then there was a din in the praetor's court and the very scheme that had been intended as a remedy, the sale and purchase of land, proved the contrary, because the faeneratores had hoarded all their money for buying land. Large-scale selling was followed by reduced prices, and the more debt a man had, the more disastrous it was for him to sell, and many were ruined. The loss of an estate destroyed dignity and reputation. Until Caesar brought help by distributing through the banks one hundred million sesterces and allowing borrowing on a large scale without interest for three years, provided the borrower gave to the people security in land equivalent to double the amount of the loan. Credit was thus restored, and gradually private lenders were found. But the purchase of land was not carried out according to the provisions of the senate's decree, rigour at the outset, as generally happens, ending in negligence."

163 Thornton, M. K., Thornton, R. L. (1990). *The Financial Crisis of A.D. 33: A Keynesian Depression?*. The Journal of Economic History. 50(3), pp. 655–662, here: p. 655.
164 The statement of Tacitus that no one of them was free of guilt must be considered hyperbolic.

It has been carefully suggested that the crisis was actually sparked by insufficient liquidity which itself came to be due to reduced building activity which was the main means of releasing cash by the state.[165] However, we find such an explanation improbable. First, our very primary sources give a different explanation as to the origins of the crisis and second, as authors of the alternative explanation themselves mention, the building programs "were near zero during the eight-year period immediately preceding the crisis of A.D. 33",[166] so there is no reason the crises should have started in 33 AD and not few years earlier or later. However, it is important to mention that despite mentioning different cause of the crises, the authors do not question the way the crisis was addressed by the Roman authorities.

As Tacitus informs us, first, the Senate tried to prop up the property prices by decreeing every senator should invest 2/3 of his property in land. However, this effort failed, and it was only the additional liquidity provided at zero interest rate that helped to solve the crisis. Moreover, we have an archaeological evidence money minting also increased in the years following the crisis and with the average production of denarii growing by eight times and that of aurei by three times in the last six years of the reign of Tiberius.[167]

There are two more points which should be briefly mentioned here. First, a huge amount of money as HS 100 million was lent out through banks and it seems that the Roman banking industry must have recuperated to absorb and process such a sum. Second, we agree with statement that there was no economic theory background behind the actions of Tiberius. He simply recognized Italian nobility lack funds and he provided them.[168]

---

165 Thornton, M. K., Thornton, R. L. (1990). *The Financial Crisis of A.D. 33: A Keynesian Depression?*. The Journal of Economic History. 50(3), pp. 655–662, here: pp. 655 and 661–662), but they do not make this statement without certain reservations, p. 660. The argument about the public spending was actually already made by Frank, T. (1935). 'The Financial Crisis of 33 A. D.'. The American Journal of Philology, 56(4), pp. 336–341, here: p. 337–341, but neither he brings enough evidence to sustain it. For critique of these approaches see Elliott, C. P. (2015). *The Crisis of A.D. 33: past and present*. Journal of Ancient History, 3(2), pp. 267–281, here: pp. 275–276).
166 Thornton, M. K., Thornton, R. L. (1990). *The Financial Crisis of A.D. 33: A Keynesian Depression?*. The Journal of Economic History. 50(3), pp. 655–662, here: p. 657.
167 Duncan-Jones, R. (1994). *Money and Government in the Roman Empire*. Cambridge: Cambridge University Press, pp. 25, 251.
168 Elliott, C. P. (2015). *The Crisis of A.D. 33: past and present*. Journal of Ancient History, 3(2), pp. 267–281, here: pp. 278–279.

Evaluation of Roman Law Measures to Resolve Financial Crises

As we have seen Roman state had to deal with the financial crises and it did so with varied success. It introduced various measures, but some of these measures were more effective than the others. For example, the increase in liquidity either by the means of coining new money or by provision of additional loans proved to be a potent remedy. The decrease in the debt burden by simple cancellation of the part of the debt also helped debtors, but at the same time naturally harmed creditors. The effect of some other measures like orders to invest in the land thus propping up its prices seems rather limited if effective at all. The same applies to the orders of Caesar according to which creditors were to accept the property of debtors at pre-crisis valuation. This only discouraged the creditors from further lending.[169] The restrictions on hording were of negligible effect as it was difficult to enforce them.

It is also worth pointing out how the measures imposed by Roman state limited the property rights of its subjects. It is rather obvious that creditors were hit particularly hard by some of them as they led to at least nominal loses of their property. However, the regulations aimed at investing of certain part of property into land property in Italy, mandating how much of it could be advanced as a credit or limiting the amount of cash one was allowed to hold show that restriction of private property was a part and parcel of anti-crisis measures. That is hardly surprising. While writing about the crisis of 33 AD, Tacitus states that "the public good takes second place to private interest".[170] However, especially in the times of crisis, rights of private subjects are often limited in order to advance so-called public good. Whether this is a real public good or not is a matter of *ad hoc* value judgement. Therefore, the measures which limit the rights of other subjects including the property rights should be accessed very carefully and implemented only if they have the potential of resolving the critical situation. Other approach would be utterly disproportional.

---

169 Kay, P. (2014). *Rome's economic revolution*. Oxford: Oxford University Press, p. 264.
170 Tacitus, Annales 6.16.

Crises Caused by Pandemics and the Roman State's Reaction

As already mentioned above, during the long-lasting existence of the Roman state, many waves of contagious diseases that had a character of pandemic can be found. We can mention, e.g., the so-called Antonine plague that hit the capital in 166 AD, or the so-called Cyprian plague that spread around the middle of the third century AD.[171] Identically with the statements in the previous subchapters, a disclaimer must be made that it is not possible to discuss reactions to all outbreaks of plague that emerged.

Up to this moment, our focus was and will soon again be oriented mainly on public law measures. However, while speaking about the legal consequences of pandemics, we should not omit to mention an institution deeply connected with each private person – a Roman testament, in particular, its special form developed as the reaction to the diseases that would otherwise prevent a Roman civic to establish his last will.

Roman Law of Succession and Pandemics

At first, it is necessary to explain, how important role the *testamentum* played in the Roman world. It could be said that testament was almost a sacred matter for the Romans. Cato the Elder comments on the status of the Roman will with only slight exaggeration when he says that he regretted only three things in his life, namely entrusting his secret to a woman, sailing by boat where he could walk, and living even one day without a will in place.[172] The eminent legal historian Max Kaser commented on his words so that it was the moral obligation of a Roman father to ensure that he never lived a moment without a testament.[173]

The Roman law of succession has undergone many changes during its long development, and various types of wills have emerged over time, often differing in their particulars. However, law, as a phenomenon necessarily linked to society, must respond to the needs of society, ideally as flexibly as possible. Thus, in the

---

171 For detailed research about the impact of climate changes and diseases on the Roman Empire see: Harper, K. (2017). The Fate of Rome. Climate, Disease, and the End of an Empire. Princeton (NJ), Oxford, Princeton University Press.
172 Plutarchos, Cato 9.6.
173 Kaser, M. (1955). Das römische Privatrecht. Erster Abschnitt. Das altrömische, das vorklassische und klassische Recht. München, C. H. Beck´sche Verlagsbuchhandlung, p. 563.

life of Roman society, situations naturally arose in which the traditional regulation of wills, even with regard to the possibility of establishing military wills for soldiers, was not sufficient for the needs of testators. It was therefore necessary to create several types of wills, which were characterized by justifiable concessions compared to the ordinary one.

An urgent event that brought a testament with reliefs were a recurring epidemics of various diseases, which the Romans superficially called plague. Even the law of succession, an important part of Roman law which governs the transfer of rights and obligations from testator to heir, did not escape the response.

Because of its importance in Roman society, for the testator and the heirs themselves, the classical testament required, among other things, a certain number of witnesses to testify the creation of the last will. Over time, the number of witnesses required for the validity of a will settled down to seven competent witnesses. Further requirement for the classic testament was that all the persons needed shall be present at the same time and throughout the whole legal act (so-called *unitas actus*).[174] It was this condition that proved unsustainable in a time of contagious diseases spreading through Roman society.

From Ulpian's fragment[175] it follows that illness is classified by Roman jurists as an intervention of the so-called force majeure (*vis maior*). It was thus a sudden illness that could lead a hitherto carefree testator to an acute need to leave a will. His contagiousness, however, was an obstacle to the establishment of a proper will.

A significant response of the Roman state to the plague pandemic was the introduction of the plague testament (*testamentum pestis tempore*). It is mentioned in the constitution included in the Justinian Code, issued by the co-ruling emperors Diocletian and Maximian in 290 AD.[176] The impetus for the issuance

---

174 Heyrovský, L. (1910). Dějiny a systém soukromého práva římského. Praha: J. Otto, p. 996.
175 D. 13.6.5.4 (Ulpianus 28 ad ed.): *Quod vero senectute contigit vel morbo, vel vi latronum ereptum est, aut quid simile accidit, dicendum est nihil eorum esse imputandum ei qui commodatum accepit, nisi aliqua culpa interveniat. proinde et si incendio vel ruina aliquid contigit vel aliquid damnum fatale, non tenebitur, nisi forte, cum possit res commodatas salvas facere, suas praetulit.*
176 Cod. Iust. 6.23.8, Imperatores Diocletianus, Maximianus: *Casus maioris ac novi contingentis ratione adversus timorem contagionis, quae testes deterret, aliquid de iure laxatum est: non tamen prorsus reliqua etiam testamentorum sollemnitas perempta est. Testes enim huiusmodi morbo oppresso eo tempore iungi atque sociari remissum est, non etiam conveniendi numeri eorum observatio sublata.*

of this rescript was a letter from a certain Marcellinus, who questioned the emperor about the validity of a will made under extraordinary circumstances caused by a contagious disease.[177] The emperor thus met the legal certainty and, in the form of a constitution, laid down the conditions for such a will to be valid.

This constitution, however, differs in several modern editions of the Code, as some authors point out.[178] Others, on the other hand, call it controversial because of its unfortunate stylization.[179] The constitution to be found in the French edition is slightly different from the Berlin edition,[180] but in the end it gives a different interpretation. The interpretation differs substantially, in one case it is a will witnessed by an infected witness, in the other case it is a will made by an infected testator.[181]

Should the witness be infected, which might deter other witnesses from participating in the making of a proper will, healthy witnesses were exempted from participating in the act at the same time as contagious witnesses under one of the possible interpretations of the above constitution, but the other standard conditions for the making of a will had to be maintained. It follows from the constitution that, in order to protect the health of others, it was not necessary for all seven required witnesses to the will to be present at the same time in this extraordinary situation, so it was sufficient to call them in turn. It was thus not necessary in this case to preserve the aforementioned *unitas actus* or *unitas loci*, that is, the unity of place for all the participants.[182]

---

177 Koredczuk, J. (2021). 'Uprzywilejowane rozporządzenia ostatniej woli sporządzane podczas zarazy w prawie i orzecznictwie sądów byłego zaboru austriackiego w okresie międzywojennym'. Krakowskie Studia z Historii Państwa i Prawa, 14 (2), pp. 189–203, here: p. 190.
178 Kursa, S. P. (2020). 'Circumstances determining the preparation of a will in the event of a plague in roman law'. In Florek, I., Koroncziová, A., Zamora Manzano, J. L. (eds.). Crisis as a challenge for human rights. Bratislava: Comenius University in Bratislava, pp. 209–216, here: pp. 213–214.
179 Piętak, L. (1882). Prawo spadkowe rzymskie. Lwow: self-published, p. 237.
180 Kursa, S. P. (2020). 'Circumstances determining the preparation of a will in the event of a plague in roman law'. In Florek, I., Koroncziová, A., Zamora Manzano, J. L. (eds.). Crisis as a challenge for human rights. Bratislava: Comenius University in Bratislava, pp. 209–216, here: pp. 213, states his sources as follows: *Codex Iustinianus, Metz 1807* (translated by P.-A. Tissot) and *Corpus iuris civilis, editio stereotypa; t. II, Codex Iustinianus, rec. P. Krüger, Berlin 1959.*
181 Cf. Bonfante, P. (1932). Instituce římského práva (in original: Istituzioni di diritto romano). Transl. by Vážný, J. 9th ed. Brno: ČS. A. S. Právník, p. 638, fn. 82.
182 Koredczuk, J. (2021). 'Uprzywilejowane rozporządzenia ostatniej woli sporządzane podczas zarazy w prawie i orzecznictwie sądów byłego zaboru austriackiego w okresie

Some, however, do not support this interpretation and stress the fact that there was no obligation to become a witness to the will when called upon, and therefore a healthy testator could choose only healthy witnesses, or replace a contagious witness with another healthy one. Thus, in accordance with the Berlin edition, they see the importance in the constitution not for the infected witnesses but for the infected testator, who can thus leave a valid will even in the event of his contagious illness, although he cannot meet seven witnesses at once. S.P. Kursa thus proposes to use a more accurate term for this will – *testamentum oppressi morbo contagioso*.[183]

Other authors add that the regulation contained in the Code was already related to the earlier legal possibility of an infected testator whose last will was attested by witnesses not present in his immediate vicinity, but we are unable to date the origin of this norm.[184] Such legislation seemed to put infected testators on an equal footing with healthy ones, as well as to motivate the witnesses to the will of an infected testator to add their testimony and thus allow for the creation of a valid will.

Now, for a while, we will leave aside private law measures, law of succession in particular, as we are, chronologically, approaching the period of reign of the emperor Justinian. This is the time for which we have the most evidence regarding the issue of pandemics and, therefore, it is worth exploring this topic in depth. After a necessary introduction into the situation in sixth century AD and analysis of public law measures, we will turn back to hereditary law and the impact of pandemics on it.

Justinianic Plague

The reign of emperor Justinian I between 527 and 565 AD is usually identified with the imaginary golden age of legal science. During the study of law, probably no student missed the information that it was the emperor Justinian the Great who issued the largest codification of private law in history, later referred to as the *Corpus Iuris Civilis*, which consists of the Code, a collection of the imperial

---

międzywojennym'. Krakowskie Studia z Historii Państwa i Prawa, 14 (2), pp. 189–203, here: p. 191.
183 Kursa, S. P. (2020). 'Circumstances determining the preparation of a will in the event of a plague in roman law'. In Florek, I., Koroncziová, A., Zamora Manzano, J. L. (eds.). Crisis as a challenge for human rights. Bratislava: Comenius University in Bratislava, pp. 209–216, here: pp. 214–215.
184 Piętak, L. (1882). Prawo spadkowe rzymskie. Lwow: self-published, pp. 236–37.

decrees of virtually all the rulers of ancient Rome, the Digest, a collection of legal advice and pronouncements of classical Roman jurists, and the Institutions, a textbook of law intended for both the teaching of students and the practice of law. There is no doubt that Justinian's legislative activity has made history, nor that it was his codification that shaped the form of contemporary civil law in continental Europe and some other parts of the world. However, it is sometimes all too easy to forget that during the glory days of the emperor Justinian, Byzantium also suffered a severe blow of fate with catastrophic consequences for the whole society, the so-called Justinianic plague.[185]

It was a plague in the true sense of the word, caused by the rat-borne bacterium Yersinia pestis. The same bacterium was also behind the medieval Black Death that spread throughout Europe in the fourteenth century, and these plagues were so different from the great pandemics that had troubled the Roman Empire earlier, which led to the spread of diseases such as smallpox and measles. According to the prevailing belief, the Justinianic plague began to spread from present-day China, from where it was brought by Central Asian nomads. It probably reached Egypt via Central Africa and Ethiopia, where it was first recorded in 541 in the port of Pelusium at the eastern edge of the Nile delta and subsequently in Alexandria. From Egypt it then began to spread into the Byzantine Empire, and probably in late March and April 542 it broke out directly in Constantinople, where it raged until August.[186] But it continued to spread through Europe and the Middle East, gradually affecting Palestine, present-day Italy and even Britain. Unfortunately, the first wave of plague between 541 and 544, for which the name Justinianic plague is primarily used, did not exhaust the plague bacteria. The plague then returned many more times in subsequent waves in the following years, with 15 or 17 waves recorded between 541 and 749.[187] Emperor Justinian experienced yet a second wave of plague in Constantinople between February and July 558.

The extensive Justinian codification *Corpus Iuris Civilis* was completed several years before the outbreak of the Justinianic plague and does not provide

---

185 To Justinian's life see, e.g., Meier, M. (2004). Justinian. Herrschaft, Reich und Religion. München, C. H. Beck.
186 Stathakopoulos D. Ch. (2016). Famine And Pestilence In The Late Roman And Early Byzantine Empire: A Systematic Survey Of Subsistence Crises And Epidemics. London, New York, Routledge, pp. 114, 286–287.
187 Hays, J. N. (2005). Epidemics and Pandemics: Their Impacts on Human History. Santa Barbara, Denver, Oxford, ABC-CLIO, p. 23. Cf. also Wójcik, M. (2011). 'Plaga Justyniana. Cesarstwo wobec epidemii'. Zeszyty Prawnicze. 11 (1), pp. 377–401.

information on the impact of the pandemic and the legal measures taken by the famous emperor and the Byzantine Empire in response. What little information is given by the amendments, i.e., the imperial decrees issued after 534 AD, after the publication of the part of the Justinian codification called the Codex, which brought together the decrees issued up to that time in one place. However, extra-legal sources are a valuable source of knowledge, which, alongside a range of other information, also convey the development of the legal order and the impact of the plague on the law in force up to that time. Fortunately, several eyewitness accounts of the course of the Justinianic plague have survived to the present day. The Byzantine jurist, historian, and scholar Procopius, who came from Caesarea, the administrative center of Palestine at the time, provides relatively detailed information. By 540, he had taken part in the Byzantine campaign to Italy, and the plague caught him in Constantinople. In his essay, Books of Wars, he describes the helplessness of the city's inhabitants and their doctors, who were unable to identify the plague from its initial symptoms and subsequently to treat it.[188] It manifested itself in a variety of symptoms, including fever, hallucinations, swelling, falling unconscious and fits of madness. Although it attacked a significant number of people, the inhabitants of Constantinople at the time could not explain the key to the disease's attack on others and noted with surprise that while some died of the plague without close contact with the sick, some of the sick's caregivers survived the pandemic in good health. Interesting, then, are Procopius' references to the Justinianic plague in the Secret History of the Court of Justinian, where he discusses the more practical implications of the pandemic.[189] Probably the most extensive passage of the text compared to other eyewitness accounts is devoted to the plague by John of Ephesus, a Syrian of Monophysite persuasion, a monk, later to become a bishop. He wrote about the events in Constantinople in the second part of his Church History. Although this part of the writing has not survived in its original form, it fortunately formed a faithful model for the third book of a Syriac historiographical work dating from the late eighth century AD, known as the Chronicle of Zuqnin or Pseudo-Dionysius of Tel-Mahre Chronicle after its supposed unknown author.[190] He left

---

188 Procopius, History of the Wars 2.22. Procopius (1914). History of the wars, books I and II. With an English translation by H. B. Dewing. London, Heinemann.
189 Procopius (1896). The Secret History of the Court of Justinian: Literally and Completely Translated from the Greek for the First Time. Athens, Athenian Society.
190 Pseudo-Dionysius of Tel-Mahre (1996). Chronicle (known also as the Chronicle of Zuqnin), Part III. Translated with notes and introduction by Witold Witakonwski. Liverpool, Liverpool University Press.

accounts of immeasurable human suffering and, like Procopius, described the symptoms of disease.

Another Syrian scholar, Evagrius Scholasticus, also described the suffering he witnessed in his book Ecclesiastical History. He himself contracted the plague in his childhood and was fortunate to recover from it, but others were not so fortunate: "Thus it happened in my own case for I deem it fitting, in due adaptation of circumstances, to insert also in this history matters relating to myself that at the commencement of this calamity I was seized with what are termed buboes, while still a school-boy, and lost by its recurrence at different times several of my children, my wife, and many of my kin, as well as of my domestic and country servants; the several indications making, as it were, a distribution of my misfortunes."[191] The Byzantine historian Agathias Scholasticus then in his Histories completes the picture of the destruction by mentioning a second wave of plague, which, however, was very similar to the first wave in its manifestations and consequences. Again, he explicitly notes the erratic nature of the disease, which varied from person to person in the severity of its course and the speed of death: "People died in great numbers as though seized by a violent and sudden attack of apoplexy. Those who stood up to the disease longest barely lasted five days. (...) Some experienced no pain or fever or any of the initial symptoms but simply dropped dead while about their normal business at home or in the street or wherever they happened to be."[192] The Justinianic plague was a devastation hardly imaginable today, terrifying not only in its scale but also in its apparent mystery to the people of the time. The multiplicity of manifestations and courses of the disease, the different immune reactions, the primarily illogical way in which the infection spread – all of this only added to the fear and real impact of the pandemic on society, which had to respond to the plague with legal instruments, among other things. It goes without saying that first and foremost, the mass deaths in the cities had to be dealt with for hygiene reasons.

---

191 Evagrius Scholasticus (1846). Ecclesiastical History. A History of the Church in six books from A. D. 431 to A. D. 594. Translated by E. Walford. London, Samuel Bagster and sons, p. 224.
192 Agathias, The Histories, 5.10. Agathias (1975). The Histories. Translated with an introduction and short explanatory notes by Joseph D. Frendo. Berlin, New York, Walter de Gruyter.

Necessary Measures

Procopius of Caesarea estimates the number of dead in Constantinople at over 10,000 a day,[193] John of Ephesus even at 16,000.[194] These figures must be taken with a grain of salt in view of the difficulty with which ancient authors would have verified their authenticity. But they nevertheless make it clear that the numbers of the dead were staggering, and that Byzantium could not have been prepared in advance for the sudden death of so many people. Thus, the measures taken in response to the increasing number of dead on the streets of Constantinople were by their nature crisis-oriented and opted for the better of the bad options.

It is understandable that at the height of the pandemic, there was a growing public interest in burying the dead quickly, as the remains of the sick threatened the health of the survivors. However, this tendency was nothing new and, together with the emphasis on the inviolability of human remains, it is recognizable in the norms of Roman law even before the outbreak of the Justinianic plague. Already the Digest fragment attributed to the classical jurist Papinianus, states that it is the public interest that requires that the bodies of the dead should not be left unburied (*propter publicam utilitatem, ne insepulta cadavera iacerent*).[195] The prohibitory interdicts *de mortuo inferendo* and *de sepulchro aedificando*[196] assured the beneficiary of carrying out the burial, or building the tomb, and forbade a third party from preventing this using force. Moreover, whoever, with the help of a mob, forcibly prevented the burial was, as is expressly reported, punished on the basis of the *lex Iulia de vi publica*.[197] Ulpianus stressed the role of the provincial administrator, whose tasks included checking that burials were not prevented: "Ne corpora aut ossa mortuorum detinerentur aut vexarentur neve prohiberentur quo minus via publica transferrentur aut quominus sepelirentur, praesidis provinciae officium est."[198] The above mentioned fragment illustrates that the timely burial of human remains was central to the maintenance of public order, and that the ancient jurists were well aware of this aspect.

---

193 Procopius, History of the Wars 2.23.
194 Pseudo-Dionysius of Tel-Mahre (1996). Chronicle (known also as the Chronicle of Zuqnin), Part III. Translated with notes and introduction by Witold Witakonwski. Liverpool, Liverpool University Press, p. 86.
195 D. 11.7.43 (Papinianus 8 quaest.).
196 D. 11.8.1.5 (Ulpianus 68 ad ed.).
197 D. 48.6.5pr. (Marcianus 14 inst.).
198 D. 11.7.38 (Ulpianus 9 de omn. trib.).

The extensive matter also dealt with the determination of the persons who were obliged to perform the burial and the detailed rules for the compensation of the costs of the burial. In the first place, this obligation lay with the mandatary with whom the testator had agreed on the burial during his lifetime. Otherwise, the burial was to be arranged in turn by the testamentary heirs, by operation of law, or by blood relatives.[199]

After the actual burial of the body, the interest in the undisturbed rest of the deceased is evident from Roman law sources. The *actio sepulchri violati* of classical law was an important means of achieving this goal. Although, literally speaking, this penal action served to preserve the tomb itself as a thing consecrated, it is clear that the true purpose was to protect the human remains deposited inside. That special attention was paid to their preservation is evidenced by the very existence of this action, which was *lex specialis* to the *actio legis Aquiliae*, and to which anyone, not just, for example, the owner of the tomb, was actively entitled as *actio popularis*.[200] This *actio* for violation of the tomb also entailed *infamia*.[201] This private law tort was transformed into a public law *crimen* during the imperial period. In addition to the facts, which included various ways of damaging tombs and removing building materials, explicit mention was also made of situations in which the perpetrator removed a dead body or bones from a tomb (*corpora ipsa extraxerint vel ossa eruerint*), robbed or stripped a corpse (*cadavera spoliant*) or merely touched it (*corpora sepulta aut reliquias contrectaverint*).[202] The literal inviolability of the dead body is illustrated by Marcian's fragment from the Digest, according to which a damaged tomb could only be reconstructed in such a way that the builders did not touch the deposited bodies: "Sepulchri deteriorem condicionem fieri prohibitum est: sed corruptum et lapsum monumentum corporibus non contactis licet reficere."[203] But there were other means of protection. To prevent any illicit action in connection with tombs as consecrated things, the *interdictum ne quid in loco sacro fiat* had passage, and for cases of clandestine or violent action the *interdictum quod vi aut clam*.[204] Further, the heirs or *bonorum possessores* could defend against *inuria* if

---

199 D. 11.7.14.2 (Ulpianus 25 ad ed.), D. 11.7.12.4 (Ulpianus 25 ad ed.).
200 D. 47.12.3.12 (Ulpianus 25 ad ed. praet.).
201 D. 47.12.1 (Ulpianus 2 ad ed. praet.)
202 D. 47.12.11 (Paulus 5 sent.), D. 47.12.3.7 (Ulpianus 25 ad ed. praet.), C. 9.19.4.3 (a. 357), C. Th. 9.17.4 (a. 357).
203 D. 47.12.7 (Marcianus 3 inst.).
204 D. 47.12.2 (Ulpianus 18 ad ed. praet.), D. 43.6.1pr. (Ulpianus 68 ad ed.).

the tort was committed against the body of the deceased or to the detriment of his public reputation. Although they brought the action in their own name and felt the injury to themselves, the deceased person was also protected.[205]

Regarding the topic of burial, it is also worth mentioning another aspect this paper deals with – limitation of ownership. It might be necessary to establish the servitude of the way (*iter ad sepuchrum; servitus itineris as sepulchrum*) in case the land through which there is an approach to the tomb is not in the ownership of the person entitled to procure the tomb. From the times of the emperor Antoninus and his father, the rule was introduced, that the person who has a tomb but no right of way to it and the access was denied by a neighbor, may reach it thanks to the *precarium* (*iter ad sepulchrum peti precario et concedi solere*), moreover, such a person can request by an extraordinary process (*cognitio extra ordinem*) to be given a right of way in return for a fair price.[206] *Iter ad sepulchrum* is never lost by a nonuse (*non usu*).[207]

During the Justinianic plague, however, the normal rules for burials were not sufficient, because relatives or other legal persons were not able to take care of the burials. Emperor Justinian therefore resorted to massive public support for the removal of dead bodies from the streets and their burial. Procopius and John of Ephesus report that the emperor entrusted the organization of this activity to his secretary Theodore, whose usual tasks were to pass on imperial orders and receive requests from the population: "And it fell to the lot of the emperor, as was natural, to make provision for the trouble. He therefore detailed soldiers from the palace and distributed money, commanding Theodorus to take charge of this work... But Theodorus, by giving out the emperor's money and by making further expenditures from his own purse, kept burying the bodies which were not cared for. And when it came about that all the tombs which had existed previously were filled with the dead, then they dug up all the places about the city one after the other, buried the dead there, each one as he could, and departed."[208] Theodorus financially encouraged the inhabitants to engage in burying bodies and digging new graves, and he himself organized the work: "This man proceeded with application. He crossed (the bay) northward to the other shore called Sykai and climbed the mountain which was above the city. He took along many people, gave them much gold and had very large pits dug, in every one of which 70,000

---

205 D. 47.10.1.4 (Ulpianus 56 ad ed.).
206 D. 11.7.12pr (Ulpianus 25 ad ed.). Cf. Also D. 47.12.5 (Pomp. 6 de Plaut.)
207 D. 8.6.4 (Paulus 27 ad ed.).
208 Procopius, History of the Wars 2.23.

(corpses) were put. He placed there (some) men who brought down and turned over (the corpses), piled them up and pressed the layers one upon another as a man might heap up hay in a stack."[209] He sought out new burial sites, and after the capacity ran out, he even had the dead bodies fill the towers of the fortifications at Sycae by exposing their roofs. This practice soon backfired on the surviving inhabitants, however, when the remains began to decompose and the stench from them took over the area.

While the emperor did not hesitate to generously reward all those who took part in the removal of dead bodies, there are accounts that criticize the practice in a moralizing manner. Not only in classical Roman law, but especially in Christian culture, which was already firmly rooted in sixth-century Constantinople, not only the places where the dead and the human remains themselves were laid to rest, but also the very process of placing them in the grave, was seen as sacred. It was a service to one's neighbor, an act of Christian charity, and it could therefore be seen as problematic if one accepted money for this act, which was removed from normal human activities. John of Ephesus describes discouraging cases of people who were diligently engaged in the work of clearing away the human remains but were motivated more by greed than by a desire to help others. They did not hesitate to actively ask Theodore for a large reward, but they did not enjoy it for long because they died shortly after receiving it themselves. Certainly a logical explanation is offered that the people disposing of the dead bodies of those who died of the plague were at extreme risk of contagion and their deaths seem almost a statistical necessity; however, in these moralistic stories their deaths are referred to as divine punishment to penalize their greed: "Such was the message of that angel who was ordered to fight people with this scourge until they should spurn all matters of this world-if not of their own will, then against it-so that everybody who might incite his mind to revolt, and still covet things of this world, was by him quickly deprived of life."[210] The plague, then, was seen as an instrument of divine warning, showing that people should devote efforts to their salvation in the event of sudden death, rather than to the accumulation of possessions and fixation on the comforts of the temporal

---

209 Pseudo-Dionysius of Tel-Mahre (1996). Chronicle (known also as the Chronicle of Zuqnin), Part III. Translated with notes and introduction by Witold Witakonwski. Liverpool, Liverpool University Press, p. 91.
210 Pseudo-Dionysius of Tel-Mahre (1996). Chronicle (known also as the Chronicle of Zuqnin), Part III. Translated with notes and introduction by Witold Witakonwski. Liverpool, Liverpool University Press, p. 95.

world. As understandable as Justinian's political decision to use money to support the preservation of public health and order is, it was arguably contrary to noble moral principles.

Procopius explicitly mentions that even the traditional burial rituals, which had been prescribed by the existing legislation, could not be observed out of necessity: "At that time all the customary rites of burial were overlooked. For the dead were not carried out escorted by a procession in the customary manner, nor were the usual chants sung over them, but it was sufficient if one carried on his shoulders the body of one of the dead to the parts of the city which bordered on the sea and flung him down; and there the corpses would be thrown upon skiffs in a heap, to be conveyed wherever it might chance."[211] With regard to the dignity of the handling of human remains, it is worth noting reports that the bodies of the dead were also thrown into the sea: "What was most pressing of all was simply that everybody who was still alive should remove corpses from his house, and that also other (corpses) should disappear from the streets by being removed to the seashore. There boats were filled with them and during each sailing they were thrown overboard and the ships returned to take other (corpses)."[212] Such conduct was not explicitly considered sufficiently dignified in the sources of Roman law before the pandemic broke out. This is evidenced by a passage attributed to the classical Roman jurist Modestinus, which has in fact been interpolated to a greater extent and illustrates the rather more recent approach of Justinian law, much more sensitive to the dignified treatment of human remains.[213] It deals with the testator's wish that his body be thrown into the sea after death. In the first place, doubt is expressed about the mental health of such a testator. If it were not clearly established, the condition would not be valid. The text also commends the attitude of the heir, which is an expression of humanity, a kind of basic humane standard for the treatment of a dead body: "Laudandus est magis quam accusandus heres, qui reliquias testatoris non in mare secundum ipsius voluntatem abiecit, sed memoria humanae condicionis sepulturae tradidit."[214] Nevertheless, it must be admitted that the passage in question does not

---

211 Procopius, History of the Wars 2.23.
212 Pseudo-Dionysius of Tel-Mahre (1996). Chronicle (known also as the Chronicle of Zuqnin), Part III. Translated with notes and introduction by Witold Witakonwski. Liverpool, Liverpool University Press, pp. 88–89.
213 Levy, E., Rabel, E. (1931). Index interpolationum quae in Iustiniani Digestis inesse dicuntur, Tomus II. Weimar, Hermann Böhlaus Nachfolger, p. 205.
214 D. 28.7.27pr. (Modestinus 8 resp.).

exclude the situation where the remains would have been thrown into the sea as a matter of right, if the testator had indeed been found sane. This, however, was evidently not considered to be a frequent case.

Ownership Restrictions and Other Legal Regulations

The Justinianic plague also had a significant impact on the sphere of property law and changed property relations. Procopius does not forget to report that the increased mortality rate naturally caused many slaves to find themselves without a master. It is worth recalling that slavery was widespread in ancient Rome, and the same was true of sixth century AD Byzantium. Slaves were then not the subjects of law, but only its objects, the objects of property law serving their owner, the free man. Only in exceptional situations was it taken into account that even a slave, as a thing, was biologically human and deserved special treatment different from ordinary things. An example of such equalization of slaves and freemen are the identical rules for the disposal of their bodily remains after death, since both the body of a free man and the body of a slave made the place of their burial *res religiosa*, thus exempting it from trade and free disposal in general. During the Justinianic plague, however, many slaves survived their masters and potential heirs. They thus became *res nullius*, things without a master, incapable of any legal action, endowed with no rights, and free for anyone to occupy and appropriate: "For slaves remained destitute of masters, and men who in former times were very prosperous were deprived of the service of their domestics who were either sick or dead, and many houses became completely destitute of human inhabitants."[215]

In the general chaos and as a result of the extinction of entire families, a considerable amount of property, both movable and immovable, was left without an owner. Their free availability led to a wave of looting, which earned strong criticism from John of Ephesus. He presents a series of moralizing stories that ascribe an unflattering end to the thieves – an early death. For example, we can mention the story of the men with a small boy who decided to take advantage of an easy opportunity to make money and robbed the houses of rich deceased townspeople: "For three days they gathered only gold and silver and with it filled one large house. On the third day (when) they were carrying (the booty) and entering the house, there, inside the house, (God's) wrath came upon them. Immediately they fell and all of them except that little boy within one hour perished

---

215 Procopius, History of the Wars 2.23.

on top of (the booty) they had gathered."[216] The boy, who perhaps because of his young age and lack of moral experience survived, was nevertheless pursued by supernatural forces and spirits.

The economic consequences of the Justinian plague resulted from the sharp decline in the workforce, the chaos caused by the abandonment of large numbers of property and slaves, the destruction of property and trades, and the disruption of supply chains. A serious manifestation of this was the decline in the empire's tax revenues. However, the solution to this problem chosen by the emperor Justinian seems highly insensitive and questionable. Unlike the measures to bury the dead, where he clearly acted in the interest of the public good, he did not act as a positive hero in dealing with the decline in tax revenues, because he was more concerned with his own interest in supplying the treasury and had no regard for the taxpayers who were severely affected by the blow of fate. Procopius, in his treatise The Secret History of the Court of Justinian, describes that Justinian, even before the outbreak of the plague, was strict about tax collection and allowed no concessions. He refused to take advantage of the established custom whereby the emperor could remit part of the tax liability of the people in need, which, according to Procopius, led to the forced departure of some poor people abroad. Nor did he show sympathy for the population, which was subjected to military attacks by barbarians, sieges, and short-term occupation. He consistently demanded that they pay their taxes, even though their property was destroyed by the soldiers and some of their relatives were slaughtered or taken into slavery. "Justinian only granted this absurd remission of tribute to these people and to others who had several times submitted to an invasion of the Medes and the continuous depredations of the Huns and Saracen barbarians in the East, while the Romans, settled in the different parts of Europe, who had equally suffered by the attacks of the barbarians, found Justinian more cruel than any of their foreign foes..."[217] The plague then brought no change in Justinian's attitude, according to remaining information.[218] Although a number of farmers

---

216 Pseudo-Dionysius of Tel-Mahre (1996). Chronicle (known also as the Chronicle of Zuqnin), Part III. Translated with notes and introduction by Witold Witakonwski. Liverpool, Liverpool University Press, p. 78.
217 Procopius, The Secret History of the Court of Justinian 23. Procopius (1896). The Secret History of the Court of Justinian: Literally and Completely Translated from the Greek for the First Time. Athens, Athenian Society.
218 Sarris, P. (2006). 'Bubonic Plague in Byzantium: The Evidence of Non-Literary Sources'. In Little, L. K. (ed.). Plague and the End of Antiquity: The Pandemic of 541–750, pp. 119–134. Cambridge, Cambridge University Press.

fell victim to the plague and their estates were abandoned, Justinian refused to waive the land tax they should normally have paid. He therefore imposed their tax liability on their neighbors who managed to survive the plague.[219] The survivors were in effect punished by the emperor, and the recovery of their farming activities after the pandemic had subsided was made much more difficult.

In the sources of the law, there is evidence of Justinian's action against inflation, the growth of which was triggered by the pandemic. In the *Edictum de constitutione artificum* of 23rd March 544, which is included in the collection *Novellae* under number 122, he lamented the "avarice" of artisans, workmen, traders and farmers who increased the prices of their goods and services to double or triple the original state and forbade this practice. He ordered them to stick to the original prices according to the ancient custom: "Placuit igitur nobis per sacrum edictum omnibus eiusmodi avaritiam interdicere, neve ullus in posterum negotiator aut agricola aut artifex ex quacumque arte vel negotiatione vel agricultura maiora quam secundum veterem consuetudinem pretia mercedesve exigere."[220] But Justinian did not stop at price regulation and also tried to prevent inflation by freezing wages. He ordered that those who measure building-work, farm-work or other work shall not allow a greater amount to the workmen but shall observe the ancient custom. This was to be observed also by those who let out any work or undertake any on contract. Here too all payments were limited by the pre-Justinian plague limit. Violation of the rules contained in the edict was punishable by a fine of three times the amount required, which was determined to fisc.

Justinian was apparently inspired by emperor Diocletian's *Edictum de pretiis rerum venalium* of 301 AD, which was also intended to counteract the rise in inflation.[221] Diocletian's regulation was not to deal with the plague but with the consequences of monetary reform and the increasing financial demands on the state apparatus and the army. The edict, however, was silent on the true causes and blamed the alleged greed of merchants who were supposedly stealing from their customers by charging exorbitant prices. He took a very detailed approach to price regulation. The edict first contains an extensive justification of the regulation adopted, describing the emperor's motives and the alleged culprits. This is

---

219 Procopius, The Secret History of the Court of Justinian 23.
220 Nov. 122.
221 Graser, E. R. (1940). 'A text and translation of the Edict of Diocletian'. In Frank T. (ed.). An Economic Survey of Ancient Rome Volume V: Rome and Italy of the Empire (1st ed.). Baltimore, Johns Hopkins Press.

followed by a detailed inventory of 1,200 items, setting out the maximum prices allowed. It is the tables with this tariff that are found in archaeological excavations of former marketplaces. Massive restrictions on property rights and free trade were accompanied by draconian punishment, with violation of Diocletian's edict punishable by death. Compared to the edict of emperor Diocletian, Justinian was minimalist and did not proceed to calculate specific price limits by means of a tariff. Similarly, the punishments prescribed by Justinian fell short of the severity of his predecessor. However, the fact that Justinian resorted to price regulation at all suggests that he did not learn from the fate of Diocletian's edict, which ultimately proved counterproductive and led to its early abolition. During the reign of the emperor Diocletian, the prescribed price limits were violated on a massive scale, the low official prices caused the Roman Empire to suffer from a shortage of goods and, as a result, the price of goods on the black market rose even more dramatically. This dismal state of affairs was further exacerbated by attacks on merchants who violated Diocletian's decrees and their killing by angry customers.[222] The unfortunate consequences of Diocletian's fight against inflation were also noted by the Church Father Lucius Caecilius Firmianus Lactantius in the treatise On the Deaths of the Persecutors: "When, because of his iniquities, he made things extremely high-priced, he attempted to fix by law the price of saleable goods. Then, on account of scarcity and the low grade of articles, much blood was spilled; and because of fear nothing purchaseable appeared. Therefore, expensiveness raged much worse, until, after the death of many, the law was dissolved by sheer necessity."[223]

Leaving aside the extra-legal sources mentioning the legal regulation adopted as a result of the plague, there is only one other source of law mentioning the pandemic during the reign of emperor Justinian. This is the *Edictum Iustiniani ad Constantinopolitanos De luxuriantibus contra naturam*, included as Novella 141 in the post-Justinian collection, which led to a more consistent sanctioning of homosexual behavior. It dates from March 559 and does not respond directly to the Justinianic plague, but to the second wave of the pandemic that struck Constantinople during 558. Justinian regarded it as a divine punishment to atone for the sins of the city's inhabitants. After the pandemic had subsided, he then

---

222 Schuettinger, R. L., Butler, E. F. (1979). Forty Centuries of Wage and Price Controls: How Not To Fight Inflation. Washington D. C., The Heritage Foundation, pp. 20–26.
223 Lactantius, On the Deaths of the Persecutors VII. Lactantius (1965). The Minor Works. Washington, Catholic University of America Press, p. 143.

deemed it necessary to outlaw and punish more severely the alleged worst cases of sinful behavior, so that the second wave of plague would result in a turning away of the inhabitants from their sins and not a third wave: "Scimus enim ex sacris scripturis edocti, quale deus iustum supplicium iis qui Sodomis olim habitarunt, propter hunc in commixtione furorem intulerit, adeo ut in hunc usque diem regio illa inextincto igni ardeat, cum deus per hoc nos erudiat, ut impiam istam actionem aversemur."[224] The link between the pandemic and the punishment of homosexual behavior is sometimes questioned by pointing to earlier legislation that preceded the Justinianic plague, which also persecuted not only sexual minorities but also Jews, pagans and heretics.[225] There is no doubt that this sanction had occurred before; it was certainly not a new idea. However, it is worth pointing out that the edict itself makes a causal connection between the plague and the alleged need to impose punishment and was clearly driven by this intention.

Justinian set out for his reign following priorities: unification of state, strengthening of religious unity and reform of law.

Regarding the latter, the legislation reflecting plague found its place only in the *Novellae*, the collection of imperial constitutions issued after the publication of *Codex Iustinianus repetitae praelectionis*. The contagion that was decimating the population of the time increased the number of deaths by leaps and bounds, which raised, beside the others already mentioned, burning questions about the functionality of the existing law of succession.

The first reactions to the ongoing Justinianic plague were reflected in a constitution found in a fragment of Novellae 115 of 542 AD. This constitution significantly modified the obligatory share and thus achieved a unification of the existing legislation, which had been very fragmented. The inalienable rights of inheritance enshrined in this constitution were both formal and substantive rights of inheritance; it was therefore incumbent not only to honor the inalienable heir by mentioning him in the will, but also to provide for a certain share in the estate. It was an honor which the testator had thus shown and had to show to the heir. There was only a minor exception to this principle, namely if the heir had been duly disinherited. It was the disinheritance which was also dealt with in this constitution, and it set out exhaustively the reasons which justified

---

224 Nov. 141.
225 Stathakopoulos, D. (2006). 'Crime and Punishment. The Plague in the Byzantine Empire, 541–749'. In Lester K. Little (ed.), Plague and the End of Antiquity the Pandemic of 541–750, pp. 99–118. Cambridge: Cambridge University Press, p. 113.

such disinheritance. For each particular disinheritance, then, such a reason had necessarily to be stated and, in particular, justified. The emperor himself states in the constitution that the reason for the exhaustive statement of the grounds for disinheritance is the fragmentation of the grounds in the numerous previous provisions and the resulting legal uncertainty for the testator and the heirs. Thus, it set out 14 specific possible grounds for disinheritance of a descendant, and 8 grounds for disinheritance of an ancestor.

Justinian's generous contribution to the law of succession was the important *Novella* 118, which was adopted only a year later. Along with it, *Novella* 127 of 548 AD also contributed to changes in the law of succession. The determining kinship for the intestate succession was cognatic, i.e., by blood, as well as the equalization of men and women, married and illegitimate children, as well as *persons sui iuris* and *persons alieni iuris* who were subject to foreign power. The first class of intestate succession belonged exclusively to the descendants of the testator, i.e., in particular to the children, or to their children if the children died before the testator. In the second class, the ancestors inherited, the closer ones before the more distant ones. Full siblings were then called alongside the ancestors of the nearest degree. In the third class, full siblings were called again, but without parents. If there were no such siblings, half siblings or their children were called. The last fourth class of inheritance included other blood (cognate) relatives, where the nearer ones were called before the more distant ones; in the case of the same degree, the estate was then divided by heads.

The contagious diseases that plagued the ancient and early medieval world undoubtedly had great impact on the law. It is no coincidence that it can be seen in the field of the law of succession, which is necessarily linked to the death of the testator, and pandemics naturally increased the number of succession cases. Roman law reacted to the situation by introducing the so-called plague will, which was intended to facilitate the establishment of a valid will during a pandemic and thus protect the testator and the witnesses necessarily present. The reforms of the emperor Justinian, which were adopted even after the contagious disease had begun to spread through his empire, then amended the law of succession, unifying the existing legislation and bringing a greater degree of legal certainty.

References

Agathias (1975). The Histories. Translated with an introduction and short explanatory notes by Joseph D. Frendo. Berlin, New York, Walter de Gruyter.

Andreau, J. (1999). Banking and business in the Roman world. Cambridge, Cambridge University Press.

Andreau, J. (2008). 'The Use and Survival of Coins and of Gold and Silver in the Vesuvian Cities'. In Harris, W. V. (ed). The monetary systems of the Greeks and Romans, Oxford, Oxford University Press, pp. 208–225.

Barlow, C. T. (1978). Bankers, Moneylenders, and Interest Rates in the Roman Republic (diss., University of North Carolina), Chapel Hill.

Barlow, C. T. (1980). 'The Roman Government and the Roman Economy, 92–80 B.C.'. The American Journal of Philology, 101(2), pp. 202–219.

Baron, C. (2012). Timaeus of Tauromenium and Hellenistic Historiography. Cambridge, Cambridge University Press.

Bonfante, P. (1932). Instituce římského práva. Transl. by Vážný, J. 9th ed. Brno: ČS. A. S. Právník.

Broughton, T. R. S. (1951). The Magistrates of the Roman Republic, vol. I. New York, The American Philological Association.

Collins, A., Walsh, J. (2014). 'Fractional Reserve Banking in the Roman Republic and Empire'. Ancient Society, 44, pp. 179–212.

Collins, A., Walsh, J. (2015). 'Debt Deflationary Crisis in the Late Roman Republic'. Ancient Society, 45.

Crawford, M.H. (1985). Coinage and Money Under the Roman Republic: Italy and the Mediterranean Economy. Berkeley, Los Angeles: Univ. California Press.

Comparette, T. L. (1918). 'Aes Signatum', American Journal of Numismatics (1897–1924), 52, pp. 1–61.

Dart, Ch. J. 'The 'Italian Constitution' in the Social War: A Reassessment (91 to 88 BCE).' Historia: Zeitschrift Für Alte Geschichte, 58(2), pp. 215–224.

Decock, W. (2019). Le marché du mérite: Penser le droit et l'économie avec Léonard Lessius. Bruxelles: Zones sensibles.

Duncan-Jones, R. (1994). Money and Government in the Roman Empire. Cambridge: Cambridge University Press.

Dvorský, V. (2020). 'Ochrana vkladatelů v právu římském'. In Tauchen, J. (ed.). VIII. česko-slovenské právněhistorické setkání doktorandů a postdoktorandů: sborník z conference. Brno: MUNI press, pp. 97–107.

Elliott, C. P. (2015). 'The Crisis of A.D. 33: past and present'. Journal of Ancient History, 3(2), pp. 267–281.

Evagrius Scholasticus (1846). Ecclesiastical History. A History of the Church in six books from A. D. 431 to A. D. 594. Translated by E. Walford. London, Samuel Bagster and sons.

Evans, J. D. (1992). The Art of Persuasion: Political Propaganda from Aeneas to Brutus. Ann Arbor, University of Michigan Press.

Finley, M. I. (1985). The Ancient Economy. London: Hogarth Press.

Frank, T. (1935). 'The Financial Crisis of 33 A. D.'. The American Journal of Philology. 56(4), pp. 336–341.

Frederick, S., Loewenstein, G., O'Donoghue, T. (2002). 'Time Discounting and Time Preference: A Critical Review'. Journal of Economic Literature, 40(2), pp. 351–401.

Frederiksen M. W. (1966). 'Cicero, Caesar and the Problem of Debt'. The Journal of Roman Studies, 56, pp. 128–141.

Graser, E. R. (1940). 'A text and translation of the Edict of Diocletian'. In Frank T. (ed.). An Economic Survey of Ancient Rome Volume V: Rome and Italy of the Empire (1st ed.). Baltimore, Johns Hopkins Press.

Harper, K. (2017). The Fate of Rome. Climate, Disease, and the End of an Empire. Princeton (NJ), Oxford, Princeton University Press.

Harris, W. V. (2006). 'A Revisionist View of Roman Money'. The Journal of Roman Studies, 96, pp. 1–24

Harris, W. V. (2019). 'Credit-Money in the Roman Economy'. Klio, 101 (1), pp. 158–189.

Hays, J. N. (2005). Epidemics and Pandemics: Their Impacts on Human History. Santa Barbara, Denver, Oxford, ABC-CLIO.

Heyrovský, L. (1910). Dějiny a systém soukromého práva římského. Praha: J. Otto.

Hollander, D. B. (2007). Money in the Late Roman Republic. Leiden, The Netherlands, Brill.

Huerta de Soto, J. (2020). Money, Bank Credit, and Economic Cycles. Auburn, Ludwig von Mises institute.

Hülsmann, J. G. (2008). The ethics of money production. Auburn: Ludwig von Mises institute.

Kaser, M. (1955). Das römische Privatrecht. Erster Abschnitt. Das altrömische, das vorklassische und klassische Recht. München, C. H. Beck'sche Verlagsbuchhandlung.

Kaser, M. (1971). Das römische Privatrecht. München, C. H. Beck.

Kaser, M., Hackl, K. (1996). Das römische Zivilprozessrecht. München, C. H. Beck.

Kay, P. (2014). Rome's economic revolution. Oxford: Oxford University Press.

Koredczuk, J. (2021). 'Uprzywilejowane rozporządzenia ostatniej woli sporządzane podczas zarazy w prawie i orzecznictwie sądów byłego zaboru austriackiego w okresie międzywojennym'. Krakowskie Studia z Historii Państwa i Prawa, 14 (2), pp. 189–203.

Kursa, S. P. (2020). 'Circumstances determining the preparation of a will in the event of a plague in roman law'. In Florek, I., Koroncziová, A., Zamora Manzano, J. L. (eds.). Crisis as a challenge for human rights. Bratislava: Comenius University in Bratislava, pp. 209–216.

Lactantius (1965). The Minor Works. Washington, Catholic University of America Press.

Levy, E., Rabel, E. (1931). Index interpolationum quae in Iustiniani Digestis inesse dicuntur, Tomus II. Weimar, Hermann Böhlaus Nachfolger.

Mankiw, N. G. (2018). Principles of Economics. Boston, Cengage Learning.

Meier, M. (2004). Justinian. Herrschaft, Reich und Religion. München, C. H. Beck.

Menger, C. (2009). On the Origins of Money. Auburn, Ludwig von Mises institute, pp. 239–55.

Mises, L. von (1998). Human Action. Auburn, Ludwig von Mises institute.

Mommsen, T. (1922). Römische Geschichte. Band 3, Von Sullas Tode bis zur Schlacht von Thapsus. Berlin, Deutsche Buch-Gemeinschaft.

Moore, T. J. (1998). The Theater of Plautus. Playing to the Audience. Austin, University of Texas Press.

Omlor, S. (2014). Geldprivatrecht. Tübingen, Mohr Siebeck.

Piętak, L. (1882). Prawo spadkowe rzymskie. Lwow: self-published.

Procopius (1896). The Secret History of the Court of Justinian: Literally and Completely Translated from the Greek for the First Time. Athens, Athenian Society.

Procopius (1914). History of the wars, books I and II. With an English translation by H. B. Dewing. London, Heinemann.

Pseudo-Dionysius of Tel-Mahre (1996). Chronicle (known also as the Chronicle of Zuqnin), Part III. Translated with notes and introduction by Witold Witakonwski. Liverpool, Liverpool University Press.

Royer, J.-P. (1967). 'Le problème des dettes a la fin de la République romaine'. Revue historique de droit français et étranger. 45, pp. 191–240 and pp. 407–450.

Salmon, E. T. (1958). 'Notes on the Social War'. In Transactions and Proceedings of the American Philological Association, 89. Baltimore, Johns Hopkins University Press, pp. 159–184.

Sarris, P. (2006). 'Bubonic Plague in Byzantium: The Evidence of Non-Literary Sources'. In Little, L. K. (ed.). Plague and the End of Antiquity: The Pandemic of 541-750, pp. 119-134. Cambridge, Cambridge University Press.

Schuettinger, R. L., Butler, E. F. (1979). Forty Centuries of Wage and Price Controls: How Not To Fight Inflation. Washington D. C., The Heritage Foundation.

Sear, D. R. (1988). Roman Coins and Their Values. London, Spink Books.

Shump, S. (2011). 'The Senatus Consultum Ultimum and its Relation to Late Republican History'. Summer Research. Paper 99.

Smith, W. (1875). A Dictionary of Greek and Roman Antiquities. London, John Murray.

Stathakopoulos, D. (2006). 'Crime and Punishment. The Plague in the Byzantine Empire, 541-749'. In Lester K. Little (ed.), Plague and the End of Antiquity the Pandemic of 541-750, pp. 99-118. Cambridge: Cambridge University Press

Stathakopoulos D. Ch. (2016). Famine And Pestilence In The Late Roman And Early Byzantine Empire: A Systematic Survey Of Subsistence Crises And Epidemics. London, New York, Routledge.

Thornton, M. K., Thornton, R. L. (1990). 'The Financial Crisis of A.D. 33: A Keynesian Depression?'. The Journal of Economic History. 50(3), pp. 655-662.

Verboven, K. (1997). 'Caritas Nummorum. Deflation in the Late Roman Republic?'. Münstersche Beiträge Zur Antiken Handelsgeschichte, 16.

Verboven, K. (2003). '54-44 BCE: Financial or Monetary Crisis?'. In: Lo Caseio, E. (ed). Credito e moneta nel mondo romano. Atti degli Incontri capresi di storia dell'economia antica (Capri, 12-14 ottobre 2000). Bari: Edipuglia, pp. 49-68

Verboven, K. (2009). 'Currency, Bullion and Accounts Monetary Modes in the Roman World'. Belgisch Tijdschrift voor Numismatiek en Zegelkunde/Revue Belge de Numismatique et de Sigillograph, 155, pp. 91-121.

Watson, A. (1984). 'The Evolution of Law: The Roman System of Contracts'. Law and History Review, 2(1), pp. 1-2.

Wójcik, M. (2011). 'Plaga Justyniana. Cesarstwo wobec epidemii'. Zeszyty Prawnicze. 11 (1), pp. 377-401.

Woytek, B. (2003). Arma et Nummi, Forschungen zur römischen Finanzgeschichte und Münzprägung der Jahre 49 bis 42 v. Chr. Vienna: Verlag der österreichischen Akademie der Wissenschaften, pp. 218-310.

Zimmermann, R. (1990). The Law of Obligations: Roman Foundations of the Civilian Tradition. Cape Town, Juta.

T. Blažková and J. Šouša

Selected Aspects of the Legal Regulations of Epidemics in the Czech Lands in the Period from the Nineteenth Century to the Year 1948

Introduction

When the global pandemic of COVID-19 caused by the SARS CoV-2 type of coronavirus[1] broke out in 2020 with massive consequences for the health of the population, it not only had a significant impact on the global economy, social relations, culture, ethics, and politics,[2] but it also manifested itself in mentalities, mindsets and interpersonal relationships, and, last but not least, in the normative systems.

As for the normative systems, the covid pandemic was reflected especially in the legislation, whether referring to generally binding normative acts, individual legal acts or other legal norms, principles, and elements. It was assumed that, in this case, the legal implications were more extensive and more fundamental than in other epidemic/pandemic diseases with which humanity, and specifically the Czech lands, had to cope with during the twentieth and early twenty-first centuries. The reason may be, for instance, the extent of the disease, i.e., its pandemic character,[3] the speed of infection propagation, and the mortality of people in

---

1 Hereafter, for the sake of simplicity and brevity, we will use the term covid for the COVID-19 pandemic.
2 See also Vögele, Jörg – Schuler, Katharin. Epidemien und Pandemien – die historische Perspektive. In: Gesundheit und Gesellschaft. Beilage G+G Wissenschaft. Heft 2/21. Berlin: Wissenschaftliches Institut der AOK (WIdO), 2021 ISSN 1868-1492, p. 24.
3 It is just the spread of an epidemic that is one of the defining features distinguishing pandemics and epidemics. For example, the 1993 Encyclopaedic Dictionary defines a pandemic as a mass outbreak of an infectious disease affecting a population without spatial limitation, while an epidemic is defined in this dictionary as occurrence of an infectious disease limited in time and area. See the pandemic entry. In: Team of authors (compiled by Bradnová, Hana et al.). Encyklopedický slovník. Praha: Praha: Odeon – Encyklopedický dům, 1993, p. 801 and the epidemic entry. In: Kolektiv autorů (compiled by Bradnová, Hana et al.). Encyklopedický slovník. Praha: Odeon – Encyklopedický dům, 1993, ISBN 80-207-0438-8, p. 278. The same distinction between epidemics and

its consequence.[4] Psychologically, the fact that there has been a certain relative calm in the territory of the Czech lands in the last seventy years in terms of new epidemic/pandemic diseases with severe impacts[5] may also have an effect in our area. However, one should note the observations of Jörg Vögele and Katharina Schuler, who stated that "epidemics and pandemics have accompanied humanity since its earliest days and have had lasting effects on the society".[6] These consequences are, among other things, of a legal nature, but not only that. It can also be stated that reactions to the experience of epidemics/pandemics, the ensuing knowledge and the facts associated with them often had an impact on the transformation of various societies in the past.

Some authors link the origins of human pandemics and epidemics to demographic and economic changes, the deepening interconnectedness of the civilization, and to the coexistence of humans with other animal species. In particular, for example, the agricultural revolution around 10 000 BC, which resulted in an increase in population, the domestication of animals and the resulting greater contact between humans and human collectives, and the coexistence of human populations and animals, leading to an increase in the possibilities of modes and risks of infection.[7] However, it is reasonable to believe that the occurrence of epidemics and pandemics on Earth may have been much older.[8]

In particular, those epidemics and pandemics that had a larger number of victims, significant economic impacts and affected larger territorial areas (i.e., were not limited to one restricted specific locality or one state) acted as a significant

---

pandemics was already made in the literature of the historical period under study. See Chaloupka, Rudolf. Nakažlivé nemoci. In: Slovník veřejného práva československého. Part II, Brno: Polygrafia: Polygrafia, 1932, p. 737.

4   Hypotheses in this direction can of course be different; one can also look at the issue of the reasons for the vigorous reaction of world governments with the concept of decolonization of history.

5   Even in these years, naturally, some epidemics also occurred in the Czech lands to a lesser extent, such as the typhus epidemic in 1954 in Valašské Meziříčí, which affected 256 people. See [cit. from 12 May 2022].

6   Vögele, Jörg – Schuler, Katharin. Epidemien und Pandemien – die historische Perspektive. In: Gesundheit und Gesellschaft. Beilage G+G Wissenschaft. Heft 2/21. Berlin: Wissenschaftliches Institut der AOK (WIdO), 2021 ISSN 1868-1492, p. 24.

7   Wintersberger, Jakob. Von der Pestordnung zum Epidemiegesetz: Die Entwicklung der Seuchenbekämpfung aus rechtsgeschichtlicher Perspektive. Diplomarbeit. Linz: Johannes Kepler Universität Linz, 2021, p. 7.

8   Indeed, one scientific theory even links the extinction of the dinosaurs with an epidemic/pandemic.

catalyst which, similarly to what we are witnessing today, had transformative effects and influenced various areas of life, society, culture, and law, leading to reforms and changes that had longer lasting effects on the form of the society of that time and, in relation to that, on the legal system as well. Such epidemics and pandemics, which have left their reflection in the historical memory and even in literature and other works of art,[9] could also be encountered in the Czech lands in the nineteenth and/or in the twentieth century.[10]

As follows from the above text, epidemics and pandemics have historically had their reflection in the legal order, including in administrative law. In this paper, we will try to present selected issues of juristic regulation, especially the most important regulations and certain trends in the efforts of our ancestors to deal with issues related to pandemics and epidemics through legal norms and principles and measures of preventive and repressive administrative or other (preventive, curative) character based on them in the period from the end of the nineteenth century until 1948 within the framework of the so-called health law as a special part of the health police and their evolution.

Given the nature of this paper, we do not claim either completeness or exclusivity of our view. We see it as an introduction to the issue and as an attempt to outline issues that can be emphasized and then compared with the current situation and regulation. These questions can be the subject of further in-depth research and elaboration of their individual aspects. After all, maintaining a collective memory of crisis situations and their solutions that humanity faced in the past and which may recur, their analysis, conceptualization and diachronic comparison may help facilitate the standardization of procedures for overcoming similar crisis situations in the future. The legal science, including legal history, has an indispensable role to play in this retrospective reflection, also by means of a diachronic comparison[11] of the legal order, sectors, concepts, institutions,

---

9   One can mention, for instance, the plague column as the elements of baroque religiousness, the novel Love in the Time of Cholera by Marquez, or the Czechoslovak film You Are Beautiful from 1986. Concerning the twenty-first-century COVID-19 pandemic, see for instance the chronicle by Michal Kubal and Vojtěch Gibiš. See Kubal, Michal – Gibiš, Vojtěch. Pandemie. Anatomie krize. Praha: Kniha Zlín, 2021, ISBN 9788076622418.
10 One can mention not only the Spanish flu, but also, for example, the cholera epidemic to pandemic in the nineteenth century or the typhus epidemic in Czechoslovakia in 1945.
11 Diachronic comparison within the law means the comparison of positive, valid, and effective legal norms, principles, notions and concepts, both of individual legal institutes

norms and principles, as well as of authorities, organizations and institutions that existed or emerged in the past.[12] For although Tomáš Garrigue Masaryk classified the legal science (similarly as history) as a theoretical science (but a concrete, not an abstract one),[13] it can be stated that it is the knowledge of historical regulation, norm-setting, interpretation and application practice that can be beneficial *de lege ferenda*, either as an inspirational source or, on the contrary, as a prevention of repeating dysfunctional solution models.

Selected Aspects of the Legal Regulation of Epidemics/Pandemics in the Period in Question

As already stated above, epidemics and pandemics accompanied the Czech lands and had their consequences even in a relatively recent historical period, although the world was not as internationally connected as it is now. Therefore, our ancestors gradually began to understand that it was desirable to create a system that would enable a rapid and comprehensive response to incoming epidemics of communicable diseases. In order to do so, it was also necessary to create a legal framework to enable such a system to function. With the transition to absolutism in the Czech lands, alongside other changes, the state was gradually becoming centralized and, in connection with this, an environment began to emerge that allowed for more general legal regulation crossing the borders of states, estates, countries or provinces, as well as national organization and management of measures, whether preventive or rather repressive, against the propagation of known contagious diseases.

---

and, more broadly, of certain segments of the legal order or even the legal order as a whole with the historical legal regulation, including the accentuation of the roots of the existing legal institutes with their current form, the tracking of features, mutual agreements and differences. As to the definition and meaning of the historical comparative studies, see for example Kysela, Jan. Prosincová ústava v kontextu diachronní komparatistiky. In: Právník. Vol. 156 (2017), No. 12. Praha: Ústav státu a práva AV ČR, v. v. i., ISSN 0231-6625, 2017, pp. 1044–1045.

12 Similarly, see Šouša, Jiří. Pokusy o zavedení principu záslužovosti do státní služby a další reformy v právní úpravě státního civilního úřednictva v letech 1918 – 1938. In: Kober, Jan (ed.) et al. Republika právníků. Praha: Academia, 2021, ISBN 978-80-200-3193-8, p. 141.

13 See Gabriel, Jiří – Pavlincová, Helena – Zouhar, Jan (eds.). Masaryk, Tomáš Garrigue. Univerzitní přednášky II. Stručný nástin dějin filozofie. Dějiny antické filozofie. Praha: Ústav T.G. Masaryka – Masarykův ústav and Archiv AV ČR, 2014, ISBN 978-80-86142-50-0 (Ústav TGM) and ISBN 978-80-87782-28-6 (MÚA AV ČR), p. 30.

As early as in the seventeenth century, various so-called plague and infectious disease orders were adopted in the countries of the Habsburg monarchy, in which the landlord, among other things, laid down rules of conduct in the event of occurrence of contagious diseases,[14] including measures to fight the disease and its propagation, and penalties on life and property in the event of violations of these principles and norms.[15] Also, population health was influenced not only by advances in medical technology but also by changes in the socio-historical context,[16] strategies, innovations, psychological, social and political factors,[17] which can be considered to also include preventive, curative, educational and administrative measures and their legal regulation.

The origins of the modern legal approach to dealing with epidemics and pandemics in the Czech lands date back to the eighteenth century in connection with the development of the so-called health police and its juristic regulation. The health police are defined as a set of mechanisms relating to measures to ensure the health of individuals to maintain public welfare, order and economic growth.[18] The new view of the health service issue, and within it the fight against epidemics and pandemics, reflected the importance that the Enlightenment scholars, representing the ruling circles of the time, attached to the whole issue in the context of caring for the subjects and achieving the common good. For example, the well-known jurist and Enlightenment thinker Joseph Sonnenfels argued that disease threatened public safety in a similar way to violence or poverty, and in his works[19] he also addressed the introduction of anti-epidemic/anti-pandemic measures for this reason.[20] Gerhard van Swieten is

---

14 Given the level of medical science at that time, the term plague also covered a number of other diseases associated with epidemics and pandemics.
15 Wintersberger, Jakob. Von der Pestordnung zum Epidemiegesetz: Die Entwicklung der Seuchenbekämpfung aus rechtsgeschichtlicher Perspektive. Diplomarbeit. Linz: Johannes-Kepler-Universität Linz, 2021, p. 8.
16 Vögele, Jörg – Schuler, Katharin. Epidemien und Pandemien – die historische Perspektive, p. 27.
17 Tinková, Daniela. Zákeřná Mefitis. Zdravotnictví, policie, osvěta a veřejná hygiena v pozdně osvícenských Čechách. Praha: Argo, 2012, p. 15.
18 Tinková, Daniela. Zákeřná Mefitis. Zdravotnictví, policie, osvěta a veřejná hygiena v pozdně osvícenských Čechách. Praha: Argo, 2012, pp. 42–43.
19 E.g., in Grundsätze der Polizey, Handlung und Finanz from 1798.
20 Tinková, Daniela. Zákeřná Mefitis. Zdravotnictví, policie, osvěta a veřejná hygiena v pozdně osvícenských Čechách. Praha: Argo, 2012, p. 42.

often cited as one of the main figures striving to modernize healthcare at that time.[21]

Already the Enlightenment legislation, therefore, regulated both the organization of the so-called health police.[22] In this regard, one can mention the General Health Standard (also General Health Order) of 2 January 1770, which was in force in the Habsburg hereditary lands and, hence, in the Czech lands as well,[23] and which not only regulated the health commission and instructions for doctors, healers, pharmacists, midwives, quarantine directors and other personnel belonging to the health police, but also contained principles concerning epidemics/pandemics, which were to be followed by the nobility. For example, according to Section 2 of the guideline which was part of the aforementioned General Health Standard of 1770, the town and regional doctors (physicists) were to stay in their area of competence in the event of an outbreak of a contagious disease and take appropriate measures there. According to Section 9 of the guideline for pharmacists, in the event of a contagious disease, an assistant was to be available in the pharmacy at all times to dispense medicines to the sick. The epidemic principles in the second part of the General Health Order concerned mainly activities at the border, but also regulated in detail, for example, sanitary cordons or the handling of animals, goods (e.g., specifically wood, metals, powder and other items), etc. The turning point in the development of epidemic periods is then considered by the legal history, general history and health law

---

21 Zaremba Vladimír. Zdravotnictví a zdravotnické koncepce v Čechách v období rozkladu feudalismu a přechodu ke kapitalismu (1740 – 1848). In: Plzeňský lékařský sborník 13/1964. Supplementum. Praha: Státní nakladatelství pedagogické literatury, 1964, ISSN 0139-603X, p. 170.
22 Hlaváčková, Lidmila. Nemoci a zdravotní péče v dílech českých písmáků v druhé polovině 18. století a první polovině 19. století. In: Český lid. Vol. 63. No. 1/1976. Praha: Etnologický ústav AV ČR, 1976, p. 33.
23 The text of the transcript is published under No. 1152 in Volume VI of so-called Theresianisches Gesetzsammlung. See Sammlung aller k.k. Verordnungen und Gesetze vom Jahre 1740. bis Jahre 1780., die unter der Regierung Kaisers Josephs des II. theils noch ganz bestehen, theils zum Theile abgeändert sind, als ein Hilfs- und Ergänzungsbuch zu dem Handbuche aller unter der Regierung des Kaisers Joseph des II. für die k.k. Erbländer ergangenen Verordnungen und Gesetze in einer chronologischen Ordnung. Sechster Band. Wien: Joh. Georg Mößle, 1786, pp. 3–121. The General Health Standard was also studied by Tinková, Daniela. Zákeřná Mefitis. Zdravotnictví, policie, osvěta a veřejná hygiena v pozdně osvícenských Čechách. Praha: Argo, 2012, p. 165, or Wintersberger, Jakob. Von der Pestordnung zum Epidemiegesetz: Die Entwicklung der Seuchenbekämpfung aus rechtsgeschichtlicher Perspektive, pp. 19--0.

science to be the industrialization and the socio-economic changes that accompanied it, when, from about the 1870s onwards, the usual mortality rate of infected persons in epidemics and pandemics declined.[24] However, even so, the number of casualties could be very high in some cases. For example, the Spanish flu was reported to have as many as 50 million victims.[25]

Even in the case of the epidemics and pandemics of the nineteenth and the twentieth centuries in the Czech lands, one has to perceive the influence of the demographic development and the regrouping of people within the socio-economic and historical framework of the legal regulation, which was important not only in the potential spread of infectious diseases, but also in the organization of health administration and service and in deciding on the ways of dealing with them, including legal regulation. Thus, according to some data, there were 1,941,284 people living in Bohemia in 1754, while in 1846, less than a century later, there were already 4,347,962 people.[26] According to the period statistics, another century later, in 1930, the Bohemian and Moravian parts of the Czechoslovak Republic had 10,674,386 inhabitants.[27] Thus, the population of the Czech lands increased more than five times in about 180 years, which, on the one hand, influenced the spread of diseases and, on the other hand, it also increased the requirements for the organization of health service and the management of procedures and measures in case of epidemics/pandemics, including the normative framework of these procedures and measures.

In the context of presenting the non-normative context of the selected issues of the legal regulations of epidemics/pandemics from the nineteenth century to 1948, it can also be pointed out that epidemics and pandemics of the nineteenth and twentieth centuries in the Czech lands affected the sick within the

---

24 Vögele, Jörg – Schuler, Katharin. Epidemien und Pandemien – die historische Perspektive, p. 25 and 26.
25 Vögele, Jörg – Schuler, Katharin. Epidemien und Pandemien – die historische Perspektive, p. 27.
26 Zaremba Vladimír. Zdravotnictví a zdravotnické koncepce v Čechách v období rozkladu feudalismu a přechodu ke kapitalismu (1740 – 1848). In: Plzeňský lékařský sborník 13/1964. Supplementum. Praha: Státní nakladatelství pedagogické literatury, 1964, ISSN 0139-603X, pp. 147–148.
27 This figure for the results of the 1930 census is based on the sum of statistics on population by sex from the census of the time. See Sčítání lidu v republice Československé ze dne 1. prosince 1930. Part I. Růst, koncentrace a hustota obyvatelstva, pohlaví, věkové rozvrstvení, rodinný stav, státní příslušnost, národnost, náboženské vyznání. Praha: Státní úřad statistický. V komisi knihkupectví Bursík & Kohout, 1934 p. 36.

immunobiological rather than the social principle,[28] which, among other things, may have increased the motivation of the ruling establishment, whose members were themselves at risk of infection, to regulate the legal procedure against epidemics/pandemics more decidedly. This was both because of preventive considerations, and possibly also because of the fact that administrative-regulatory interventions (including, for example, vaccination or property interventions linked to the solution of limiting the spread of the epidemic of a contagious disease) were perceived first as an interference with the privileges of persons (of course, only the privileged ones), then, with the gradual introduction of constitutionalism in the so-called kingdoms and lands represented in the Reichstag, it was also seen as an interference with the constitutionally guaranteed rights and freedoms, and therefore had to have a transparent legal framework and, from the point of view of the persons concerned and the science of the time, limits of appropriateness, expediency, proportionality, utility, but also rationality and economy.

With regard to the contemporary considerations concerning the various limits of the legal regulation of the epidemic/pandemic measures, one can mention the fact that, for example, already at the end of the eighteenth century and at the beginning of the nineteenth century, according to some authors, the publications of Ernst Benjamin Gottlieb Hebenstreit were influential in the Habsburg monarchy, of which the Czech lands were then a part, in which he criticized, among other things, the excessive coercive elements in the regulations of the health police.[29] It is just the different views and approaches in comparing and weighing proportionally and rationally the different aspects in the introduction and implementation of measures against pandemics/epidemics that can be perceived since the nineteenth century. These debates were reflected very highly at the time of the Spanish influenza pandemic[30] and also in dealing with the issue of vaccination, in particular the question of whether it should be compulsory or voluntary.

Until the beginning of the twentieth century, the legal regulation of measures against pandemics and epidemics in the Czech lands, as well as in the rest of the Habsburg Monarchy, was fragmented in several legal regulations of a statutory

---

28 Hlaváčková, Lidmila. Nemoci a zdravotní péče v dílech českých písmáků v druhé polovině 18. století a první polovině 19. století. In: Český lid. Vol. 63. No. 1/1976. Praha: Etnologický ústav AV ČR, 1976, p. 35.
29 Tinková, Daniela. Zákeřná Mefitis. Zdravotnictví, policie, osvěta a veřejná hygiena v pozdně osvícenských Čechách. Praha: Argo, 2012, p. 46.
30 See the respective passage in this paper.

and sub-statutory nature, where some regulations contained, for example, partial restrictive measures against individual epidemic or pandemic waves of specific diseases. There was neither specific nor more general epidemic law. Already in the middle of the nineteenth century, the organization of health service was reorganized in the context of public administration organization modernization in the Austrian Empire.[31] In particular, Act No. 68/1870 RGBl., on the public health service organization in the state, which was in force in the wording of amendments throughout the entire period under examination (from the nineteenth century to 1948) and was derogated from only by Act No. 103/1951 Sb., on uniform preventive and curative care, played an important role in regulating the organization of the public health service, which was also responsible for preventing, suppressing, containing the spread of and assisting in the treatment of contagious diseases, including in the event of an epidemic/pandemic.

The Public Health Service Act of 1870 provided in Section 1, among other things, that "The supreme supervision of all health system and the supreme management of medical affairs shall be vested in the state administration," and, further, regulated the division of competences between the state and local governments, the organization of the health police and care, as well as individual state officials and health police authorities. Within this division of competences, the above-mentioned Act of 1870 entrusted the state administration with the task of implementing the regulations on contagious diseases, epidemics and pandemics of humans and animals as well as quarantine, and to manage vaccination,[32] while local measures for the prevention and containment of the propagation of contagious diseases and participation in vaccination per this Act was carried out by the municipality in a delegated competence.[33] The second tier of public administration, i.e., the local government, namely the municipalities, on the other hand, was responsible, for example, for the care of drinking, utility, stagnant and running water, for the health police in places intended for public assembly or at cattle markets, cattle drives and also in the establishment and

---

31 One can mention, for example, Decree No. 376/1850 of the Imperial Code, which placed the health police in charge of the Ministry of the Interior, and Decree No. 10/1853 of the Imperial Code, regulating the lower levels of the healthcare administration. See Wintersberger, Jakob. Von der Pestordnung zum Epidemiegesetz: Die Entwicklung der Seuchenbekämpfung aus rechtsgeschichtlicher Perspektive. Diplomarbeit. Linz: Johannes Kepler Universität Linz, 2021, p. 21.
32 Section 2(c)(d) of Act No. 68/1870 RGBl.
33 Section 4(a)(d) of Act No. 68/1870 RGBl.

management of cattle burial grounds.[34] But the organization of health administration and services and the fight against epidemics/pandemics was fragmented further by the implementation regulations of the individual lands.[35] The competences of municipalities as to the health police were also regulated by municipal systems and other regulations concerning municipalities.[36] For example, Decree of the Ministry of the Interior No. 22881 of 15 September 1893 corroborated and concretized that measures were to be taken if an epidemic threatened and then checked for being carried out by the state administration, with municipalities implementing them in a delegated competence.[37] It was just the question of the division of competences, unification and nationalization of the health system also for epidemics/pandemics that was the subject of discussions and reform efforts in interwar Czechoslovakia.

Some examples can be provided to get an idea as regards the above-mentioned sectional arrangement of measures in the matters of epidemics and pandemics. For example, in 1879, Regulation of the Ministries of the Interior, Finance and Trade No. 15/1879 RGBl.[38] prohibited the import or transit of the goods listed in Clauses 1 to 3 of the Regulation from Russia because of the prevailing epidemic of contagious diseases in Astrakhan (probably also cholera). In 1892, Regulation of the Ministry of the Interior and Trade No. 154/1892 RGBl., on healthcare facilities in case of a cholera epidemic outbreak in the interior[39] was issued, restricting the export of specified goods, as well as prohibiting certain forms of internal trade and specifying the length of the restriction and potential

---

34 Section 3(a)(e)(f) of Act No. 68/1870 RGBl.
35 See Wintersberger, Jakob. Von der Pestordnung zum Epidemiegesetz: Die Entwicklung der Seuchenbekämpfung aus rechtsgeschichtlicher Perspektive. Diplomarbeit. Linz: Johannes Kepler Universität Linz, 2021, p. 22.
36 For example, in Art. V, Clause 5, of Act No. 18/1862 RGBl., on the general municipal establishment, or Acts No. 9/1888 z.z., No. 28/1884 mor.z.z., and No. 31/1896 slez.z. z, on the health service in municipalities
37 Chaloupka, Rudolf. Nakažlivé nemoci. In: Slovník veřejného práva československého. Part II, Brno: Polygrafia: Polygrafia, 1932, p. 738.
38 Regulation of the Ministries of the Interior, Finance and Trade No. 15/1879 RGBl., prohibiting to import or transit some goods from Russia due to the epidemic broken out in Astrakhan Province.
39 A more accurate Czech translation of the official German-language text would be "on healthcare measures in case of a cholera epidemic outbreak in the interior", but we have used the Czech period translation of the title in the Imperial Code of Law, as well as in other period regulations, if they existed. We work with the text, however, as with an official one, i.e., German.

penalties. It may be noted at this point that one of the sanctions was seizure and destruction of the goods in question, i.e., interference with property rights by the intervening state authorities. This legislation can be included in the set of legal rules and principles introducing the regulation of the movement of goods in the context of efforts to protect against the spread of epidemic/pandemic-tending communicable diseases.

At the end of the nineteenth century, sources of international law also began to appear, concerning measures related to the fight against epidemics and pandemics, such as the multilateral intergovernmental convention on joint measures for the protection of public health during cholera epidemics. This convention was ratified and published in the wording binding on the Czech lands in the Imperial Code of Law under No. 69/1894 and was concluded for a period of five years with automatic renewal for five years at a time and was valid for the high contracting party, unless it withdrew from it during the last six months before the end of the five-year period.[40] In 1897, an international convention against plague was negotiated in Venice and issued in the Imperial Code of Law under No. 13/1901.[41] This international legislation on plague, cholera and yellow fever was summarized and amended at the International Health Conference held in Paris in 1903. The convention thereunder was published for the Czech lands under No. 81/1911 RGBl..[42] During the First Czechoslovak Republic, international convention No. 15/1929 Sb. z. a n. was signed concerning not only plague, cholera and yellow fever, but also epidemic typhus and smallpox.[43] One can also mention the bilateral conventions signed with Germany in 1933 or with Poland in 1897 and 1926.[44] In this context, we can also recall the establishment of the International Office of Public Health in Paris according to the international

---

40 International Convention No. 69/1894 RGBl. between Austria-Hungary, Germany, Belgium, France, Italy, Luxembourg, Montenegro, the Netherlands, Russia, and Switzerland on common measures for public health protection at the time of an outbreak of cholera.
41 See Chaloupka, Rudolf. Nakažlivé nemoci. In: Slovník veřejného práva československého. Part. II, Brno: Polygrafia, 1932, p. 749.
42 See Chaloupka, Rudolf. Nakažlivé nemoci. In: Slovník veřejného práva československého. Part. II, Brno: Polygrafia, 1932, p. 749.
43 Chaloupka, Rudolf. Nakažlivé nemoci. In: Slovník veřejného práva československého. Part. II, Brno: Polygrafia, 1932, p. 750.
44 Chaloupka, Rudolf. Nakažlivé nemoci. In: Slovník veřejného práva československého. Part. II, Brno: Polygrafia, 1932, p. 750.

convention of 1907, which was later joined by Czechoslovakia.[45] According to Article 4 of the Statutes of the International Office of Public Health, "the main task of the Office was to collect and monitor for the states involved, events and documents of general interest relating to public health and especially to contagious diseases, namely cholera, plague, and yellow fever, as well as the measures taken to combat these diseases."

However, despite all the progress in the management, organization and regulation of issues related to the protection, prevention, or other limitation of the spread of contagious diseases that could reach epidemic or pandemic proportions, it was not until shortly before the outbreak of the First World War that a unified law was created that constituted a unitary general basis for the regulation of anti-epidemiological measures, although this does not mean that many issues were not regulated by special normative acts during the period under review. Thus, the legislation on epidemics and pandemics can be regarded as rather fragmented during the period. Indeed, until the middle of the twentieth century, the particularization of the legal order was one of the features of public law in the Czech lands.

That key milestone, the legislation concerning the basic legal regulation of epidemics and pandemics in general in the Czech lands in the period in question, was Act No. 67/1913 RGBl., on the prevention and suppression of communicable diseases (hereinafter referred to as the Epidemic Diseases Act of 1913), which generalized and basically unified the so far fragmented legal regulation concerning contagious diseases.[46] The Epidemic Diseases Act of 1913 followed Act No. 177/1909 RGBl., on the prevention and suppression of contagious animal diseases, which had been adopted four years earlier.[47] Animal monitoring was also very important for the prevention of various contagious diseases. In the Czech lands, the Epidemic Diseases Act of 1913 was in force until 1948, when

---

45 Act No. 131/1923 Sb. z. a n., international regulation on the establishment of the Office of Public Health in Paris. In: Chaloupka, Rudolf. Nakažlivé nemoci. In: Slovník veřejného práva československého. Part. II, Brno: Polygrafia: Polygrafia: Polygrafia, 1932, p. 750.
46 Wintersberger, Jakob. Von der Pestordnung zum Epidemiegesetz: Die Entwicklung der Seuchenbekämpfung aus rechtsgeschichtlicher Perspektive. Diplomarbeit. Linz: Johannes Kepler Universität Linz, 2021, p. 31.
47 Amended later with Government Regulation No. 74/ 1927 Sb., complementing the implementation provisions to Act No. 177 of 6 August 1909, on the prevention and suppression of contagious animal diseases, as regards protective vaccination against rabies.

it was replaced by Act No. 60/1948 Sb., on combating diseases communicable to humans, and Act No. 61/1948 Sb., on certain protective measures against tuberculosis. It should be noted here, for the sake of international comparative interest, that the Epidemic Diseases Act of 1913 was re-enacted under No. 186/1950 BGBl., as amended for the territory of the Republic of Austria, under the name of the Epidemic Act, and that this Epidemic Act is still part of the legal system in force in Austria today.

In its original version, the Epidemic Diseases Act of 1913 was divided systematically into 5 chapters and 51 sections to deal with the identification of reportable diseases, pandemic/ epidemic measures, compensation for costs incurred in connection with epidemic/pandemic measures, and also contained law violation penalties.[48] As it followed from the previous legislation and did not include some of the proposed changes (e.g. sanitation issues or compulsory vaccination), it was criticized by some authors.[49]

An important milestone, though not legal but subject-matter-oriented, in terms of the fight against epidemics and pandemics was the multiplication of the tasks of the state at the end of the nineteenth century in the social, health and economic spheres, as well as the creation of Czechoslovakia, with one of the pillars being the development in the social and economic spheres, but also in the administrative sphere, with which the development of instruments relating to public health, education, etc. was associated.[50] The legal science of the time spoke of the tasks of public administration, of which one was to be the protection of the life and health of people within the assurance of public welfare, not only by the mere formulation of principles in normative texts but also by the real implementation of these principles in everyday life;[51] therefore, in Roscoe

---

48 Wintersberger, Jakob. Von der Pestordnung zum Epidemiegesetz: Die Entwicklung der Seuchenbekämpfung aus rechtsgeschichtlicher Perspektive. Diplomarbeit. Linz: Johannes Kepler Universität Linz, 2021, p. 32. The contents of the law are reflected in more detail further in the text.

49 Wintersberger, Jakob. Von der Pestordnung zum Epidemiegesetz: Die Entwicklung der Seuchenbekämpfung aus rechtsgeschichtlicher Perspektive. Diplomarbeit. Linz: Johannes Kepler Universität Linz, 2021, p. 32.

50 On the character of the First Republic, see, for example, Šouša, Jiří. Právní úprava amnestie v letech 1918 – 1953 v českých zemích. Pelhřimov: Nová tiskárna Pelhřimov, 2019, p. 96.

51 Vacek, B. Organizace zdravotní služby v Československu. In: In: Albert, B. - Basař, S. - Břeský, E. - Gruschka, Th. - Gutwirth, Al. - Jirásek, Arnold - Kafka, Fr. - Pelc, H. - Procházka, Lad. P. - Prošek, V.J. - Vacek, B. - Veselý, Jos. - Ziel, R. Zdravotnictví a sociální politika. Praha: Sociální ústav ČSR, 1934, pp. 11–12.

Pound's words, not only within the law in books but also within the law in action.[52] One can thus perceive here a continuation and further deepening of progressive views, of which some elements already appeared in the Enlightenment. Also, in regard to the legal regulation of epidemics at the time of establishment of the Czechoslovak state, there was the principle of material continuity of the existing legal regulation and organization of administration stipulated in Articles 2 and 3 of Act No. 11/1918 Sb. z. a n., on the foundation of independent Czechoslovak state (so-called Reception Act of 1918).[53] The Reception Act of 1918 also resulted in the existence of legal dualism in the legal regulation of epidemics and pandemics, i.e., in the fact that there was a different legal regulation of this issue in the Czech lands and a different one in Subcarpathian Ruthenia. However, the legal regulations were based on similar principles.[54]

Czechoslovakia, in view of the expanding concept of the tasks of states also in the social, health and economic spheres, strengthened the tasks of the state also in the area of the so-called health police,[55] which, per Section 4(8) of Act No. 332/1920 Sb. z. a n., through which the state took over the health-police tasks, also covered the *"measures and fight against contagious diseases and folk illnesses."* However, Section 19 of Act No. 332/1920 Sb. z. a n. determined explicitly that "the specific duties imposed on municipalities per the legal regulations on the prevention and suppression of contagious diseases were not affected by the law."[56] An important change was that public municipal and district doctors, who were usually the first of the official medical staff to come into contact with an epidemic/pandemic, became civil servants.[57] A specific instruction was issued for the state, municipal, district and town doctors and district medical officials (physicians) through Decree of the Ministry of Public Health No. 10991 of 10

---

52 See, for instance, Roscoe, Pound. Law in Books and Law in Action. In: American Law Review. Vol. 44. Issue 1 (January-February 1910). 1910, pp. 12–36.
53 For more details as to the law, see, for instance, the recent work of: Vojáček, Ladislav. První československý zákon. Pokus o opožděný komentář. Praha: Wolters Kluwer, 2018.
54 Chaloupka, Rudolf. Nakažlivé nemoci. In: Slovník veřejného práva československého. Part. II, Brno: Polygrafia: Polygrafia, 1932, p. 738.
55 Sections 3–5 of Act No. 332/1920 Sb. z. a n.
56 Chaloupka, Rudolf. Nakažlivé nemoci. In: Slovník veřejného práva československého. Part. II, Brno: Polygrafia, 1932, p. 738.
57 Chaloupka, Rudolf. Nakažlivé nemoci. In: Slovník veřejného práva československého. Part. II, Brno: Polygrafia, 1932, p. 738.

April 1925 on the basis of Act No. 236/1922 Sb. z. a n. in connection with Government Regulation No. 24/1923 Sb. z. a n.[58]

As already mentioned above, one of the main sources of the legal regulation of epidemics/pandemics in the period from the second half of the nineteenth century to 1948 in the Czech lands, i.e., also in the Czechoslovak Republic from its establishment until 1948, was the so-called Epidemic Diseases Act of 1913, which was classified by the contemporary jurisprudence mainly among the administrative-repressive instruments of the state.[59] Its content will be discussed in more detail in the following passages. For example, the diseases considered contagious in the Czech lands at the end of the nineteenth and at the beginning of the twentieth century and *de facto* diseases with the possibility of epidemic (and even pandemic) development are provided in Section 1 of Act No. 67/1913 RGBl., which contains a list of reportable diseases. It included, for example, scarlet fever, typhoid fever, dysentery, smallpox, cholera,[60] plague, leprosy, anthrax, and even also animal diseases transmissible and dangerous to humans, such as rabies or glanders.[61] In addition to these dangerous diseases, which threatened to affect a wider area of the territory and a wider range of people with their contagiousness, the contemporary science also included measles, fever, distemper, or tuberculosis.[62]

The epidemics and pandemics striking the Czech lands in the period under study included, among others, the epidemic or spotted fever[63] (e.g., in the years

---

58 Chaloupka, Rudolf. Nakažlivé nemoci. In: Slovník veřejného práva československého. Part. II, Brno: Polygrafia, 1932, p. 738.
59 Vacek, Bohumil. Organizace zdravotní služby v Československu. In: In: Albert, B. – Basař, S. – Břeský, E. – Gruschka, Th. – Gutwirth, Al. – Jirásek, Arnold, Kafka, Fr. – Pelc, H. – Procházka, Lad. P. – Prošek, V.J. – Vacek, B. – Veselý, Jos. – Ziel, R. Zdravotnictví a sociální politika. Praha: Sociální ústav ČSR, 1934, p. 15.
60 At that time, it was still referred to as Asian cholera after the area from where it came to Europe. Here we can mention the tendency of a part of the Euro-Atlantic political representation to use adjectives that are supposed to indicate the origin of the disease just in the designation of COVID.
61 Glanders (malleus) is a contagious bacterial disease of odd-toed ungulates transmissible to humans. See the entry "glanders" at https://cs.wikipedia.org/wiki/Vozhřivka [cit. dated 4 May 2022].
62 Vacek, Bohumil. Zákony a nařízení jakož i důležitá rozhodnutí o organisaci zdravotní a epidemické služby v Čechách a na Moravě. Praha: Nákladem Spolku českých lékařů, 1916, pp. X–XVII.
63 Epidemic fever or "*Spotted fever is an acute infectious fatal disease caused by an intracellular parasitic bacterium called Rickettsia prowazekii.*" See Horáková, Eliška. Epidemie skvrnitého tyfu na konci druhé světové války v Terezíně. Bachelor thesis. Charles

1805–1806, 1812–1814 and 1945),[64] smallpox (e.g., 1800–1801),[65] cholera, Spanish influenza (1918–1920) and typhoid fever (e.g., 1803–1805, 1813–1815 and 1847–1848).[66] Some contagious epidemic diseases were already considered historical, but just as covid appeared in Europe in the twenty-first century, cholera was considered a "new" disease, whose identifiable epidemic or pandemic in the Czech lands occurred as late as in the nineteenth century. The disease first occurred regionally in Asia, only to be spread to Europe due to the development of world trade[67] and the gradual conquest of large areas of Asia by European powers in the context of colonialism and expansion (e.g., of the Indian subcontinent, in particular, by the United Kingdom and of areas in Asia by the Russian Empire). The first epidemic or even perhaps pandemic of cholera occurred in Europe in the period 1830–1837;[68] of this wave, the authors mention the occurrence of cholera in the Czech lands in 1831–1832.[69] Other cholera waves affected Europe in 1863, 1861–876 and 1885–1910.[70] At that time, the consequences of the infection and the outbreak of communicable disease in the wider population were characterized by relatively high mortality rates.[71] Concerns about cholera and efforts to prevent its spread can be traced, for example, in the variety of information materials distributed within the government offices

---

University. Faculty of Education, 2018, p. 18. It is a disease different from typhoid fever or febris putrida in Latin. See Horáková, Eliška. Epidemie skvrnitého tyfu na konci druhé světové války v Terezíně. Bachelor thesis. Praha: Charles University. Faculty of Education, 2018, p. 19.

64 Zaremba Vladimír. Zdravotnictví a zdravotnické koncepce v Čechách v období rozkladu feudalismu a přechodu ke kapitalismu (1740–1848). In: Plzeňský lékařský sborník 13/1964. Supplementum. Praha: Státní nakladatelství pedagogické literatury, 1964, ISSN 0139-603X, p. 150.
65 Ibid.
66 Zaremba Vladimír. Zdravotnictví a zdravotnické koncepce v Čechách v období rozkladu feudalismu a přechodu ke kapitalismu (1740–1848), pp. 150–151.
67 Vögele, Jörg – Schuler, Katharin. Epidemien und Pandemien – die historische Perspektive, p. 27.
68 Wiesner, Antonín. Cholera a ochrana proti ní. Praha: J. Otto, 1910, p. 4.
69 Hlaváčková, Lidmila. Nemoci a zdravotní péče v dílech českých písmáků v druhé polovině 18. století a první polovině 19. století. In: Český lid. Vol. 63. No. 1/1976. Praha: Etnologický ústav AV ČR, 1976, p. 34.
70 Wiesner, Antonín. Cholera a ochrana proti ní. Praha: J. Otto, 1910, p. 4.
71 For example, in the wave during the 1880s and 1890s, according to some data, about 42.3% of the population of Hamburg died within three months. See Wiesner, Antonín. Cholera a ochrana proti ní. Praha: J. Otto, 1910, p. 5.

to educate about the symptoms and possibilities of transmission of the disease in order to prevent its spread.[72]

Waves of cholera came to Europe and then within Europe to the Czech lands from various centers and directions (just as covid in the present day); as the statistical data shows, cholera went from being originally a seasonal affair to becoming in later waves a contagious disease that persisted in the population of Europe for a longer period of time before it was essentially eradicated in the twentieth century thanks to technical-medical advances as well as socio-economic and other changes and education in the Czech lands. As for the direction of the epidemic/pandemic spread directly to the Czech lands, for example, it was traditionally said that cholera was brought to Bohemia by the Prussian troops in the 1860s during the Austro-Prussian War.[73] It was the efforts to eradicate cholera, especially the attack in the 1870s and 1890s, which also contributed to the development of sanitary reforms such as sewerage and other infrastructure, etc.,[74] but also influenced significantly the nature of the national and international health law (see below).

One should also mention the Spanish flu affecting the Czech lands in 1918–1920 or the spotted fever epidemic in 1945, the former of which, unlike the latter, can also be considered a "new" disease. In the case of the Spanish influenza epidemic of 1918–1920, despite its name, it is not still known precisely when the epidemic began and ended or where it originated, but it is reported to occur in four waves (early summer 1918, August-November 1918, January-February 1919, and the wave of 1920), differing from one another in pandemic intensity and mortality.[75] It is interesting that, apart from the aforementioned Act of 1920, the Spanish influenza did not bring any major recodification of epidemic regulations with the force of law to the Czechoslovak legal system.

---

72 National Archive, collection of the Provincial National Committee in Prague 1874–1928, sign. 1054/3, card 2396, Instruction of the Chief Health Councillor on Cholera from 5 August 1886.
73 Wiesner, Antonín. Cholera a ochrana proti ní. Praha: J. Otto, 1910, pp. 3–5; similarly: Dobiáš, Václav. Přehledné dějiny všeobecného a vojenského lékařství. Praha: Naše vojsko, 1958, p. 156.
74 Vögele, Jörg – Schuler, Katharin. Epidemien und Pandemien – die historische Perspektive, p. 28.
75 Salfellner, Harald. Pandemie španělské chřipky 1918/19 se zvláštním zřetelem na České země a středoevropské poměry. Doctoral thesis. Charles University. First Faculty of Medicine. Praha: Charles University, 2017, p. 95.

The development of the legal regulation of epidemics from the nineteenth century to 1948 in the Czech lands can therefore be seen as a rather gradually evolving set of norms and principles, with the adoption of major generally binding normative acts being the result of this continual evolution. As to the spotted fever epidemic in 1945, it can be noted that, as the text above pointed to the influence of population concentration on the easier spread of contagious diseases, this, together with inadequate sanitary conditions, malnutrition and other causes, was one of the reasons for the spotted fever epidemic in Terezín in 1945 when the population practically doubled in the limited spaces of the ghetto and of the Small Fortress.[76]

What methods of action and measures against contagious diseases were offered by the legislation in the period from the nineteenth century until 1948? The traditional method of state intervention introducing and implementing counter-epidemiological measures, which emerged quite early and continued into the nineteenth century, was the attempt to capture and record the occurrence of a disease in terms of a reporting duty. This reporting duty was regulated, for example, in Court Decree No. 16135 of 3 November 1808, laying down instructions for medical practitioners in the event of an epidemic, including the duty to report the occurrence immediately to the local superior authority and, if the latter was slow in carrying out its duty, then also to the regional authority.[77] Already in the Middle Ages there was an effort to register the infected by marking their houses with a white cross.[78] In this context, it should be noted that in 1715–1716 the last epidemic of bubonic plague took place in the Czech lands, which may have included spotted fever and which left about 50.000 dead.[79] As early as from the late eighteenth and early nineteenth centuries, state physicians in areas (still regions then) recorded reports on the movement of people, diseases of people and animals and on the number of deaths for the purpose of early identification of situations that might indicate the seeds of an epidemic/pandemic and,

---

76 See Horáková, Eliška. Epidemie skvrnitého tyfu na konci druhé světové války v Terezíně. Bachelor thesis. Praha: Charles University. Faculty of Education, 2018, p. 28.
77 Fischer, Luděk – Veselý, Václav (ed.). Zákonná ustanovení o potírání nakažlivých chorob. Praha: Mladá generace lékařů při Ústř. Jednotě Čs. Lékařů, 1928, p. 7.
78 Vögele, Jörg – Schuler, Katharin. Epidemien und Pandemien – die historische Perspektive, p. 24.
79 Zaremba Vladimír. Zdravotnictví a zdravotnické koncepce v Čechách v období rozkladu feudalismu a přechodu ke kapitalismu (1740 – 1848), p. 149.

after evaluation, for the purpose of warnings and measures to be taken against human and animal epidemics.[80]

The reporting duty of the competent authorities regarding the risk of cholera was incorporated, for example, in Czech Governorate Decree No. 64/1892. Per Section 1 of Act No. 67/1913 RGBl, the listed diseases were subject to the reporting duty. Of the unlisted diseases, others could be subject to the reporting duty if, according to their symptoms or circumstances (e.g., if they occurred in medical institutions, boarding schools, etc.), there was a fear of their dangerous spread. The reporting duty was gradually extended to other diseases during the period in question.[81] The Epidemic Diseases Act of 1913 also regulated how the notification was to be implemented. Every suspected disease, diagnosed disease, death from a disease and suspected death from a reportable disease was to be reported immediately to the competent authority at the moment the person having the reporting duty knew or could have assumed that it was a case of the above disease. The notification should have included the name, age, residence of the sick or dead person and, if ascertainable, the designation of the disease being reported.[82] The notification form was annexed to Decree of the Ministry of the Interior No. 103/1914 RGBl.[83]

The information was to be reported by the mayor to the district political office as quickly as possible, i.e., using modern means of communication (e.g., at that time, via telegraph, telephone, or express messenger). Part of the information duty, although included as a separate measure in the Epidemic Diseases Act of 1913, was to keep the population sufficiently informed about the epidemic/

---

80 For example, according to the court decree of 16 October 1806 or the decree of the Czech Provincial Governorate of 9 May 1811. See Tinková, Daniela. Zákeřná Mefitis. Zdravotnictví, policie, osvěta a veřejná hygiena v pozdně osvícenských Čechách. Praha: Argo, 2012, p. 64.
81 For example, measles, pertussis, mumps, German measles by Ministry of the Interior Regulation in agreement with the Ministry of Trade No. 103/1914 RGBl., malaria by Ministry of the Interior Regulation No. 490/1912 RGBl., smallpox by Government Regulation No. 50/1920 Sb. z. a n., influenza by Government Regulation No. 239/1920 Sb. z. a n., polio by Government Regulation No. 161/1927 Sb. z. a n., etc. See Chaloupka, Rudolf. Nakažlivé nemoci. In: Slovník veřejného práva československého. Part. II, Brno: Polygrafia, 1932, p. 739.
82 Section 2 of the Epidemic Diseases Act of 1913.
83 Chaloupka, Rudolf. Nakažlivé nemoci. In: Slovník veřejného práva československého. Part. II. Brno: Polygrafia, 1932, p. 739.

pandemic[84] and about the measures taken to combat the contagious disease which had to be followed. For it was also the personal responsibility of every individual on which the success of the entire anti-epidemiological/anti-pandemic effort of all authorities in fact depended to a great extent. Thus, according to the Epidemic Diseases Act of 1913, this information was to be announced both in each municipality of the affected district in the usual manner and in the newspapers, i.e., in the form of the mass media of the time.[85]

In Cisleithania with the exception of Dalmatia and Carniola, the reporting duty did not exist as a general statutory reporting duty of every individual but as one of the subjects appointed by the legal regulations, such as municipalities, doctors, midwives, authorities, house and flat owners, caretakers, guesthouse owners or their officially authorized representatives, heads of school facilities towards the students and employees of such facilities, etc.[86] According to the implementation circular of the Imperial and Royal Governorate for the Kingdom of Bohemia, any lay person without medical training, who by law had a duty to report, was negligent in reporting only if he or she had demonstrable knowledge that the case was reportable, while a doctor was liable even for negligence alone, i.e. if it was proved that he or she could conclude from his training with even a mere suspicion that the case was a contagious disease which he or she was legally obliged to report.[87] It should be noted here that because influenza was not explicitly listed as a reportable disease in the Epidemic Diseases Act of 1913 or in any

---

84 Mayerhofer, Ernst. Handbuch für den politischen Verwaltungsdienst in den im Reichsrathe vertretenen Königreichen und Ländern mit besonderer Berücksichtigung der diesen Ländern gemeinsamen Gesetze und Verordnungen. Dritter band. Das Sanitärswesen. Das Polizeiwesen. 5. Auflage. Wien: Manzsche k. u. k. Hof- Verlags und Universitätsbuchhandlung, 1897, p. 360.
85 Section 6 of the Epidemic Diseases Act of 1913.
86 Mayerhofer, Ernst. Handbuch für den politischen Verwaltungsdienst in den im Reichsrathe vertretenen Königreichen und Ländern mit besonderer Berücksichtigung der diesen Ländern gemeinsamen Gesetze und Verordnungen. Dritter band. Das Sanitärswesen. Das Polizeiwesen. 5. Auflage. Wien: Manzsche k. u. k. Hof- Verlags und Universitätsbuchhandlung, 1897, p. 345. See also Section 3 of the Epidemic Diseases Act of 1913.
87 National Archive, collection of the Provincial National Committee in Prague 1874–1928, sign. 1054/3, card 2484, Decree of the Governorate for the Kingdom of Bohemia, Ref. No. 22 B 1.621 of 7 July 1913, Governorate No. (m.č.) 212 523. See also Vacek, Bohumil. Zákony a nařízení jakož i důležitá rozhodnutí o organisaci zdravotní a epidemické služby v Čechách a na Moravě. Praha: Nákladem Spolku českých lékařů, 1916, p. 149.

other legislation at the beginning of the twentieth century (it was not until Government Decree No. 239/1920 Sb. z. a n., on compulsory influenza reporting), there were discussions held at the beginning of the Spanish influenza pandemic in the Czech lands, not only in public but also within the competent authorities, as to whether to apply the reporting system to this disease as well.

In the note of the Imperial and Royal Governorate for the Kingdom of Bohemia on 29 October, it was stated – and repeated by the Provincial Administration Committee on 8 January 1919 – that the general influenza reporting duty based on the Epidemic Act should be waived, "since the isolation of the sick is not feasible in a large-scale epidemic and no special, more effective protective measures can follow the notification.[88]

As part of the registration process, mayors first submitted weekly and, from 1921, semi-monthly name reports on the status and course of illnesses and deaths due to epidemic diseases to the district authorities, which further processed them statistically and forwarded them to the superior administrative authorities.[89] In addition, monthly reports were submitted on other major health issues.[90]

The control, registration, notification, and reporting practices as important, legally established measures in the fight against communicable diseases with epidemic/pandemic potential were not limited to the national level during the period under review. According to the above-mentioned International Cholera Convention No. 69/1894 RGBl, each contracting party to the Convention was obliged not only to report the occurrence of cholera to the other contracting parties, but also to report the area of occurrence, the time of disease outbreak, the number of clinically diagnosed cases, and the number of deaths. After the initial

---

88 See Salfellner, Harald. Pandemie španělské chřipky 1918/19 se zvláštním zřetelem na České země a středoevropské poměry. Doctoral thesis. Charles University. First Faculty of Medicine. Praha: Charles University, 2017, p. 147. Here, the author refers to the National Archive, Provincial Committee Prague, 1874–1928, collection number 1054, card 2485.
89 Based on Regulation No. 103/1914 RGBl., Decree of the Governorate for Bohemia No. 159240 of 20 May 1914, Decree of the Governorate for Moravia No. 39975 of 1 June 1914, Decree of the Ministry of Public Health No. 13730 of 11 December 1920 and Decree of the Ministry of Public Health No. 1329/I of 6 February 1920. See Chaloupka, Rudolf. Nakažlivé nemoci. In: Slovník veřejného práva československého. Part. II, Brno: Polygrafia, 1932, p. 740.
90 According to Decree of the Governorate for Bohemia No. 22 B 2510, Governorate No. (m.č.) 223 037 of 9 July 1914. See Vacek, Bohumil. Zákony a nařízení jakož i důležitá rozhodnutí o organisaci zdravotní a epidemické služby v Čechách a na Moravě. Praha: Nákladem Spolku českých lékařů, 1916, p. 175.

notification, further notifications to the other contracting parties were to follow at regular intervals so that their governments would have up-to-date information where possible. The information was to include, for example, the patient isolation and quarantine issues, and states directly bordering each other could specifically agree to exchange information.[91] Similar information duties were laid down in the aforementioned unification convention No. 81/1911, which, due to its extended scope, also imposed a duty to report the existence of plague and increased mortality in mice and rats.[92] It was also important to provide information on protective measures taken in the areas of infection.[93] Thus, the international multilateral conventions provided not only a framework but also for coordination of actions over a wider area than the state, including the so much needed informedness of other states for the purposes of functional preventive measures.

Early and rapid diagnosis by the medical officer who acted on the notification was also important for the anti-epidemic measures. The competent medical officers were obliged to verify the facts and diagnose the disease immediately. [94]

Isolation (and, naturally, quarantine)[95] and the closure of entire areas were used extensively as tools, especially in earlier times. Quarantine in its original form included both isolation and quarantine and often applied to the district affected by the epidemic/pandemic and to all persons from that district. With regard to the preventive closure or restriction of public spaces, the closure of territorial districts, quarantine and isolation, the so-called 'border stations' and 'sanitary cordons' were known in the eighteenth century in the context of quarantine/isolation and restriction of the movement of persons, including the use

---

91 Title II. of an annex to Convention No. 69/1894 RGBl.
92 Art. 2 of Convention No. 81/1911 RGBl.
93 Art. 10 of Convention No. 81/1911 RGBl.
94 Section 5 of the Epidemic Diseases Act of 1913.
95 Per Section 2(6)(7)(64) of Act No. 258/2000 Sb., on public health protection and on the amendment of some related laws, as amended, the term "quarantine" as one of the quarantine measures (quarantine, medical surveillance and increased medical surveillance) "*means separation of a healthy individual who, during the incubation period, has been in contact with an infectious disease or has resided in the area of disease outbreak... from other individuals and the medical examination of such individual to prevent the transmission of the infectious disease during the period when the disease could spread*," and the term "isolation" means "*separation of an individual who has contracted an infectious disease or is showing symptoms of such a disease from other individuals*", depending on the nature of the infectious disease.

of containment periods for persons and goods.[96] In the section concerning contagious diseases, the above-mentioned General Health Standard of 1770 dealt mainly with activities in connection with the state borders, especially with the Ottoman Empire.[97] According to Section 1 of the second part of this standard, containment stations were to be set up, with persons, animals and goods travelling across the border being subject to health measures. The period of containment was relatively long then, namely 21 days according to Section 2 of the second part of the General Health Standard of 1770, and, moreover, in the event of an increased risk, it was extended under other provisions up to twice as long.

The nineteenth century in the Czech lands also initially followed this older concept of quarantines and cordons.[98] In the years 1831–1832 of the period in question, the health administration in Bohemia[99] strived to prevent the introduction of cholera into Bohemia by creating a so-called sanitary cordon and, at the same time, by administratively dividing the then administrative regions into so-called cholera districts and establishing cholera hospitals, where medical personnel – doctors, surgeons[100] and medical students[101] – were assigned. In

---

96 Tinková, Daniela. Zákeřná Mefitis. Zdravotnictví, policie, osvěta a veřejná hygiena v pozdně osvícenských Čechách. Praha: Argo, 2012, pp. 164–165.
97 Sammlung aller k.k. Verordnungen und Gesetze vom Jahre 1740. bis Jahre 1780., die unter der Regierung Kaisers Josephs des II. theils noch ganz bestehen, theils zum Theile abgeändert sind, als ein Hilfs- und Ergänzungsbuch zu dem Handbuche aller unter der Regierung des Kaisers Joseph des II. für die k.k. Erbländer ergangenen Verordnungen und Gesetze in einer chronologischen Ordnung. Sechster Band. Wien: Joh. Georg Mößle, 1786, p. 33 an.
98 The aforementioned General Health Order contained, among other things, instructions on the sanitary cordon. See Sammlung aller k.k. Verordnungen und Gesetze vom Jahre 1740. bis Jahre 1780., die unter der Regierung Kaisers Josephs des II. theils noch ganz bestehen, theils zum Theile abgeändert sind, als ein Hilfs- und Ergänzungsbuch zu dem Handbuche aller unter der Regierung des Kaisers Joseph des II. für die k.k. Erbländer ergangenen Verordnungen und Gesetze in einer chronologischen Ordnung. Sechster Band. Wien: Joh. Georg Mößle, 1786, p. 39 an. In Section 5, the sanitary cordon instruction described as to how to proceed when detecting an effort of unauthorized breaking through a cordon.
99 Protomedikus Ignác Nádherný. Hlaváčková, Lidmila. Nemoci a zdravotní péče v dílech českých písmáků v druhé polovině 18. století a první polovině 19. století. In: Český lid. Vol. 63. No. 1/1976. Praha: Etnologický ústav AV ČR, 1976, p. 35.
100 Then, physicians at a lower level of hierarchy.
101 Hlaváčková, Lidmila. Nemoci a zdravotní péče v dílech českých písmáků v druhé polovině 18. století a první polovině 19. století. In: Český lid. Vol. 63. No. 1/1976. Praha: Etnologický ústav AV ČR, 1976, p. 35.

the first half of the nineteenth century, as part of the fight against the epidemics and pandemics of infectious diseases, the authorities were obliged to seal off infected localities in relation not only to persons but also to goods that were to be exported from or transported through the locality, with particular attention being paid to the most common long-distance transport means at the time, namely by rail and waterways.[102] Furthermore, infected persons were to be isolated in healthcare facilities, and if there was a lack of space in such facilities, the sick were to be isolated at home.[103]

However, this approach changed over time, as reflected in the legislation from the end of the nineteenth century onwards, and in particular the Epidemic Diseases Act of 1913. As regards isolation in the period under review, it continued to apply to the sick and also to persons "suspected to be ill", i.e., in principle the term "isolation" included quarantine in the today's sense of the word. Such isolation/quarantine was to be carried out in the sick person's home or, if that was not possible, in a hospital or other suitable room. However, the patient could only be transported out of such isolation with official authorization, which could only be granted if this did not endanger the public interest and if it was necessary to transport the patient.[104] A very detailed regulation regarding isolation, as well as restrictions on visits to school facilities, public assembly events, public spaces or the prohibition of the use of public transport means was contained in Regulation of the Ministry of the Interior in agreement with the Ministry of Culture and Education No. 39/1915 RGBl. and the decrees issued by the Governorate thereunder (No. 22 B 376, Governorate No. (m.č.) 53490 of 2 March 1915 for Bohemia and No. 10463 of 29 March 1915 for Moravia).[105] They concerned rooms, contacts between persons, nursing staff, means of transport and the specificities of individual communicable diseases.[106] Additional implementation standards were adopted for individual diseases. For example, in the case of dysentery, the patient was to be isolated in a hospital or, if that was not possible, in an isolation room, separated from other persons and from items or food that might

---

102 Wiesner, Antonín. Cholera a ochrana proti ní. Praha: J. Otto, 1910, p. 15.
103 Wiesner, Antonín. Cholera a ochrana proti ní. Praha: J. Otto, 1910, p. 15.
104 Section 7 of the Epidemic Diseases Act of 1913.
105 See Chaloupka, Rudolf. Nakažlivé nemoci. In: Slovník veřejného práva československého. Part. II, Brno: Polygrafia: Polygrafia, 1932, p. 741.
106 Vacek, Bohumil. Zákony a nařízení jakož i důležitá rozhodnutí o organisaci zdravotní a epidemické služby v Čechách a na Moravě. Praha: Nákladem Spolku českých lékařů, 1916, pp. 212–231.

come into contact with other persons, not transported in public transport, their clothing, bedding, water, feces had to be disinfected/treated, etc.[107]

Strict isolation of the sick and quarantine (restriction of movement of healthy persons) was also used due to the circumstances in the case of the typhus epidemic, for instance, in Terezín in 1945.[108] If someone left Terezín, they were obliged to report for a period of three consecutive weeks to a doctor at the place of their new residence in order to check their health, as a possible outbreak of the disease could not be ruled out.[109]

However, the closure of public spaces, establishments, districts, etc., as well as quarantine, had significant economic impacts; especially in the nineteenth and twentieth centuries when the economy was based on the production of goods, services and trade, the closure of entire districts was considered counterproductive.[110] The health conferences held in Constantinople in 1866, in Vienna in 1874 and in Rome in 1885 repeatedly relativized the functionality of sanitary cordons and pointed out their harmfulness in terms of their economic impacts, e.g., on trade or employment growth, arguing that effective measures should not be based on stereotypes but always had to be adapted to the specific conditions.[111]

Therefore, the authorities started to seek other solutions, and in the second half of the nineteenth century the above-mentioned area closures and sanitary cordons were replaced by monitoring/reporting traffic and movement including the arrival of foreigners from risky areas, control and disinfection, along with the closure of alternative border crossings (mountain passes), for example.[112] The

---

107 Vacek, Bohumil. Zákony a nařízení jakož i důležitá rozhodnutí o organisaci zdravotní a epidemické služby v Čechách a na Moravě. Praha: Nákladem Spolku českých lékařů, 1916, pp. 290–297.
108 Horáková, Eliška. Epidemie skvrnitého tyfu na konci druhé světové války v Terezíně. Bachelor thesis. Praha: Charles University. Faculty of Education, 2018, p. 48.
109 Horáková, Eliška. Epidemie skvrnitého tyfu na konci druhé světové války v Terezíně. Bachelor thesis. Praha: Charles University. Faculty of Education, 2018, p. 48.
110 Vögele, Jörg – Schuler, Katharin. Epidemien und Pandemien – die historische Perspektive, p. 28.
111 Mayerhofer, Ernst. Handbuch für den politischen Verwaltungsdienst in den im Reichsrathe vertretenen Königreichen und Ländern mit besonderer Berücksichtigung der diesen Ländern gemeinsamen Gesetze und Verordnungen. Dritter band. Das Sanitärswesen. Das Polizeiwesen. 5. Auflage. Wien: Manzsche k. u. k. Hof- Verlags und Universitätsbuchhandlung, 1897, p. 355 and 358.
112 Mayerhofer, Ernst. Handbuch für den politischen Verwaltungsdienst in den im Reichsrathe vertretenen Königreichen und Ländern mit besonderer Berücksichtigung der diesen Ländern gemeinsamen Gesetze und Verordnungen. Dritter band.

reporting of travelling persons and their health examinations due to a typhus epidemic were imposed, for instance, by Decree of the Ministry of the Interior for political offices No. 42 643 of 26 December 1896. Especially on the principle of surveillance was also based Regulation of the Ministry of the Interior No. 148/ 1893 RGBl., declaring rules for controlling navigation on waterways to prevent cholera propagation. According to the above-mentioned international convention No. 69/1894 RGBl.[113] and international convention No. 81/1911 RGBl.,[114] sick travelers only could be detained at borders and not allowed to enter the territory of the other contracting party. For the others, the procedure and medical intervention had to be limited to state of health check and, if found to be healthy, such passengers had to be allowed to enter the country, but they were to be subjected to a five-day check at their destination, which can be considered as a quarantine *sui generis* in the today's sense of the word. On the other hand, there were groups of persons towards whom governments could adopt a different regime.[115]

The restriction of movement or quarantine of persons had to take place where there was a risk of infection.[116] For example, the Epidemic Diseases Act of 1913 allowed the occupants of houses where a disease was present to be excluded from school facilities, and, similarly, in the case of certain diseases, allowed to restrict or prohibit the use of bathhouses, public washrooms, public toilets, grocery stores, funerals, schools, organization of public meetings, door-to-door sales, trade in certain items, or even to restrict or prohibit the operation of businesses if they would pose an increased risk of spreading an epidemic/pandemic and if continued operation would create an urgent and severe threat to employees or

---

Das Sanitärswesen. Das Polizeiwesen. 5. Auflage. Wien: Manzsche k. u. k. Hof- Verlags und Universitätsbuchhandlung, 1897, p. 356.

113 Mayerhofer, Ernst. Handbuch für den politischen Verwaltungsdienst in den im Reichsrathe vertretenen Königreichen und Ländern mit besonderer Berücksichtigung der diesen Ländern gemeinsamen Gesetze und Verordnungen. Dritter band. Das Sanitärswesen. Das Polizeiwesen. 5. Auflage. Wien: Manzsche k. u. k. Hof- Verlags und Universitätsbuchhandlung, 1897, p. 350.

114 Art. 37–44 of Convention No. 81/1911 RGBl.

115 These were mainly marginalized people and immigrants. See Title V. of the annex to Convention No. 69/1894 RGBl.

116 Mayerhofer, Ernst. Handbuch für den politischen Verwaltungsdienst in den im Reichsrathe vertretenen Königreichen und Ländern mit besonderer Berücksichtigung der diesen Ländern gemeinsamen Gesetze und Verordnungen. Dritter band. Das Sanitärswesen. Das Polizeiwesen. 5. Auflage. Wien: Manzsche k. u. k. Hof- Verlags und Universitätsbuchhandlung, 1897, pp. 323–325.

the spread of the disease.[117] From the end of the nineteenth century, it was possible to defend oneself against the actions of the state authorities in this respect through administrative courts.[118] There is evidence, for example, of a decision of the Supreme Administrative Court of 13 February 1895, in which the court set out requirements for the closure of a private well for risk and protection against an infectious disease.[119]

During the Spanish influenza pandemic, it was widely believed that restricting contacts between people, e.g., by banning gatherings, public events, etc., could not in itself stop the epidemic/pandemic, and the effectiveness of such measures also in relation to the economy was subject to debate and controversy.[120] As a consequence of different views, as well as the influence of the particularization of the tasks within the organization of health administration in Cisleithania, i.e., also in the Czech lands and later in Czechoslovakia, among other things, schools, theaters, cinemas, public houses, etc. were closed, restrictions on public events or bans on visits to health establishments at the height of the most intense wave of the Spanish flu pandemic were introduced gradually and differently in individual towns and districts, and these measures were the subject of discussion and controversy.[121] Also, as a result of fears of social tension in a society suffering from the hardships of war for the fourth year in a row, various half-measures were also implemented, such as occupying every other seats in theaters or increasing

---

117 Sections 9–26 of the Epidemic Diseases Act of 1913.
118 The Supreme Administrative Court was established under Act No. 36/1876 RGBl., on administrative court establishment.
119 Mayerhofer, Ernst. Handbuch für den politischen Verwaltungsdienst in den im Reichsrathe vertretenen Königreichen und Ländern mit besonderer Berücksichtigung der diesen Ländern gemeinsamen Gesetze und Verordnungen. Dritter band. Das Sanitärswesen. Das Polizeiwesen. 5. Auflage. Wien: Manzsche k. u. k. Hof- Verlags und Universitätsbuchhandlung, 1897, p. 326.
120 Salfellner, Harald. Pandemie španělské chřipky 1918/19 se zvláštním zřetelem na České země a středoevropské poměry. Doctoral thesis. Charles University. First Faculty of Medicine. Praha: Charles University, 2017, p. 48.
121 For more details see Salfellner, Harald. Pandemie španělské chřipky 1918/19 se zvláštním zřetelem na České země a středoevropské poměry. Doctoral thesis. Charles University. First Faculty of Medicine. Praha: Charles University, 2017, pp. 129–130 and 147.

the intervals between theater performances.[122] Here, too, the contemporary man can perceive certain similarities with the events of the recent past.

Along with the registration and restriction of movement of the sick, the restrictive measures also applied to items from epidemic- or pandemic-affected areas. The aforementioned Regulation of the Ministry of the Interior and Trade No. 154/1892 RGBl, on healthcare facilities in case of a cholera epidemic outbreak in the interior, stipulated that if a cholera epidemic was declared in a political district or a city with its own status, the export of meat from slaughtered animals, milk, butter, fruit and vegetables was prohibited, as was the collection of rags and the door-to-door and street sales of the aforementioned foodstuffs and goods,[123] under a penalty of up to 100 florins or jail from 6 hours to 14 days with destruction of the seized items.[124] Here, one can undoubtedly perceive a significant administrative interference with the property rights of the owners of the movable assets in question. For that matter, the "provisions of Sections 71 and 72 of Act No. 177/1909 RGBl, on the prevention and suppression of contagious animal diseases, also made it possible for infected animals, animal raw materials or other objects to be declared forfeited by the court or prosecutor, not only if infected but also if there was a risk of contagion or if the standards laid down in the law were simply violated."[125]

But the roots of legislation concerning the disposal of livestock and other animals in connection with contagious diseases and efforts to prevent their spread, especially dead ones at first, can be found in the Czech lands much earlier.[126] The Epidemic Diseases Act of 1913, for example, also provided for the destruction of items that were subject to disinfection and for which effective disinfection would either be impossible or too costly in relation to the value of the particular item.[127] Also, the Epidemic Diseases Act of 1913 allowed as a penalty to seize articles

---

122 Salfellner, Harald. Pandemie španělské chřipky 1918/19 se zvláštním zřetelem na České země a středoevropské poměry. Doctoral thesis. Charles University. First Faculty of Medicine. Praha: Charles University, 2017, p. 150.
123 Section 1 of Regulation of the Ministry of the Interior and Trade No. 154/1892 RGBl.
124 Section 2 of Regulation of the Ministry of the Interior and Trade No. 154/1892 RGBl.
125 Blažková, Tereza – Šouša, Jiří. Konfiskace jako důsledek sankce od roku 1918 do roku 1938 za podmínek nikoliv mimořádných – koncepční východiska. In: Sborník VIII. Česko-slovenské právněhistorické setkání doktorandů a postdoktorandů. Brno: Polygrafia: Polygrafia: 2020, p. 21.
126 In Bohemia, it was, for instance, the Act of the Czech Provincial Governorate dated 13 March 1771. See Tinková, Daniela. Zákeřná Mefitis. Zdravotnictví, policie, osvěta a veřejná hygiena v pozdně osvícenských Čechách. Praha: Argo, 2012, p. 64.
127 Section 8 of the Epidemic Diseases Act of 1913.

whose storage, handling, or use would violate or circumvent the law or the implementation anti-epidemic regulations. Invariably seized and forfeited (here, unlike the previous situation, there was no discretion on the part of the decision-making authority) were those articles which violated the anti-epidemiological restrictions on foreign trade. The fate of the seized items was then either to be destroyed or sold at public auction. The seizure and forfeiture were carried out independently of the imposition of penalties under the Epidemic Diseases Act of 1913.[128] If there was a suspicion that the disease was being concealed or that items or animals suspected of being infected were being hidden, a house search could be carried out pursuant to Sections 3 and 5 of Act No. 88/1862 RGBl, on the protection of inviolability of home.[129]

The legislation of the period also set out the duration of the restrictions.[130] A similar measure against things was the disinfection of items and rooms as well as the contents of passengers' luggage, certain goods under specified conditions, etc. This was provided for in the aforementioned international convention No. 69/1894 RGBl, which assigned the decision on the place and disinfection measures within the limits mentioned above to the competent authorities of the contracting parties, but completely excluded correspondence from disinfection.[131] A similar regulation was also included in international convention No. 81/1911 RGBl.[132] It can be assumed that this was primarily due to the high risk of the documents being devalued, perhaps also in view of the already constitutionally guaranteed secrecy of letters. Similarly, disinfection was provided for in Section 8 of the Epidemic Diseases Act of 1913, but older legislation contained more detailed provisions on disinfection.[133]

One of the elements that accompanied the administrative/repressive measures and was of a repressive nature was the regulation of acts that violated the

---

128 Section 41 of the Epidemic Diseases Act of 1913.
129 Chaloupka, Rudolf. Nakažlivé nemoci. In: Slovník veřejného práva československého. Part. II, Brno: Polygrafia, 1932, p. 741.
130 For example, according to Regulation of the Ministry of the Interior and Trade No. 154/1892 RGBl., on healthcare facilities in case of a cholera epidemic outbreak, restrictions ended four weeks after the complete subsidence of the epidemic.
131 Title IV of the annex to Convention No. 69/1894 RGBl.
132 Art. 11–19 of Convention No. 81/1911 RGBl.
133 For example, Decree of the Ministry of the Interior No. 20662 of 16 August 1887 and Decree of the Ministry of the Interior No. 491 of 16 August 1893. See Chaloupka, Rudolf. Nakažlivé nemoci. In: Slovník veřejného práva československého. Part. II, Brno: Polygrafia, 1932, p. 742.

legislation regulating the fight against epidemics/pandemics and providing sanctions for such offences against health law. Originally, the penalties were quite severe; in the case of plague, for instance, such violations could even be punished by death penalty.[134] During the late nineteenth century, the first Czechoslovak Republic and the period up to 1948 in the Czech lands, the code of substantive criminal law regulating penalties was Act No. 117/1852 RGBl, on crimes, misdemeanors and offences (hereinafter referred to as the Criminal Act), which superseded the substantive part of the Act on Crimes and Serious Police Offences of 3 December 1803 and which regulated criminal offences in the field of epidemics/pandemics in Title IX (misdemeanours and offences against health),[135] namely in Sections 393–397.[136] Title IV of the Epidemic Diseases Act of 1913 was significant in this respect, as it contained the penalty provisions. Violation of the reporting and registration duties was punishable either by a fine of up to 100 crowns or imprisonment for up to eight days, the liberating grounds being if the notification was made by a person closest to the obliged one but was made in time.[137] Notwithstanding the offence above, an act or omission by which a person violated the Epidemic Diseases Act of 1913 was punishable by a penalty of either a fine of up to 200 crowns or imprisonment for up to fourteen days.[138]

In addition to the penalty for violation of the reporting duty, penalties for violation of the Epidemic Diseases Act of 1913 were imposed when the criminal law

---

134 Tinková, Daniela. Zákeřná Mefitis. Zdravotnictví, policie, osvěta a veřejná hygiena v pozdně osvícenských Čechách. Praha: Argo, 2012, p. 165. One can mention, for instance, Section 31 of the instruction on quarantine directors and their duties of the General Health Order. Sammlung aller k.k. Verordnungen und Gesetze vom Jahre 1740. bis Jahre 1780., die unter der Regierung Kaisers Josephs des II. theils noch ganz bestehen, theils zum Theile abgeändert sind, als ein Hilfs- und Ergänzungsbuch zu dem Handbuche aller unter der Regierung des Kaisers Joseph des II. für die k.k. Erbländer ergangenen Verordnungen und Gesetze in einer chronologischen Ordnung. Sechster Band. Wien: Joh. Georg Mößle, 1786, p. 81.
135 Mayerhofer, Ernst. Handbuch für den politischen Verwaltungsdienst in den im Reichsrathe vertretenen Königreichen und Ländern mit besonderer Berücksichtigung der diesen Ländern gemeinsamen Gesetze und Verordnungen. Dritter band. Das Sanitärswesen. Das Polizeiwesen. 5. Auflage. Wien: Manzsche k. u. k. Hof- Verlags und Universitätsbuchhandlung, 1897, p. 129.
136 See Wintersberger, Jakob. Von der Pestordnung zum Epidemiegesetz: Die Entwicklung der Seuchenbekämpfung aus rechtsgeschichtlicher Perspektive. Diplomarbeit. Linz: Johannes Kepler Universität Linz, 2021, p. 30.
137 Section 39 of the Epidemic Diseases Act of 1913.
138 Section 40 of the Epidemic Diseases Act of 1913.

did not apply. However, section 48 of the Epidemic Diseases Act 1913 repealed Sections 393 to 397 of the Criminal Act, and Section 49 of the Epidemic Diseases Act 1913 amended the Criminal Act by inserting new Section 393, which regulated the single offence of endangering health by communicable diseases. Under this provision, anyone who acted or omitted to act, with knowledge that such act or omission was likely to cause the spread of a communicable disease and thereby endanger the life and health of the public, committed the offence specified. The punishment was a fine of a relatively certain rate of 10 to 1000 crowns or imprisonment from 3 days to 3 months. If the consequence of such an act or omission was severe damage to the health or death of a person, the penalty, with reference to Section 335 of the Criminal Act, was imprisonment for six months to one year. If the offence was committed under particularly dangerous circumstances, the penalty was imprisonment for a term of between six months and two years and, in the case of the death of the victim, imprisonment for up to three years.[139] The special amount of punishment concerned persons in special positions.[140]

The so-called preventive and curative measures were also included as part of the anti-epidemiological measures in the nineteenth century and in the first half of the twentieth century. They were measures to ensure that medical care was provided, as far as possible, to the widest possible range of people and to the widest possible extent. Such measures included, for example, sanitary surveillance, surveillance of wells, scavenging sites, slaughterhouses, swamps and similar places posing risk factors,[141] as well as the use of disinfection to prevent the propagation of diseases and other ways of assuring the cleanliness of streets and public spaces, and efforts to prevent or remove potential contamination of waters[142] as regulated in the cholera-fighting instructions, for example.[143] Disinfection and

---

139 Section 393 in association with Sections 335, 85(c), 87 and 89 of Act No. 117/1852 RGBl.
140 Section 393 in association with Sections 432 and 85(c) of Act No. 117/1852 RGBl.
141 Tinková, Daniela. Zákeřná Mefitis. Zdravotnictví, policie, osvěta a veřejná hygiena v pozdně osvícenských Čechách. Praha: Argo, 2012, p. 166.
142 Wiesner, Antonín. Cholera a ochrana proti ní. Praha: J. Otto, 1910, p. 15; see also Mayerhofer, Ernst. Handbuch für den politischen Verwaltungsdienst in den im Reichsrathe vertretenen Königreichen und Ländern mit besonderer Berücksichtigung der diesen Ländern gemeinsamen Gesetze und Verordnungen. Dritter band. Das Sanitärswesen. Das Polizeiwesen. 5. Auflage. Wien: Manzsche k. u. k. Hof- Verlags und Universitätsbuchhandlung, 1897, p. 357.
143 Instruction for Bohemia No. 67/1886 z.z., re-published under No. 43/1892 z.z., Instruction for Moravia No. 69/1886 mor. z. z., re-published under No. 61/1892 mor. z.

hygiene also applied to the transport means and persons who came into contact with the infected.[144] For example, the precautions taken during the Spanish flu period included avoiding handshaking, wearing protective drapes or masks and, above all, increased attention to cleanliness and disinfection.[145]

Among the preventive measures against contagious diseases from the nineteenth century to 1948, which were regulated in the legal system in force in the territory of the Czech lands during this period, one can also include vaccination against contagious diseases depending on the level of medical development that gradually became established in the period under study. Vaccination was understood to mean

> an intervention which, either by injecting certain specific substances into an organism, is intended to awaken it to the production of protective antibodies and thereby protect the organism against infection, or, in the case of a disease which has already arisen, by injecting ready-made antibodies to effectively support the sick organism in its fight against the disease.[146]

Vaccination was carried out on a recommended basis, and it was only later that a range of compulsorily vaccinated diseases began to appear in the Czech lands.[147] The year 1821 is sometimes considered to be the start of vaccination in the Czech lands,[148] but some authors note that first vaccination was introduced

---

z. and Instruction for Silesia No. 31/1886 slez. z. z., re-published under No. 47/1892 slez. z. z.

144 Mayerhofer, Ernst. Handbuch für den politischen Verwaltungsdienst in den im Reichsrathe vertretenen Königreichen und Ländern mit besonderer Berücksichtigung der diesen Ländern gemeinsamen Gesetze und Verordnungen. Dritter Band. Das Sanitärswesen. Das Polizeiwesen. 5. Auflage. Wien: Manzsche k. u. k. Hof- Verlags und Universitätsbuchhandlung, 1897, p. 361.

145 Salfellner, Harald. Pandemie španělské chřipky 1918/19 se zvláštním zřetelem na České země a středoevropské poměry. Doctoral thesis. Charles University. First Faculty of Medicine. Praha: Charles University, 2017, pp. 49–50.

146 Sucharda, Karel. Očkování In: Slovník veřejného práva československého. Part. II, Brno: Polygrafia, 1932, p. 1050.

147 Tinková, Daniela. Zákeřná Mefitis. Zdravotnictví, policie, osvěta a veřejná hygiena v pozdně osvícenských Čechách. Praha: Argo, 2012, p. 64.

148 For instance, see Kolářová, Marie. Jak je to v Česku doopravdy s povinným očkováním. Co říká legislativa a jak se mají při očkování chovat lékaři. Available at: https://www.em.muni.cz/vite/5924-jak-je-to-v-cesku-doopravdy-s-povinnym-ockovanim [cit. from 7 May 2022]

through a regulation of 12 March 1807[149] on vaccination with cowpox virus, with the nobility and civil servants to be an example to and to motivate the population (then mostly living in the country in bondage)[150] and that the Cowpox Vaccination Order was already in place for the whole territory of the monarchy from 27 January 1808.[151] The follow-up vaccination orders from 1812 and 1836 provided for free vaccination of the poor.[152] For example, Court Decree No. 13192 of 9 July 1836, which was the third vaccination order in the Czech lands and was relevant to the period of this text, not only regulated the system of managing the population vaccination process, which interlinked the public administration from the central authorities to the local ones but also laid down requirements for quality vaccines, including their "freshness", the establishment of a vaccination proving document, the keeping of records of the vaccinated, and the need for education to be performed by respected persons such as parish priests and teachers.[153] Court Decree No. 17742 of 30 July 1840 then introduced the experience-based re-vaccination institute.[154] However, vaccination should never limit or replace other necessary health-policing protective and restrictive measures but should be implemented alongside them.[155] Although the smallpox epidemic of 1873, for example, also affected vaccinated persons, they were those who had received

---

149 Zaremba Vladimír. Zdravotnictví a zdravotnické koncepce v Čechách v období rozkladu feudalismu a přechodu ke kapitalismu (1740 – 1848), p. 152.
150 Tinková, Daniela. Zákeřná Mefitis. Zdravotnictví, policie, osvěta a veřejná hygiena v pozdně osvícenských Čechách. Praha: Argo, 2012, p. 253.
151 Tinková, Daniela. Zákeřná Mefitis. Zdravotnictví, policie, osvěta a veřejná hygiena v pozdně osvícenských Čechách. Praha: Argo, 2012, pp. 253–254.
152 Tinková, Daniela. Zákeřná Mefitis. Zdravotnictví, policie, osvěta a veřejná hygiena v pozdně osvícenských Čechách. Praha: Argo, 2012, p. 255.
153 Mayerhofer, Ernst. Handbuch für den politischen Verwaltungsdienst in den im Reichsrathe vertretenen Königreichen und Ländern mit besonderer Berücksichtigung der diesen Ländern gemeinsamen Gesetze und Verordnungen. Dritter band. Das Sanitärswesen. Das Polizeiwesen. 5. Auflage. Wien: Manzsche k. u. k. Hof- Verlags und Universitätsbuchhandlung, 1897, pp. 284–303.
154 Mayerhofer, Ernst. Handbuch für den politischen Verwaltungsdienst in den im Reichsrathe vertretenen Königreichen und Ländern mit besonderer Berücksichtigung der diesen Ländern gemeinsamen Gesetze und Verordnungen. Dritter band. Das Sanitärswesen. Das Polizeiwesen. 5. Auflage. Wien: Manzsche k. u. k. Hof- Verlags und Universitätsbuchhandlung, 1897, p. 312.
155 See, for instance, Vacek, Bohumil. Zákony a nařízení jakož i důležitá rozhodnutí o organisaci zdravotní a epidemické služby v Čechách a na Moravě. Praha: Nákladem Spolku českých lékařů, 1916, p. 421.

the vaccine some time earlier and, therefore, it was decided to carry out revaccination. According to some authors, it was just vaccination, among other things, that caused the rapid decline in smallpox mortality.[156] It should be noted that already in the past, vaccination and its legal basis were the subject of ideological disputes: "Vaccination itself, but especially forced vaccination, has always had its opponents, who are divided into two camps: 1. opponents of vaccination in general, 2. opponents of forced vaccination."[157]

During the whole period of the Austrian monarchy, vaccination was not compulsory in the Czech lands, although such a concept was considered. The demand for ordering compulsory vaccination against smallpox, for example, appeared during the preparation of the Epidemic Diseases Act of 1913, but it failed to be included in the text of the law.[158] For example, if there was a situation where the father of a family refused vaccination for himself and for the members of his household,[159] he was not forced to do otherwise but was advised of the importance of vaccination and of the risks of not being vaccinated, and a protocol was drawn up about it.[160] In the case of the Spanish influenza pandemic, for example, the efforts to strengthen the immunization of the population by vaccination in Czechoslovakia in the period from 1918 to 1920 were ineffective, primarily due to the unclear etiology of the disease, and it was not until the discovery of the causative agent of influenza that preventive vaccination could be introduced.[161] Compulsory vaccination against smallpox was established in Czechoslovakia in

---

156 Tinková, Daniela. Zákeřná Mefitis. Zdravotnictví, policie, osvěta a veřejná hygiena v pozdně osvícenských Čechách. Praha: Argo, 2012, p. 257.
157 Sucharda, Karel. Očkování In: Slovník veřejného práva československého. Part. II, Brno: Polygrafia, 1932, p. 1051.
158 Wintersberger, Jakob. Von der Pestordnung zum Epidemiegesetz: Die Entwicklung der Seuchenbekämpfung aus rechtsgeschichtlicher Perspektive. Diplomarbeit. Linz: Johannes Kepler Universität Linz, 2021, p. 32.
159 He could do so on the basis of the still surviving institution of paternal and conjugal power.
160 Mayerhofer, Ernst. Handbuch für den politischen Verwaltungsdienst in den im Reichsrathe vertretenen Königreichen und Ländern mit besonderer Berücksichtigung der diesen Ländern gemeinsamen Gesetze und Verordnungen. Dritter band. Das Sanitärswesen. Das Polizeiwesen. 5. Auflage. Wien: Manzsche k. u. k. Hof- Verlags und Universitätsbuchhandlung, 1897, p. 312.
161 Salfellner, Harald. Pandemie španělské chřipky 1918/19 se zvláštním zřetelem na České země a středoevropské poměry. Doctoral thesis. Charles University. First Faculty of Medicine. Praha: Charles University, 2017, p. 46.

1919[162] under Act No. 412/1919 Sb. z. a n., on compulsory vaccination against smallpox. The compulsory smallpox vaccination act was implemented through Government Regulation No. 298/1920 S. z. a n., on implementation of Act No. 412 Sb. z. a n. of 15 July 1919, on compulsory vaccination against smallpox. The vaccination process was controlled by the state administration authorities, vaccinating and re-vaccinating children in the first, seventh, and fourteenth year of their age; unlike the previous case, their parents and all other persons entrusted with the child's care were responsible for meeting this obligation.[163] The state administration kept lists of vaccinated persons for these purposes, with vaccination schedules being set up.[164]

As one of the measures to suppress the smallpox epidemic, the law also provided that in territories threatened by smallpox infection or those with smallpox occurrence the state authorities should introduce compulsory vaccination, tests, and re-vaccination of the entire population.[165] The obligation arose for the population as soon as the competent authorities declared their area endangered or infested and encouraged the population by public notice to participate in the necessary vaccination. In justified cases, the vaccination obligation could be imposed on certain groups of the population only.[166]

In some occupations subject to an increased risk of infection, vaccination and re-vaccination against smallpox could be required prior to employment, thus being actually a precondition of employment.[167] This general provision of the 1919 compulsory smallpox vaccination act was implemented, for instance, through Government Regulation No. 191/1923 Sb. z. a n., on compulsory vaccination of railway and postal employees against smallpox, and Act No. 116/1934 Sb. z. a n, on compulsory vaccination of the members of the army and gendarmerie and of some other persons against infectious diseases. However, during the period of the interwar Czechoslovak Republic, the insurance company was

---

162 Kolářová, Marie. Jak je to v Česku doopravdy s povinným očkováním. Co říká legislativa a jak se mají při očkování chovat lékaři. Available at: https://www.em.muni.cz/vite/5924-jak-je-to-v-cesku-doopravdy-s-povinnym-ockovanim [cit. from 7 May 2022]
163 Sections 1 and 4–5 of Act No. 412/1919 Sb. z. a n., on compulsory vaccination against smallpox. Cf. also Tinková, Daniela. Zákeřná Mefitis. Zdravotnictví, policie, osvěta a veřejná hygiena v pozdně osvícenských Čechách. Praha: Argo, 2012, p. 255.
164 Sections 7–13 of Government Regulation No. 298/1920 S. z. a n., implementing Act No. 412 Sb. z a n. of 15 July 1919 on compulsory vaccination against smallpox
165 Section 6 of Act No. 412/1919 Sb. z. a n., on compulsory vaccination against smallpox
166 Section 7 of Act No. 412/1919 Sb. z. a n., on compulsory vaccination against smallpox
167 Section 8 of Act No. 412/1919 Sb. z. a n., on compulsory vaccination against smallpox

not legally obliged to carry out protective vaccinations in the event of an imminent epidemic of diphtheria, scarlet fever, typhus, etc., and disputes were held as to whether, in such cases, vaccination was to be paid from the public funds.[168] On the other hand, in the case of rabies vaccination, the Court Decree of 1916 regulated at least the reimbursement of the medical fee. The owner of the rabid dog was primarily responsible for this, but if he was indigent or undetected, the municipality paid one third and the state two thirds of the costs.[169]

From the legal point of view, the Czechoslovak legal science also classified social insurance among similar preventive and curative measures.[170] For instance, it was Jan Melič, notable Czech physician at the turn of the eighteenth and nineteenth centuries,[171] who was among the first to support social insurance as a preventive and curative tool.[172] In the period of the First Czechoslovak Republic, according to the statistical data at the time, approximately 3.5 million people were insured, which, together with their family members, accounted for about one half of the population.[173] The preventive and curative tools also included hygiene in the wider sense of the word, encompassing care of healthy nutrition,

---

168 Břeský, Edvard. Sociální pojištění ve svém vztahu k veřejnému zdravotnictví a dborovolné péči. In: Albert, B. – Basař, S. – Břeský, E. – Gruschka, Th. – Gutwirth, Al. – Jirásek, Arnold – Kafka, Fr. – Pelc, H. – Procházka, Lad. P. – Prošek, V.J. – Vacek, B. – Veselý, Jos. – Ziel, R. Zdravotnictví a sociální politika. Praha: Sociální ústav ČSR, 1934, p. 50.
169 Sucharda, Karel. Očkování In: Slovník veřejného práva československého. Part. II, Brno: Polygrafia, 1932, p. 1057.
170 Procházka, Ladislav P. Zdravotnictví a sociální politika. In: Albert, B. – Basař, S. – Břeský, E. – Gruschka, Th. – Gutwirth, Al. – Jirásek, Arnold – Kafka, Fr. – Pelc, H. – Procházka, Lad. P. – Prošek, V.J. – Vacek, B. – Veselý, Jos. – Ziel, R. Zdravotnictví a sociální politika. Praha: Sociální ústav ČSR, 1934, p. 6.
171 Zaremba Vladimír. Zdravotnictví a zdravotnické koncepce v Čechách v období rozkladu feudalismu a přechodu ke kapitalismu (1740 – 1848). In: Plzeňský lékařský sborník 13/1964. Supplementum. Praha: Státní nakladatelství pedagogické literatury, 1964, ISSN 0139-603X, p. 210-213.
172 Dobiáš, Václav. Přehledné dějiny všeobecného a vojenského lékařství. Praha: Naše vojsko, 1958, p. 95.
173 Břeský, Edvard. Sociální pojištění ve svém vztahu k veřejnému zdravotnictví a dborovolné péči. In: Albert, B. – Basař, S. – Břeský, E. – Gruschka, Th. – Gutwirth, Al. – Jirásek, Arnold – Kafka, Fr. – Pelc, H. – Procházka, Lad. P. – Prošek, V.J. – Vacek, B. – Veselý, Jos. – Ziel, R. Zdravotnictví a sociální politika. Praha: Sociální ústav ČSR, 1934, p. 46.

sanitation activities, school health services, physical and health education[174] and, in general, regulation of the public health service as part of caring for people and their welfare by the public administration.[175]

It was also the care for hygiene in this concept that helped prevent epidemics/pandemics of communicable diseases, with its importance being gradually accentuated with the understanding of the adverse impact of epidemics/pandemics on the economy and, on the other hand, with the overcoming of Malthusianism.[176] At present, sanitation is seen mainly from an architectural and cultural point of view, being perceived by the historical memory as important architectural and constructional restoration and modernization of cities, but what should also be pointed out is its health aspect connected with the effort to sanitize the environment, increase the purity of soil, drinking and utility water and modernize sewage systems as preventive tools to avert the emergence and spread of contagious diseases.[177] Well known in this respect is just the sanitation of Prague based mainly on Act No. 22/1892 RGBl., on nationalization to control the sanitation district of the Royal Capital City of Prague.[178] Recommended for

---

174 Vacek, B. Organizace zdravotní služby v Československu. In: Albert, B. - Basař, S. - Břeský, E. - Gruschka, Th. - Gutwirth, Al. - Jirásek, Arnold - Kafka, Fr. - Pelc, H. - Procházka, Lad. P. - Prošek, V.J. - Vacek, B. - Veselý, Jos. - Ziel, R. Zdravotnictví a sociální politika. Praha: Sociální ústav ČSR, 1934, p. 15 and Chaloupka, Rudolf. Nakažlivé nemoci. In: Slovník veřejného práva československého. Part. II, Brno: Polygrafia, 1932, p. 737.
175 Vacek, B. Organizace zdravotní služby v Československu. In: Albert, B. - Basař, S. - Břeský, E. - Gruschka, Th. - Gutwirth, Al. - Jirásek, Arnold - Kafka, Fr. - Pelc, H. - Procházka, Lad. P. - Prošek, V.J. - Vacek, B. - Veselý, Jos. - Ziel, R. Zdravotnictví a sociální politika. Praha: Sociální ústav ČSR, 1934, p. 12.
176 Dobiáš, Václav. Přehledné dějiny všeobecného a vojenského lékařství. Praha: Naše vojsko, 1958, p. 89.
177 Wintersberger, Jakob. Von der Pestordnung zum Epidemiegesetz: Die Entwicklung der Seuchenbekämpfung aus rechtsgeschichtlicher Perspektive. Diplomarbeit. Linz: Johannes-Kepler-Universität Linz, 2021, p. 31.
178 Out of the literature concerning this topic, see for instance: Bečková, Kateřina - Benešová, Marie - Hrůza, Jiří - Míka, Zdeněk - Pařík, Arno - Voděra, Svatopluk - Wurzer, Rudolf. Pražská asanace. K 100.výročí vydání asanačního zákona pro Prahu. Acta Musci Pragensis. Svazek 93. Praha: Muzeum hlavního města Prahy, 1993, Giustino, Cathleen M. Za Prahu zdravější. Modernizace města a politická moc (kolem roku 1900). In: Dějiny a současnost Kulturně historická revue. Vol. 2005. No. 11, Praha: Občanské sdružení pro podporu historické literatury a časopisu Dějiny a současnost v produkci NLN, s. r. o., 2005, ISSN 0418-5129, pp. 21-23, and Asanace král. hlavního města Prahy. (Text zákona v příčině osvobození nových staveb a

health reasons was also the sanitation of the Artillery Barracks in the epidemic typhus period in Terezín.[179]

In the collections of the Provincial National Committee in the National Archives, one can find, among other things, a number of circulars relating to the sanitation in the sense mentioned above. For example, according to the instructions of the I&R Governorate for Bohemia, district governors were to report regularly on the sanitation works simultaneously with sending their periodic reports on the state of health. They were to supervise compliance with measures to protect drinking water, the dealing with the problem of overcrowding in certain, especially industrial areas, the drainage of sewers and sewage disposal, etc. All these measures were intended mainly to prevent or slow down the cholera epidemic/pandemic.[180]

Given the above-mentioned concept of preventive and curative measures, the legal regulations relating to the solution of pandemics and epidemics can be deemed to include, for instance, the social insurance laws relevant to the subject period, such as Act No. 268/1919 Sb. z. a n., amending the regulations of the act on health insurance of workers, Act No. 221/1924 Sb. z. a n., on employee insurance against illness, disability and old age, and its implementation regulation – Government Regulation No. 200/1925 Sb. z. a n.; later in the period in question, also Government Regulation No. 279/1942 Sb. z a n., on public medical services and related legal regulations – Government Regulation No. 188/1944 Sb. z. a n., amending Government Regulation No. 279, on public medical services, some provisions of Act No. 164/1946 Sb. z. a n., on caring for disabled ex-servicemen and for the victims of war and fascist persecution, and Act No. 49/1947 Sb. z. a n., on advisory healthcare, as well as Act No. 99/1932 Sb. z. a n., on reimbursement for occupational diseases, etc.

The health-policing tasks, which included those related to epidemics and pandemics, were carried out, as already mentioned above, mainly by state, municipal and district doctors.[181] As also mentioned above, in interwar Czechoslovakia, the

---

přestaveb od činžovní daně domovní a zákona o vyvlastnění za účelem regulace v asanačním obvodu). Praha: Národní tiskárna a nakladatelstvo, 1893.

179 Horáková, Eliška. Epidemie skvrnitého tyfu na konci druhé světové války v Terezíně. Bachelor thesis. Praha: Charles University. Faculty of Education, 2018, p. 50.

180 National Archives, collections of the Provincial National Committee in Prague 1874–1928, sign. 1054/3, card 2396, Circular of the I&R Governorate in Prague of 22 August 1892.

181 Vacek, B. Organizace zdravotní služby v Československu. In: Albert, B. – Basař, S. – Břeský, E. – Gruschka, Th. – Gutwirth, Al. – Jirásek, Arnold – Kafka, Fr. – Pelc,

tasks of the health police in preventing epidemics and pandemics remained particularized among the individual authorities, but the medical staff was "nationalized" through Act No. 332/1920 Sb. z. a n., by which the state took over the health police operations. Thus, the Government committed itself to providing sufficient medical staff, which had not been provided by the state until then.[182] Under this legal regulation, a whole number of specific instructions and service orders were started being issued for the state, municipal and district doctors.[183]

The overall organization of the health administration in the Czechoslovak Republic consisted of 1) district authorities, 2) provincial authorities and 3) the Ministry of Public Health and Physical Education, where expert assistance, advice, initiative and control was also provided for epidemics and pandemics by the National Institute of Public Health,[184] which had also experts in the field of epidemiology.[185]

The gradual formation of hospitals (polyclinics) can also be regarded as a turning point in the field of preventive and curative care aimed at eliminating the causes of pandemic diseases and their treatment, or at least at professional supervision of the sick and the provision of medical assistance at an appropriate level corresponding to the state of medical science at the time and to the concepts of health and medical care. These multifunctional institutions replaced the older concept of hospitals and other facilities operated since the Middle Ages. The roots of the building of hospitals can be traced back to the Enlightenment, when Joseph II adopted the first directive rules.[186]

H. – Procházka, Lad. P. – Prošek, V.J. – Vacek, B. – Veselý, Jos. – Ziel, R. Zdravotnictví a sociální politika. Praha: Sociální ústav ČSR, 1934, p. 17.

182 This was regulated by Act No. 236/1922 Sb. z. a n., complementing and partially implementing the provisions of Act No. 332 Sb. z. a n. of 15 April 1920, through which the state assumed the health-police operations.

183 Fischer, Luděk – Veselý, Václav. (ed.) Zákonná ustanovení o potírání nakažlivých chorob. Praha: Mladá generace lékařů při Ústř. Jednotě Čs. Lékařů, 1928, p. 37.

184 Established under Act No. 218/1925 Sb. z. a n., on the establishment, competence and organization of the National Institute of Public Health of the Czechoslovak Republic

185 Vacek, B. Organizace zdravotní služby v Československu. In: Albert, B. – Basař, S. – Břeský, E. – Gruschka, Th. – Gutwirth, Al. – Jirásek, Arnold – Kafka, Fr. – Pelc, H. – Procházka, Lad. P. – Prošek, V.J. – Vacek, B. – Veselý, Jos. – Ziel, R. Zdravotnictví a sociální politika. Praha: Sociální ústav ČSR, 1934, p. 20-22.

186 Tinková, Daniela. Zákeřná Mefitis. Zdravotnictví, policie, osvěta a veřejná hygiena v pozdně osvícenských Čechách. Praha: Argo, 2012, p. 52, see also Zaremba Vladimír. Zdravotnictví a zdravotnické koncepce v Čechách v období rozkladu feudalismu a přechodu ke kapitalismu (1740 – 1848). In: Plzeňský lékařský sborník 13/1964.

In the nineteenth century, hospitals assumed significance also during pandemics/epidemics when isolating infected people.[187] Important organizational anti-epidemic tasks were also fulfilled by the health and social advisory centers as social hygiene facilities not intended to provide curative services.[188] In terms of epidemics and pandemics, they were especially the so-called tuberculosis clinics, with the first anti-tuberculosis dispensary being established in the Czech lands by a French model in 1904/1905 in Prague, not yet state-owned at that time. Although with its decree of 2 January 1917 the Austrian Ministry of the Interior intended to open tuberculosis clinics, they started emerging as late as after the formation of the Czechoslovak Republic, with the principal organizational regulation being Decree of the Ministry of Public Health and Physical Education No. 35 137 of 28 December 1927, setting up a framework scheme, working methods, and a uniform administration.[189] But, in the end, no anti-tuberculosis law was passed in interwar Czechoslovakia,[190] leaving the regulation of different tuberculosis propagation containment measures to remain particularized. They were mostly various sub-legislation regulations or even recommendation of authorities.[191] The clinics were replaced under Act No. 49/1947 Sb., on healthcare advisory services, by national institutes of health established by district

---

Supplementum. Praha: Státní nakladatelství pedagogické literatury, 1964, ISSN 0139-603X, p. 191.
187 Wiesner, Antonín. Cholera a ochrana proti ní. Praha: J. Otto, 1910, p. 15.
188 Prošek, V.J. Lékaři a zdravotnický personál. In: Albert, B. – Basař, S. – Břeský, E. – Gruschka, Th. – Gutwirth, Al. – Jirásek, Arnold – Kafka, Fr. – Pelc, H. – Procházka, Lad. P. – Prošek, V.J. – Vacek, B. – Veselý, Jos. – Ziel, R. Zdravotnictví a sociální politika. Praha: Sociální ústav ČSR, 1934, s. 37 a Gutwirth, Alois. Poradny zabývající se sociálními chorobami. In: Albert, B. – Basař, S. – Břeský, E. – Gruschka, Th. – Gutwirth, Al. – Jirásek, Arnold – Kafka, Fr. – Pelc, H. – Procházka, Lad. P. – Prošek, V.J. – Vacek, B. – Veselý, Jos. – Ziel, R. Zdravotnictví a sociální politika. Praha: Sociální ústav ČSR, 1934, p. 94.
189 Gutwirth, Alois. Poradny zabývající se sociálními chorobami. In: Albert, B. – Basař, S. – Břeský, E. – Gruschka, Th. – Gutwirth, Al. – Jirásek, Arnold – Kafka, Fr. – Pelc, H. – Procházka, Lad. P. – Prošek, V.J. – Vacek, B. – Veselý, Jos. – Ziel, R. Zdravotnictví a sociální politika. Praha: Sociální ústav ČSR, 1934, pp. 94–97.
190 For more detail see Stiglerová, Pavla. Zdravotně sociální péče v Čechách v první polovině 20. století na příkladu středočeských léčeben tuberkulózy. Diploma thesis. Pardubice: University of Pardubice. Faculty of Arts and Philosophy, 2016, p. 138.
191 National Archives, collections of the Provincial National Committee in Prague 1874–1928, sign. 1054/3, card 2234, Decree No. 29949 of the Chairman of I&R Ministry as Administrator of the Ministry of the Interior of 14 July 1902.

national committees as their executive facilities in medical affairs.[192] In terms of epidemics and pandemics, these institutes were important for prevention and education as they monitored the state of health of people and their social and health conditions, and they were supposed to carry out health education. One of their tasks was to help prevent the spread of infectious diseases.[193] Efforts to increase the requirements for relevant education and qualifications of physicians can also be considered to be part of the effort to create a comprehensive antiepidemic solution to infectious diseases.[194].

Also, suppression of venereal diseases cannot be overlooked in the context of the control of and fight against contagious human diseases. The fragmented and incomplete legislation was unified by Act No 241/1922 Sb. z. a n., on the suppression of venereal diseases, covering syphilis, gonorrhea, and soft ulcer. Patients suffering from any of these diseases were obliged to let themselves be treated privately or in a public hospital for as long as their disease was transmittable.[195] Act No 241/1922 Sb. z. a n. of 11 July 1922, on the suppression of venereal diseases, was implemented through Government Regulation No. 193/1923 Sb. z. a n. This Government Regulation regulated the specific aspects of the mandatory treatment of patients suffering from venereal diseases. These included the possibility of forced medical examination of persons suspected of being infected or even forced treatment in institutions. Combating contagious venereal diseases also had its own special institutional arrangements. According to Government Regulation No. 15 of 19 December 1919, a standing advisory board for combating venereal diseases and prostitution was set up within the Ministry of Public Health and Physical Education. The Committee was to provide the Ministry with expert scientific opinions and its own proposals on the issues of combating venereal diseases and prostitution.

As already mentioned above, the Epidemic Diseases Act of 1913 remained valid in our country until 1948. The general regulation which derogated it and got over the so-called Czechoslovak legal dualism, i.e., unified the until then uncoordinated legislation of the Czech lands and Slovakia, was Act No. 60/1948 Sb.,

---

192 Section 3 of Act No. 49/1947 Sb.
193 See Stiglerová, Pavla. Zdravotně sociální péče v Čechách v první polovině 20. století na příkladu středočeských léčeben tuberkulózy. Diploma thesis. Pardubice: University of Pardubice. Faculty of Arts and Philosophy, 2016, p. 138.
194 Tinková, Daniela. Zákeřná Mefitis. Zdravotnictví, policie, osvěta a veřejná hygiena v pozdně osvícenských Čechách. Praha: Argo, 2012, p. 67.
195 Fischer, Luděk – Veselý, Václav. (ed.) Zákonná ustanovení o potírání nakažlivých chorob. Praha: Mladá generace lékařů při Ústř. Jednotě Čs. Lékařů, 1928, p. 33.

on combating diseases communicable to humans (the Communicable Disease Control Act). It was adopted at a meeting of the Constituent National Assembly held on 20 March 1948. At the same time as the Communicable Disease Control Act, a generally binding regulation with the force of law was finally adopted to regulate measures against tuberculosis, namely Act No. 61/1948 Sb., on certain protective measures against tuberculosis. Although the title might suggest that it was a partial regulation, the content and, above all, the context of the previous developments made it impossible to view this legislation in this way. It regulated the reporting duty (in the terminology of the time, the "obligation to report"), the tasks of anti-tuberculosis clinics, and measures similar to the epidemic laws mentioned above.

Communist Member of Parliament Ladislav Bláha, who as a reporter presented the two bills mentioned above, stressed the importance of both bills for the health policy, but at the same time he emphasized that that only was a small part of it and that, moreover, the health policy had other, more important tasks. He also stressed the importance of the regulation since he saw illness and sickness rate as a manifestation of the social background: "The sickness rate always results from a certain social and economic basis and is largely an expression or reflection of it."[196]

The Communicable Disease Control Act was obviously based on and followed the previous regulation of the Epidemic Diseases Act of 1913. At first, in the provisions of Section 1, it listed the communicable diseases that were subject to the reporting duty and then regulated the manner in which they were to be reported. The reporting duty newly applied to doctors, veterinarians, and pharmacists only and was therefore narrowed down. The sick person or, if he or she was unable to do so, the person who cared for him or her, had to report changes in the place of residence and stay for a period exceeding one month.[197] As against the Epidemic Diseases Act of 1913, the range of reportable diseases was significantly broader. The extension of the list reflected, among others, the development of the legal regulation following the adoption of the Epidemic Diseases Act of 1913. The Communicable Disease Control Act also contained empowerment

---

196 Common Czech and Slovak Parliament Library. Digital Library. Constituent National Assembly of Czechoslovak Republic 1946–1948. Stenographic protocol on the meeting of the Constituent National Assembly of 20 April 1948, see https://www.psp.cz/eknih/1946uns/stenprot/099schuz/s099007.htm (cited at 10 May 2022).
197 Section 3(1)(2) of Act No. 60/1948 Sb., on combating diseases communicable to humans.

for the Ministry of Health to amend the reporting duty in any other communicable disease should the public interest require so.[198]

Both laws contained sets of measures to be taken in the event of the occurrence of a contagious disease. Both also provided for the isolation of the sick, disinfection, prohibition of activities or occupations for persons affected by the disease, restrictions on trade and mobility in the affected areas, and the marking of houses and flats where the disease was thought to be present.[199] Both epidemic laws also regulated compensation for damages in a relatively comprehensive manner.[200] They defined the range of beneficiaries and the method of compensation – for example, for confiscated items or lost earnings. The Communicable Disease Control Act regulated compensation in a somewhat broader way. It also granted compensation to certain doctors over and above the previous regulation and regulated the so-called infectious disease allowance. This was an award to certain persons who had assisted in the suppression of the epidemic.[201] On the other hand, the Communicable Disease Control Act did not regulate so comprehensively the measures consisting in seizure and forfeiture of things, being only limited to a somewhat terse definition of the "items that were handled in contradiction with the provisions of this law or with the regulations issued hereunder."[202] Such items could be seized by the national committee on the basis of criteria not specified further. Both laws regulated identically the fines imposed for the offence of violating the reporting duty.[203] The retributive

---

198 Section 1(2) of Act No. 60/1948 Sb., on combating diseases communicable to humans.
199 Sections 7 to 19 of Act No. 60/1948 Sb., on combating diseases communicable to humans, and the provisions of Sections 6 to 28 of Act No. 67/1913 RGBl., on prevention and suppression of communicable diseases.
200 The provisions of Sections 20 to 29 of Act No. 60/1948 Sb., on combating diseases communicable to humans, and the provisions of Sections 28 to 38 of Act No. 67/1913 RGBl., on prevention and suppression of communicable diseases.
201 The provisions of Section 34 of Act No. 60/1948 Sb., on combating diseases communicable to humans, and the provisions of Sections 6–28 of Act No. 67/1913 RGBl., on prevention and suppression of communicable diseases.
The provisions of Sections 20-29 of Act No. 60/1948 Sb., on combating diseases communicable to humans, and the provisions of Section 29 of Act No. 67/1913 RGBl., on prevention and suppression of communicable diseases.
202 The provisions of Section 41 of Act No. 67/1913 RGBl., on prevention and suppression of communicable diseases.
203 The provisions of Section 33 of Act No. 60/1948 Sb., on combating diseases communicable to humans, and the provisions of Section 39 of Act No. 67/1913 RGBl., on prevention and suppression of communicable diseases.

measures introduced by the Epidemic Diseases Act remained unaffected by the Communicable Disease Control Act.[204] It is possible to encounter minor differences in the two laws; however, apart from the unification of the legislation with Slovakia, the changes were not so revolutionary. In terms of structure and basic concept, the Communicable Disease Control Act followed the previous legislation continually, being based on similar principles. In some respects, the original Austrian legislation was even more carefully formulated.

Conclusion

The current statements containing an assessment of the recent covid pandemic reflect well a kind of shock, the psychological reflection already mentioned in the introduction to this text, of the fact that in the territory of the Czech lands there has been a certain relative calm in the last seventy years in terms of new severe-impact epidemic/pandemic diseases: "The coronavirus pandemic and the related anti-epidemic measures represent an unprecedented negative shock to the world economy in the form of a dramatic decline in economic activities."[205] It can be stated that this view also reflects the level of the general living memory of the humanity concerning epidemics and pandemics, as, regarding the level of globalization, the interconnection of the world following therefrom, the modern technologies and other factors, the covid pandemics has really hit the world and the society from the economic, social, mental and legal points of view, shocking them much more than any other epidemic or pandemic occurring in about the last hundred years.

However, it would also be appropriate to perceive not only the effect of existence at the given moment, but also the effect of the reality evaluation criteria set up by every present. The knowledge of the past, in this respect, could not only influence such perception, help understand and absorb the facts which already occurred in history, but also, in some cases, perhaps facilitate or at least speed up the search for solutions. As already mentioned at the beginning of this paper, a number of different waves of epidemics and/or pandemics can be tracked in the territory of the Czech lands in the period from the nineteenth century to

---

204 The provisions of Section 35(2) of Act No. 60/1948 Sb., on combating diseases communicable to humans
205 Assessing the impact of the pandemic on the world's major economies: Crisis of supply or demand? see https://www.cnb.cz/cs/o_cnb/cnblog/Vyhodnoceni-dopadu-pandemie-na-hlavni-ekonomiky-sveta-Krize-nabidky-nebo-poptavky/ (cited at 10 May 2022).

the year 1948 and, in connection with them, to learn the legal regulations of the measures which strived not only to deal with such epidemics and pandemics during their occurrence but also to prevent them. These included the regulation of preventive, repressive, curative, and educational measures, which included, for example, interference with rights, including property rights, namely not only generally binding legal regulations of various legal force but also individual legal acts of varying, also administrative nature. The creation of the health police as a starting point for health administration and service was an important step. Industrialization was also an important step forward, bringing new circumstances and conditions (including those of a demographic, technological and medical nature), which required legislation to respond to these factors. However, the regulation of epidemic issues remained in the regime of partial and particulate legislation. It was not until the adoption of the Epidemic Diseases Act of 1913 that a more uniform basis for the general regulation of the institutes of this legal area in our territory was established. The extension of the tasks of the state in the field of public health was also important, and considerable importance was attached in the period under review to the regulation of the related aspects such as hygiene in the broader sense of the word, efforts to prevent the causes of disease occurrence or the necessary education, and also to the international regulation of the coordination of epidemics and pandemics. The Communicable Disease Control Act followed the previous legislation on anti-epidemic measures and continued its development, also in the light of the scientific (etiological and medical) progress. The unification of legislation throughout the territory and the efforts to overcome the particularization of the organization of the prevention and control of epidemics/pandemics and the strengthening of preventive and modernization of treatment procedures in the health service can also be considered to be positive outcomes.

However, if one focuses on the issue of epidemics as a period with a significantly higher concentration of one particular disease affecting a large number of people, which has very substantial economic, social, but also normative impacts, it must be stated that similar situations, although of course with unquestionable differences, have basically affected the humanity since time immemorial. However, it must never be forgotten that every legal regulation is conditioned by place, time, and other circumstances. It is always possible to find something in the definitional system of a particular period that distinguishes it and makes it unique. No two historical stages will ever exhibit such a degree of similarity that one could responsibly declare that there is nothing unprecedented about one or the other. And the legislation corresponds to this.

Finally, one cannot ignore the fact that epidemics are traditionally accompanied by a necessary response that brings with it society-wide changes in the economy, health, thinking, social relations and, last but not least, in the field of law.

The issue of the legal regulation of epidemics and pandemics, of the legal instruments and other measures to deal with them is a very broad topic, which could not have been fully exhausted in this paper for the period being reviewed, and it directly encourages further – not only legal and historica – research. The main intention of this paper, therefore, was to consolidate and conceptualize the selected issues of the legal regulation of epidemics and pandemics for the period and thus to enable certain comparison that presents itself in terms of concepts, institutes, legal norms, principles or institutions and organizations in this respect from the present perspective. To what extent this has been achieved, we leave to the discretion of the kind reader.

References

Fischer, Luděk, Veselý, Václav (ed.). Zákonná ustanovení o potírání nakažlivých chorob. Praha: Mladá generace lékařů při Ústř. Jednotě Čs. Lékařů, 1928.

Gabriel, Jiří-Pavlincová, Helena – Zouhar, Jan (eds.). Masaryk, Tomáš Garrigue. Univerzitní přednášky II. Stručný nástin dějin filozofie. Dějiny antické filozofie. Praha: Ústav T.G. Masaryka – Masarykův ústav and Archiv AV ČR, 2014.

Horáková, Eliška. Epidemie skvrnitého tyfu na konci druhé světové války v Terezíně. Bachelor thesis. Praha: Charles University. Faculty of Education, 2018.

Hlaváčková, Ludmila. Nemoci a zdravotní péče v dílech českých písmáků v druhé polovině 18. století a první polovině 19. století. In: Český lid. Vol. 63. No. 1/1976. Praha: Etnologický ústav AV ČR, 1976.

Chaloupka, Rudolf. Nakažlivé nemoci. In: Slovník veřejného práva československého. Part II, Brno: Polygrafia: Polygrafia, 1932, p. 738–739.

Mayerhofer, Ernst. Handbuch für den politischen Verwaltungsdienst in den im Reichsrathe vertretenen Königreichen und Ländern mit besonderer Berücksichtigung der diesen Ländern gemeinsamen Gesetze und Verordnungen. Dritter band. Das Sanitärswesen. Das Polizeiwesen. 5. Auflage. Wien: Manzsche k. u. k. Hof- Verlags und Universitätsbuchhandlung, 1897.

Salfellner, Harald. Pandemie španělské chřipky 1918/19 se zvláštním zřetelem na České země a středoevropské poměry. Doctoral thesis. Charles University. First Faculty of Medicine. Praha: Charles University, 2017.

Sucharda, Karel. Očkování In: Slovník veřejného práva československého. Part. II, Brno: Polygrafia, 1932, p. 1057–1062.

Tinková, Daniela. Zákeřná Mefitis. Zdravotnictví, policie, osvěta a veřejná hygiena v pozdně osvícenských Čechách. Praha: Argo, 2012,

Vacek, Bohumil. Zákony a nařízení jakož i důležitá rozhodnutí o organisaci zdravotní a epidemické služby v Čechách a na Moravě. Praha: Nákladem Spolku českých lékařů, 1916

Wintersberger, Jakob. Von der Pestordnung zum Epidemiegesetz: Die Entwicklung der Seuchenbekämpfung aus rechtsgeschichtlicher Perspektive. Diplomarbeit. Linz: Johannes-Kepler-Universität Linz, 2021.

Zaremba Vladimír. Zdravotnictví a zdravotnické koncepce v Čechách v období rozkladu feudalismu a přechodu ke kapitalismu (1740 – 1848). In: Plzeňský lékařský sborník 13/1964. Supplementum. Praha: Státní nakladatelství pedagogické literatury, 1964

J. Balounová and G. Prokopová

Administrative Measures in the Times of Pandemics

Introduction

By way of introduction, we should define what the term "administrative-legal measures in the time of a pandemic" actually means. The definition is not easy at all, even if we divide the collocation, which is the title of this chapter, into its individual parts.

The term "pandemic" is usually understood to be a large spread of a particularly contagious disease, or a mass outbreak of an infectious disease in humans without any spatial limitation.[1] In the context of this chapter, the term "pandemic" especially means that of the COVID-19 disease caused by the SARS-CoV-2 coronavirus by which (not only) the Czech Republic has been affected since March 2020, and the administrative-legal measures taken in connection therewith.

The subject of this chapter only covers those measures in the times of a pandemic that are administrative-legal by nature. The administrative law can be broadly characterized as a set of public law norms that regulate, in particular, the organization and activities of public administration.[2] Therefore, administrative-legal can be considered those measures which are issued (taken) in the sphere of public administration by the competent public administration authorities, usually by way of the procedures envisaged and regulated by the administrative law.

Although the inclusion (or non-inclusion) of a particular measure within the boundaries of the administrative law may seem relatively straightforward at first glance, the pandemic has raised a number of theoretical and practical issues that have had to be addressed. Largely discussed in the Czech law was, for instance, the nature of the state of emergency to be declared and of the emergency

---

1 Internet Language Reference Book [online]. Czech Language Institute of the Czech Academy of Sciences [cit. 11 Feb 2022]. Available at: https://prirucka.ujc.cas.cz/?slovo=pandemie.
2 Cf., for instance Hendrych, D. Správní právo. In Hendrych, D. et al. *Správní právo. Obecná část*. Ed 9. Praha: C. H. Beck, 2016, p. 9, or Sládeček, V. *Obecné správní právo*. Ed. 4 (amended). Praha: Wolters Kluwer ČR, 2019, p. 43.

measures issued by the Government to follow the state of emergency declared. In particular, the question of whether the Government acts as an administrative body (or as a public administration body or as an executor of public administration) when adopting a resolution on declaring a state of emergency and a resolution on adopting emergency measures, or whether these are "acts of governing", had to be answered. The answer to that question, i.e., whether it concerns one or the other classification, has significant consequences, especially regarding the application of the requirement of legality and scrutiny.[3] A practical and illustrative example of this problem can be seen in the possibilities of judicial review.

In this particular question, the Constitutional Court of the Czech Republic concluded that, in case of the decision on the state of emergency, it was primarily a political act of the Government and, unless the decision on the state of emergency itself contained specific emergency measures, then its direct and "isolated" review by the Constitutional Court was basically excluded.[4] However, the situation with the Government's emergency measures is a bit more complicated; the Czech (especially the administrative) courts seem to have settled on the opinion that it is first necessary to determine the nature of the Government's emergency measure, while the Government's emergency measures may, depending on their content, either take the form of a *sui generis* legal regulation, an individual administrative act, or a purely internal act.[5] This then determines whether a given emergency measure can be subjected to direct judicial review or whether its review by the administrative courts or by the Constitutional Court can be considered.[6]

A rather complicated situation also arises with the term *measure*. For that matter, Josef Staša, to introduce his article in which he went into the meaning of the term "measure" in the administrative law regulations, stated that the reliability of the legal terminology is the prerequisite of legal language comprehensiveness, while adding immediately afterwards that "to illustrate as to how the

---

3   Staša J. Krizová opatření a kontrola jejich zákonnosti. In: Hlinka, T., Szakácz, A. (eds). *Aktuálne výzvy pre správne súdnictvo*. Zborník príspevkov z medzinárodnej vedeckej konferencie Bratislavské právnické fórum 2021. Bratislava: Comenius University in Bratislava, Faculty of Law, 2021, pp. 91–99.
4   Resolution of the Constitutional Court of 22 April 2020, File No. Pl. ÚS 8/20.
5   Cf., for instance, the judgement of the Extended Senate of the Supreme Administrative Court of 30 June 2021, Ref. No. 9 As 264/2020-51, No. 4232/2021 Sb. NSS.
6   Cf., for instance, the judgement of the Extended Senate of the Supreme Administrative Court of 30 June 2021, Ref. No. 9 As 264/2020-51, No. 4232/2021 Sb. NSS, or the Resolution of the Constitutional Court of 22 April 2020, File No. Pl. ÚS 8/20.

current administrative law deviates from the desirable state one can use the so frequented term "measure"."[7] The term "measure" occurs frequently in the contemporary Czech administrative law and is used quite widely. In the Code of Administrative Procedure, for instance, one can refer to measures needed to ensure the equality of certain persons,[8] preliminary measures,[9] public order measures,[10] measures against inactivity,[11] measures of a general nature,[12] or corrective measures taken in attending to complaints.[13] Phrases expressing authority or obligation to impose or take measures are contained in a whole number of laws;[14] in special regulations, measures are frequently, but not exclusively, associated with various tasks of prevention or correction.[15] In a specific sense, the term "measure" is used in the legal regulation of state supervision over the exercise of the competences of local self-government units.[16] The term "measure" is also used by the legislation governing the different institutes whose common attribute is their purpose to be applied when an undesirable situation threatening an interest protected by law arises,[17] e.g., the emergency measures relevant for this chapter[18] or the extraordinary measures against an epidemic and the danger

---

7   Staša, J. *Nad významy termínu "opatření" v předpisech správního práva*. Právní rozhledy, 2017, No. 22, p. 777.
8   Esp. Section 7 of Act No. 500/2004 Sb., the Code of Administrative Procedure (the "CAP").
9   Esp. Section 61 of the CAP.
10 Esp. Sections 62, 63 and 143 of the CAP.
11 Esp. Section 80 of the CAP.
12 Esp. Section 171 et seq. of the CAP.
13 Esp. Section 175 of the CAP.
14 For more see, for instance, Staša, J. *Nad významy termínu "opatření" v předpisech správního práva*. Právní rozhledy, 2017, No. 22, p. 777.
15 One could refer, for instance, to the measures imposed by the Czech Trade Inspection Authority under Act No. 64/1986 Sb., on the Czech Trade Inspection Authority, or by the Czech Environmental Inspectorate under Act No. 282/1991 Sb., on the Czech Environmental Inspectorate.
16 For instance, Section 126 et seq. of Act No. 128/2000 Sb., on municipalities (municipal establishment).
17 For more see, for instance, Staša, J. *Nad významy termínu "opatření" v předpisech správního práva*. Právní rozhledy, 2017, No. 22, p. 777.
18 Act No. 240/2000 Sb., on crisis management and on the amendment of certain laws (the "Crisis Act").

of its outbreak.[19] But the term "measure" is also used (not only by the legislation) in connection with the politics (in the sense of *policy*).[20]

The term "measure" as used in the applicable law, therefore, appears either alone or as part of established or prescribed phrases.[21] It covers both relatively well-established and specific legal institutes and a special category of unspecified acts of the public administration in order to address specific situations.[22] While the today's Czech language understands the term "measure" especially as "*an activity or procedure to ensure something*",[23] the meaning taken by the administrative law is not too distant, understanding it as an activity or procedure of the *public administration* to ensure something. At this point, however, it must be admitted that such a definition of the term "measure" is perhaps too broad, as it covers essentially all public administration activities, whether carried out through forms of public or private law. On the other hand, such a broad definition is essentially a reflection and consequence of the terminology of the administrative-legal law. Thus, not only can measures not be identified with one single category of forms of administrative activities traditionally distinguished by the administrative science (where measures can have the nature of several of them), but they can also be considered in terms of non-governmental administration.

---

19 Act No. 258/2000 Sb., on public health protection and on the amendment of some related laws (the "Public Health Protection Act").
20 Cf., for instance, the ruling of the Constitutional Court of 25 September 2007, File No. Pl. ÚS 5/04: "Indeed, the broader concept of "measure", which is found in our legal system, raises considerable interpretative difficulties and could significantly affect the position of the Constitutional Court and its relations with other institutions. Our legislation uses the term 'measures' very frequently and very broadly, for example, in the sense of setting up programs, restructuring industry, ensuring health and safety, ensuring border protection, or transferring funds (budgetary measures). However, provisions of primary and secondary European Community law, direct support and additional payments are also defined as measures (cf. Section 2(a) of Act No. 252/1997 Sb., on agriculture, as amended in Act No. 128/2003 Sb. and Act No. 441/2005 Sb.)."
21 Staša, J. *Nad významy termínu "opatření" v předpisech správního práva*. Právní rozhledy, 2017, No. 22, p. 777.
22 Cf., mainly, Svoboda, T., Hejč, D. *K povaze "krizových opatření", odpovědnosti za škodu a ochraně subjektivních práv* (1. část). Právní rozhledy, 2021, No. 9, p. 315.
23 Internet Language Reference Book [online]. Czech Language Institute of the Czech Academy of Sciences [cit. 11. 2. 2022]. Available at: https://prirucka.ujc.cas.cz/?slovo=opat%C5%99en%C3%AD.

Types of Administrative-Legal Measures

In the time of the COVID-19 pandemic, the administrative-legal measures can be split by more criteria. Division according to the following points of view can be taken into account:

Regulative and non-regulative measures. As a rule, the administrative-legal measures interfere with the rights and obligations of people, and the laws assume such interferences to happen.[24] A typical interference with rights and freedoms in the time of a pandemic may be, for example, the interference with freedom of movement or the right to property. However, there are also measures that do not directly interfere with the rights and obligations of persons. These include, in particular, those of an internal nature, directed within the public administration, in particular various organizational or technical measures.[25] However, one can also consider the non-regulatory measures directed outside the public administration.[26]

Forms of administrative activities. Pandemic measures do not take a single form of administrative measures, as distinguished by the administrative law theory, but may fall into different categories. Mostly, they will have the form of an abstract act[27] or of a measure of a general nature,[28] but one can also consider the category of (individual) administrative acts, factual and non-regulative tasks.

---

24 This follows, for instance, from the definition of an emergency measure in Section 2(c) of the Crisis Act, according to which, for the purposes of the Crisis Act, an emergency measure means an organizational or technical measure intended to address an emergency situation and eliminate its consequences, *including measures that interfere with the rights and obligations of persons.*

25 Cf., especially, Svoboda, T., Hejč, D. *K povaze "krizových opatření", odpovědnosti za škodu a ochraně subjektivních práv* (Part 1). Právní rozhledy, 2021, No. 9, p. 315.

26 For example, Tomáš Svoboda and David Hejč provide examples of non-regulative measures focused outwardly: property-law actions of crisis management authorities or their corresponding public entities in the form of purchases of medical devices, as well as various variants or modifications of so-called public services in the context of a pandemic, e.g., provision of voluntary testing for the presence of the disease. Cf., especially, Svoboda, T., Hejč, D. *K povaze "krizových opatření", odpovědnosti za škodu a ochraně subjektivních práv* (Part 1). Právní rozhledy, 2021, No. 9, p. 315. Various recommendations and information acts can also be considered to be the non-regulatory acts of public administration.

27 Especially the emergency measures taken by the Government under the Crisis Act.

28 Again, the emergency measures of the Government or, for instance, the extraordinary measures taken under the Public Health Protection Act and under the Pandemic Act. Interesting is the resolution of the Supreme Administrative Court of 13 October

Body authorized to issue. There are several bodies authorized to issue measures in the time of a pandemic. In the first place, one has to mention the Government, the Ministry of Health, the Regional Public Health Authorities and the Public Health Authority of the Capital City of Prague. Certain powers to issue pandemic measures are also held by the Ministries of Defense and of the Interior,[29] the regional council governors,[30] and the Mayor of the Capital City of Prague.

Measure issuance regimes. A distinction can be made between measures that are (can be) taken regardless of whether any state of emergency is declared[31] and those conditioned by a certain state of emergency. In the latter case, a further distinction could be made between measures that are conditional on the declaration of a state of emergency[32] and those conditioned by a state of danger.[33] A specific situation is represented by measures that are conditioned by a state of pandemic alert.[34]

Administrative-Legal Measures in Practice

In connection with the theoretical definition of the term "administrative-legal measures" and the possibility of their division, the following chapter will be devoted to selected administrative-legal measures from a practical point of view, i.e., to those administrative-legal measures that have already been adopted in the time of the pandemic, or whose adoption is assumed by the applicable laws.

2020, Ref. No. 4 As 258/2020-60, in which the SAC identified the "regulation" to be a "measure of a general nature"; for more see Footnote No. 62.

29 For instance, Section 83 of the Public Health Protection Act.
30 For instance, Section 14 of the Crisis Act.
31 For instance, the extraordinary measures in the event of an epidemic or danger of its occurrence pursuant to Section 69 of the Public Health Protection Act or protective measures against the introduction of highly contagious infectious diseases from abroad pursuant to Section 68 of the Public Health Protection Act.
32 For instance, the emergency measures of the Government taken per Section 6(3) of the Crisis Act.
33 For instance, the measures taken by the regional council governor per Section 14(4) 4 of the Crisis Act.
34 The state of pandemic alert was declared through Act No. 94/2021 Sb., on extraordinary measures during the COVID-19 epidemic (hereinafter, the "Pandemic Act"), which regulates mainly the authorization of the Ministry of Health and of the Regional Public Health Authorities to impose extraordinary measures to eradicate the COVID-19 epidemic or the danger of its recurrence.

a) Administrative-Legal Measures under the Crisis Act

The Crisis Act is one of the important legal regulations to govern the possibility to issue administrative-legal measures in the time of a pandemic. In Section 2(c), it defines the term "emergency measure", which means, for the purposes of this act, "organizational or technical measures designed to deal with an emergency situation and to eliminate its consequences, including measures that interfere with the rights and obligations of persons."

The authority to issue emergency measures under the Crisis Act is vested in the Government and is linked to either the duration of the state of emergency or the duration of the state of threat to the state. In the context of the COVID-19 pandemic, a state of emergency was declared several times on the territory of the Czech Republic, with the last state of emergency being in force from 26 November to 25 December 2021. The general extent of potential restrictions in a state of emergency is defined by Section 5 of the Crisis Act,[35] while the emergency measures the Government is authorized to take in a state of emergency are listed in Section 6 of the Crisis Act.

The provisions of the Crisis Act follow from the Constitutional Act on the Security of the Czech Republic,[36] which defines the extraordinary states, namely the state of emergency, the state of threat and the state of war. In Section 6(1), the Constitutional Act on the Security of the Czech Republic stipulates, among other things, that, together with the declaration of a state of emergency, the Government must define which rights set out in the special law are restricted and to what extent in accordance with the Charter of Fundamental Rights and Freedoms, and which obligations are imposed and to what extent. The details are laid down by law, which is the Crisis Act.

One of the many emergency measures taken by the Government under the Crisis Act was that through which the Government banned and restricted a number of activities with reference to Sections 5(c) to (e) and 6(1)(b) of the Crisis

---

35 Under Section 5(c) and (e) of the Crisis Act, it is, for instance, possible to restrict the freedom of movement and residence in a defined area of the territory threatened or affected by an emergency situation for a strictly necessary period of time and to the strictly necessary extent during a state of emergency, or the right to carry out business activities that would endanger the emergency measures being carried out or disrupt or prevent their implementation.
36 Constitutional Act No. 110/1998 Sb., on the security of the Czech Republic (hereinafter also the "Constitutional Act on the Security of the Czech Republic").

Act.[37] For example, the operation of Advent and Christmas markets (the occasional markets set up for the pre-Christmas period) and the sale or consumption of alcoholic beverages in publicly accessible places was prohibited, and the operation of retail stores selling goods and services and of establishments providing such services was substantially restricted. Although the Crisis Act introduces significant interferences with the fundamental human rights and freedoms and the consequent broad powers of the Government to restrict them, it does not explicitly state in what form the Government has to do so, i.e., whether the emergency measure is to be adopted, for instance, through a government regulation, a measure of a general nature or a mere government resolution, which only is an internal decision by nature.[38] The legal nature of emergency measures taken by the Government was thus addressed by the Constitutional Court in the context of the review of the Government's emergency measures, and it concluded that the government resolution on the adoption of emergency measures under Sections 5 and 6 of the Crisis Act had the nature of a different legal regulation within the sense of the Constitutional Court Act, as it also had the nature of a general normative legal act.[39] Subsequently, however, the Constitutional Court admitted that emergency measures in the form of a government resolution are of a diverse nature (they may be not only a legal regulation, but also a decision or other intervention of a public authority), and the Constitutional Court has to assess the nature of the emergency measure in each individual case according to its content.[40]

As the Crisis Act neither stipulates the legal form of the emergency measures[41] nor the process of their adoption or publication, as well as the associated ambiguities occurring in connection with their adoption, it is undoubtedly advisable

---

37 Resolution of the Government of the Czech Republic of 25 November 2021 No. 1066 on the adoption of an emergency measure.
38 Resolution of the Constitutional Court of 30 April 1998, File No. I. ÚS 482/97.
39 Resolution of the Constitutional Court of 22 April 2020, File No. Pl. ÚS 8/20. Concerning the legal nature of emergency measures taken by the Government, cf. also Fronc, J. *Usnesení vlády jako právní předpis: terminologický zmatek sui generis*. Jurisprudence, 2021, No. 1, p. 33–38.
40 Esp. the Resolution of the Constitutional Court of 5 May 2020, File No. Pl. ÚS 10/20.
41 Interesting is that Section 8 of the Crisis Act determines that "*decisions on emergency measures referred to in Section 6(1) to (3) and Section 7 shall be published in the mass media and promulgated in the same way as a law. They take effect at the moment specified in the decision.*" However, the term decision is generally understood to be an individual administrative act regulating the rights and obligations of designated persons, but an emergency measure is undoubtedly not such a decision.

that at least Sections 5 and 6 of the Crisis Act be amended to reflect mainly the reproofs based especially on the resolution of the Constitutional Court.[42]

Other administrative-legal measures that can be ordered during a pandemic are those that the governor of a region is authorized to order during a state of danger.[43] In a state of danger, the governor of a region, for instance, is authorized to order a work obligation, work assistance or the provision of material means to deal with an emergency situation or a ban on entry, stay and movement of persons in a defined place or territory. Even in this case, the Crisis Act does not stipulate in what form the governor should take or order such an administrative-legal measure; in view of the above-mentioned conclusions of the Constitutional Court, it can also be stated that this would be a legal regulation of its kind.[44]

b) Administrative-Legal Measures under the Pandemic Act

Another law that stipulates the possibility of issuing administrative-legal measures during a pandemic is the Pandemic Act, which was adopted in 2021,[45]

---

42 See, for instance, just the Resolution of the Constitutional Court of 22 April 2020, File No. Pl. ÚS 8/20, or the Resolution of the Constitutional Court of 21 April 2020, File No. Pl. ÚS 7/20.
43 A state of danger may be declared as an urgent measure if lives, health, property, or the environment are threatened, unless the intensity of the threat reaches a significant scale ... The state of danger for the territory of a region or its part is declared by the regional council governor and, in Prague, by the Mayor of the Capital City of Prague; cf. Section 3(1) to (3) of the Crisis Act.
44 However, opinions on this issue are not uniform; according to Tomáš Svoboda and David Hejč, for example, the prohibition of entry, stay and movement of persons in a defined place or territory ordered by the governor in a state of danger under Section 14(4) of the Crisis Act will have the nature of a "mixed administrative act"– cf. Svoboda, T., Hejč, D. *K povaze "krizových opatření", odpovědnosti za škodu a ochraně subjektivních práv* (Part 1). Právní rozhledy, 2021, No. 9, p. 315.
45 It applies per Section 1(1) of the Pandemic Act that it regulates measures to cope with the COVID-19 epidemic caused by the new coronavirus identified as SARS CoV-2 and its impacts on the territory of the Czech Republic. The Act came into effect on 27 February 2021, but it (the provisions of Sections 1 to 8) was limited until 30 November 2022. At first, the effect of the said provisions was limited (only) to 28 February 2022 but Act No. 39/2022 Sb. amended Section 22 of the Pandemic Act, extending the effect of selected provisions to 30 November 2022. The Pandemic Act amendment was discussed in the Parliament of the Czech Republic as parliament publication 127. The motion approved by the Chamber of Deputies was rejected by the Senate subsequently. In the follow-up reading of the bill, the Chamber of Deputies insisted on its original

particularly because the Public Health Protection Act did not offer a sufficient range of tools for dealing with the epidemic caused by COVID-19 within the framework of the extraordinary measures defined therein, and the procedural arrangements for issuing such measures were also assessed negatively.[46] Unlike the Crisis Act and the Public Health Protection Act, the Pandemic Act is directly linked to the COVID-19 pandemic to regulate measures for managing (just only) the COVID-19 epidemic and its impact on the territory of the Czech Republic.[47]

The Pandemic Act provides for the possibility of issuing so-called extraordinary measures, which can be ordered either by the Ministry of Health or by the Regional Public Health Authorities or by the Public Health Authority of the Capital City of Prague in order to eradicate the COVID-19 epidemic or the danger of its recurrence.[48] By way of an extraordinary measure, the authority ordering it may prescribe certain activities contributing to the fulfilment of that purpose, or prohibit or restrict certain activities or services the performance of which could spread COVID-19, or impose conditions on the performance of such activities or the provision of such services.[49]

Extraordinary measures include, but are not limited to, restricting the operation of a commercial or manufacturing establishment or the operation of a shopping center; setting conditions for their operation; prohibiting or restricting the organization of public or private events at which persons are concentrated in one place or setting conditions for their organization that reduce the danger of COVID-19 transmission; and restricting the teaching or other operation of a university or setting conditions for the teaching or other operation of a university.[50]

The possibility to order extraordinary measures under Section 2 of the Pandemic Act is tied to the period of pandemic alert, a concept that has been

---

motion and, on 25 February 2022, the Act was issued in the Collection of Laws. Cf. https://www.psp.cz/sqw/historie.sqw?t=127.

46 Cf. the explanatory report to the governmental bill of act on extraordinary measures during the COVID-19 epidemic and on the amendment of some related laws. Parliament of the Czech Republic, Chamber of Deputies, election period VIII, parliament publication 1158.

47 Section 1(1) of the Pandemic Act.

48 The Ministry can order an extraordinary measure to cover the whole state or several regions. The Regional Public Health Authority can order an extraordinary measure for its administrative district only.

49 Section 2(1) of the Pandemic Act.

50 Section 2(2) of the Pandemic Act.

introduced into the legal system just by the Pandemic Act. A state of pandemic alert was declared on the day of the Act coming into force.[51]

The legal regulation of the adoption of extraordinary measures under the Pandemic Act is considerably more sophisticated compared to the Crisis Act, but this does not mean that problematic issues do not arise in practice in connection with the new legal regulation or that such extraordinary measures could not be subsequently annulled by the courts for various reasons.

Extraordinary measures are issued by the Ministry of Health or by the regional public health authorities as measures of a general nature, without any procedure being held concerning the proposal for such a measure.[52] The possibility for persons who may be affected by an extraordinary measure to defend themselves against the extraordinary measure before it is issued is thus explicitly excluded by the Pandemic Act.

Extraordinary measures are posted on the official boards of the Ministry of Health and of the regional public health authorities. On its website, the Ministry of Health also publishes information on the valid and effective extraordinary measures, not only on those issued under the Pandemic Act but also under the Public Health Protection Act, if their purpose is to eliminate the COVID-19 epidemic or the danger of its recurrence.[53]

c) Administrative-Legal Measures under the Public Health Protection Act

Administrative-legal measures to control or eliminate a pandemic can also be ordered under the Public Health Protection Act. This Act is a general legal regulation governing (not only) the general procedures to be held in the event of a pandemic or danger of its occurrence.

Extraordinary measures that may be ordered in the time of a pandemic or of the danger of pandemic occurrence are, for example, prohibition or restriction of production, processing, storage, transport, import, export and sale; prohibition or restriction of contact of groups of individuals suspected of being infected with other individuals, in particular restriction of travel from certain areas and

---

51 Section 1(1) of the Pandemic Act.
52 Section 3(6) of the Pandemic Act. According to the general rules, an extraordinary measure comes into effect on the fourth day of the day of being posted on the official board of the ministry or of the regional public health authority.
53 Section 3(6) and Section 5(1)(d) of the Pandemic Act.

restriction of transport between certain areas; prohibition or restriction of festivals, theater and film performances, sports and other gatherings and markets; and prohibition or ordering of certain other activities to eradicate the epidemic or to eliminate the danger of its occurrence.[54]

In the event of an epidemic and of the danger of its occurrence, extraordinary measures are ordered by the Ministry of Health as measures of a general nature, without any procedure being held concerning the proposal of such a measure.[55] In particular, the Public Health Protection Act was followed in the early stages of the 2020 coronavirus pandemic until the Pandemic Act came into force. In relation to the Pandemic Act, the Public Health Protection Act is in a relationship of subsidiarity, as it applies unless the Pandemic Act provides otherwise.[56]

The Pandemic Act, as a separate legal regulation to the Public Health Protection Act, also established the rule[57] stipulating that an extraordinary measure under Section 69(1)(b) or (i) of the Public Health Protection Act, the purpose of which is to eradicate the COVID-19 epidemic or the danger of its recurrence and which is valid for the whole territory of the state, may only be ordered in the time of pandemic alert.[58] Thus, the Ministry of Health may only order an extraordinary measure per Section 69(1)(b) or (i) as one to fight the COVID-19 epidemic in the time of pandemic alert, while using the procedure set forth in the Pandemic Act.[59]

When the pandemic alert ends, such extraordinary measures cease to be valid. However, this rule only applies to the emergency measures issued under Section 69(1)(b) and (i) of the Public Health Protection Act and, in the sense of Section 2(4) of the Pandemic Act, the validity and effectiveness of earlier extraordinary

---

54 Section 69(1)(a)(b) and (i) of the Public Health Protection Act.
55 Section 94(a)(2) of the Public Health Protection Act; identically also the ruling of the Constitutional Court of 22 April 2020, File No. Pl. ÚS 8/20 (Clauses 50-54).
56 Section 1(2) of the Pandemic Act.
57 Section 2(4) of the Pandemic Act.
58 Section 1(3) of the Pandemic Act.
59 For it applies per Section 4 of the Pandemic Act that, when imposing extraordinary measures per Section 69(1)(b) or (i) of the Public Health Protection Act whose purpose is to eradicate the COVID-19 pandemic or the danger of its recurrence and which have nationwide coverage, Section 3(1) to (5) and Section 9 of the Pandemic Act are used similarly.
60 Such an extraordinary measure, for instance, is that of the Ministry of Health of 5 January 2022, Ref. No. MZDR 461/2022-1/MIN/KAN, which imposed, among other

measures issued under the Public Health Protection Act are not affected by this rule.[61]

According to the Public Health Protection Act, extraordinary measures in the event of an epidemic or of the danger of epidemic occurrence may also be ordered by the regional public health authorities.[62] Such extraordinary measures can be taken for the administrative territory of a regional public health authority or its part by way of a legal regulation issued by it and identified as a regulation of the regional public health authority.[63] This, however, is inconsistent with the wording of Section 94a(2) of the Public Health Protection Act, which provides, among others, that measures under Section 82(2)(m) that concern a generally defined range of addressees are to be issued by the competent public health protection authority as measures of a general nature. The Public Health Protection Act, therefore, expressly provides that such a measure takes the form of one of a general nature, without any procedure being held concerning the proposal of such a measure.[64]

Another administrative-legal measure under the Public Health Protection Act available to the Ministry of Health during a pandemic is one against the introduction of highly contagious infectious diseases from abroad.[65] The protective measures are similar in nature to the extraordinary ones taken in the event of an epidemic or of the danger of its occurrence, but their purpose is somewhat different as they are intended to protect against the introduction of a particular disease (as opposed to the extraordinary measures, which deal with direct intervention by the competent public health authority in the event of an

---

things, the obligation to test all employees. – https://www.mzcr.cz/mimoradne-opatreni-testovani-zamestnancu-a-dalsich-osob-s-ucinnosti-od-17-1-2022/
61 Hejč, D., Svoboda, T. *Zákon o mimořádných opatřeních při epidemii onemocnění COVID-19. Komentář.* Ed. 1. Praha: C. H. Beck, 2021, p. 50.
62 Section 82(2)(m) of the Public Health Protection Act.
63 Section 85(1) and (3) of the Public Health Protection Act.
64 Cf. the judgement of the Supreme Administrative Court of 13 October 2020, Ref. No. 4 As 258/2020-60. Regarding this issue, the Supreme Administrative Court stated, among others, that: "*The wording of Section 85 of the Public Health Protection Act, according to which extraordinary measures in the event of an epidemic and the danger of its occurrence are laid down in the form of an ordinance as a legal regulation of a regional public health authority, must, according to the "lex posterior derogat priori" rule, give way to the later legislation represented by Section 94a(2) of the same Act, which provides that such extraordinary measures are issued as ones of a general nature.*"
65 Section 68(1) of the Public Health Protection Act.

epidemic or the danger of its occurrence). The Public Health Protection Act does not contain any list of protective measures that the competent public health authority is entitled to order, as is the case with the extraordinary measures; since the beginning of the COVID-19 pandemic, protective measures have been used to regulate entry into the Czech Republic, including, for example, the designation of countries or territories with a low, medium, high and very high danger of COVID-19 occurrence.[66] Protective measures are also issued in the form of ones of a general nature.[67]

Judicial Review of Administrative-Legal Measures in the Time of a Pandemic

The individual administrative measures taken during a pandemic usually result in a significant interference with human rights and freedoms. In view of this, it is essential, in accordance with the fundamental attributes of the legal state, that judicial review of these measures be ensured. In the context of a judicial review, and particularly at the beginning of the pandemic when measures that were among the first to be adopted were being challenged, the courts had to deal with a number of problematic issues relating in particular to the form of the administrative-legal measure and the associated method of judicial review. The possibilities of judicial defense and subsequent judicial review depend just on the nature of the administrative-legal measure in question.

As already mentioned above, the Constitutional Court concluded that the Government's resolution on the adoption of emergency measures per Sections 5 and 6 of the Crisis Act usually had the nature of a different legal regulation in the sense of the Constitutional Court Act,[68] namely the material nature of a different legal regulation in the sense of Art. 87(1)(b) of the Constitution or Section 64(2) of the Constitutional Court Act.[69] A motion to repeal such a different legal regulation may be filed by the entities listed in Section 64(2) of the Constitutional Court Act. Such a motion may be filed separately by the Government or by a group of at least 25 members of the Parliament or by a group of at least 10 senators. A natural person or a legal entity may only file such a motion together

---

66 For instance, the protective measure of the Ministry of Health of 23 December 2021, Ref. No. MZDR 20599/2020-139/MIN/KAN.
67 Cf. Section 94(a)(2) in conjunction with Section 80(1)(h) and Section 68(1) of the Public Health Protection Act.
68 Act No. 182/1993 Sb., on the Constitutional Court.
69 Resolution of the Constitutional Court of 22 April 2020, File No. Pl. ÚS 8/20.

with a constitutional complaint against a final decision or other interference by a public authority with his or her constitutionally guaranteed fundamental rights and freedoms, if the application of such a decision or other interference by a public authority has given rise to the fact which is the subject of the constitutional complaint.[70] For this reason, a number of constitutional complaints filed directly against the Government's resolution on the adoption of an emergency measure have been rejected by the Constitutional Court on the grounds that the motion was filed by someone who was manifestly unauthorized to do so. Therefore, natural persons or legal entities who wish to challenge directly a Government's resolution on the adoption of an emergency measure must be a party to a constitutional complaint procedure, and in their constitutional complaint they must claim a specific interference with their fundamental rights in the form of a decision, measure or other intervention made by the public authority; they may then combine their constitutional complaint with a motion for the annulment of a different legal regulation. The same procedure of judicial review should also be applied to the measures which, according to the Crisis Act, the governor of a region is entitled to order in a state of danger, since, in view of the above and, in particular, of the reasoning of the Constitutional Court, it can be concluded that such measures will also be, by their nature, legal regulations of their kind.

The extraordinary measures adopted under the Pandemic Act regime are those of a general nature and protection against them can therefore be sought through the administrative courts in proceedings for the annulment of a measure of a general nature or part thereof. A motion for annulment of a measure of a general nature or of parts thereof may be lodged by an entity which claims to have been deprived of their rights by a measure of a general nature issued by an administrative authority.[71] In doing so, the petitioner must claim in a logical, consequent and conceivable manner the possibility of affection of their legal sphere by the measure in question[72] and, at the same time, their rights affected by the measure must be of certain quality.[73] When reviewing the pandemic measures, which are those of a general nature, the administrative courts then proceed in accordance

---

70 Cf. Section 64(2)(d) and Section 74 of the Constitutional Court Act and, identically, for instance, the Resolution of the Constitutional Court of 5 May 2020, File No. Pl. ÚS 10/20.
71 Section 101(a) of Act No. 150/2002 Sb., the Code of Administrative Justice.
72 Cf. the Resolution of the Extended Senate of the Supreme Administrative Court of 21 July 2009, Ref. No. 1 Ao 1/2009-120.
73 Cf., for instance, the judgement of the Supreme Administrative Court of 21 May 2021, Ref. No. 6 Ao 22/2021-44.

with the algorithm defined by the Supreme Administrative Court, which consists of five successive steps.[74]

However, in contrast to the general rules under the Code of Administrative Justice, the Pandemic Act sets out a number of differences.

The Supreme Administrative Court has jurisdiction to hear a motion to cancel an extraordinary measure pursuant to the Pandemic Act or extraordinary measures pursuant to Section 69(1)(b) or (i) of the Public Health Protection Act in a state of pandemic alert, the purpose of which is to eradicate the COVID-19 epidemic or the danger of its recurrence nationwide, provided that the measure was issued by the Ministry of Health. In other cases, e.g., if an extraordinary measure issued by the Ministry of Health does not have nationwide coverage or if it is issued by a regional public health authority, the regional court has jurisdiction to hear the motion.[75] Subsequently, the Supreme Administrative Court summarized that its in-rem jurisdiction was established by the Pandemic Act to hear a motion for annulment of an extraordinary measure under Section 2 of the Pandemic Act or under Section 69(1)(b) or (i) of the Public Health Protection Act on the precondition only that the following four statutory conditions were met cumulatively: the purpose of the measure is to eradicate the COVID-19 epidemic or the danger of its recurrence; the measure was issued by the Ministry of Health; the measure has nationwide coverage; and it was issued in a state of pandemic alert, i.e. only with the Pandemic Act being in force.[76]

---

74 Esp. the judgement of the Supreme Administrative Court of 27 September 2005, Ref. No. 1 Ao 1/2005-98, according to which the algorithm of the judicial review of a measure of a general nature consists in five steps; *first, in a review of the authority of the administrative authority to issue a measure of a general nature; second, in a review of whether the administrative authority has exceeded the limits of its statutory competence in issuing the measure of a general nature (ultra vires action); third, in a review of whether the measure of a general nature was adopted in accordance with the procedure laid down by law; fourth, in a review of the content of a measure of a general nature in terms of whether the measure of a general nature (or part of it) is contrary to the law (substantive criterion); fifth, in a review of the content of a measure of a general nature issued in terms of its proportionality.* However, this algorithm is not applicable in its entirety and without further notice since the court is bound by the scope and grounds of the motion when deciding on the application for annulment of a measure of a general nature or part thereof.
75 Section 13(1) of the Pandemic Act.
76 Cf., for instance, the judgements of the Supreme Administrative Court of 23 March 2021, Ref. No. 9 Ao 1/2021-4, or of 23 March 2021, Ref. No. 7 Ao 1/2021-32.

Another significant difference is the time limit for filing such a motion. It can only be filed within one month from the date on which the contested measure of a general nature came into force. This one-month time limit serves in particular to ensure a rapid and objective review. The purpose of the time limit is to concentrate all applications for annulment of the same measure of a general nature in a single period, so that the addressees affected by the contested measure of a general nature can be assured with certain legal certainty that the measure will not be annulled by a court later. At the same time, however, the addressees of the measure must be able to have access to the courts, so that justice is not denied.[77]

A special rule of judicial review for this category of administrative-legal measures is also provided for situations where the motion is manifestly unfounded. In such a case, the motion shall be rejected by the court through a resolution made outside an oral hearing without the presence of the parties.[78]

The Pandemic Act also explicitly foresees the cases in which an extraordinary measure expires during the course of the procedure. Such a fact does not preclude further proceedings, since if the court concludes that the measure of a general nature, or parts thereof, was contrary to the law, or that the entity which issued it exceeded the limits of its competence and authority, or that the measure of a general nature was not issued in the manner prescribed by law, it will state so in its verdict.[79] Such a declaratory judgment by which the court would pronounce the conclusion above has effects against all (*erga omnes*). In subsequent proceedings for a declaration that the same measure of a general nature, or part thereof, which has already been declared unlawful, is unlawful, the subject-matter of the proceedings will therefore be materially emptied, since no claimant could achieve a better result than the declaration of unlawfulness which has already been made. The court will reject such motions.[80]

The Pandemic Act thus introduced an exception to the rule, or rather to the established practice of the administrative courts, according to which proceedings on a motion for annulment of a measure of a general nature are preconditioned by the existence of the contested act, as the annulment of a measure of a general nature constitutes an irremovable obstacle to the proceedings. However,

---

77 Resolution of the Supreme Administrative Court of 17 June 2021, Ref. No. 5 Ao 20/2021-15.
78 Section 13(3) of the Pandemic Act.
79 Section 13(4) of the Pandemic Act.
80 Resolution of the Supreme Administrative Court of 11 June 2021, Ref. No. 8 Ao 9/2021-43.

during the COVID-19 pandemic, the administrative courts, in response to the fact that measures were repealed and replaced by substantively similar measures at a time interval which effectively prevented the possibility of judicial review of the (originally challenged) measure, concluded that in such a case it was possible to allow an amendment of the original motion. In such a situation, the failure to allow the amendment of the original motion and its rejection on the grounds of an irremediable defect in the procedural conditions would constitute an infringement of the right to a fair trial and the right to effective judicial protection of rights in the sense of Article 36(2) of the Charter.[81] Such a procedure, i.e., an amendment of the motion, is also possible in the case of the pandemic measures which are not covered by the rules of the Pandemic Act. On the other hand, in the case of measures covered by the Pandemic Act, i.e., extraordinary measures issued pursuant to the Pandemic Act and extraordinary measures of a nationwide coverage issued pursuant to Section 69(1)(b) or (i) of the Public Health Protection Act in a state of pandemic alert for the purpose of eradicating the COVID-19 epidemic or the danger of its recurrence, as laid down in Section 13(4) of the Pandemic Act, the above-described exception to the general rule applies. Thus, where such an extraordinary measure has lapsed because it has been replaced by a new measure of a similar content, there is no need to amend the motion in relation to the new measure, since the subject-matter of the proceedings has not been removed or the subject-matter of the proceedings has not changed, since it remains the legality of the same extraordinary measure. The Court will therefore continue the proceedings and, where appropriate, declare the measure unlawful.[82]

Last but not least, the Pandemic Act stipulates that no cassation complaint is admissible against a decision in a case pursuant to Section 13(1), first sentence (i.e., in cases where the Supreme Administrative Court has jurisdiction). That rule may be regarded as superfluous, since a cassation complaint is an appeal against a final decision of a regional court in the administrative justice system.[83] On the other hand, with reference to the general provisions of the Code of Administrative Justice, it is obvious that a cassation complaint is admissible against

---

[81] Cf., for instance, the judgement of the Supreme Administrative Court of 4 June 2020, Ref. No. 6 As 88/2020-44.

[82] Cf., for instance, the judgement of the Supreme Administrative Court of 14 April 2021, Ref. No. 8 Ao 1/2021-13.

[83] Section 102 of the Code of Administrative Justice.

a decision of the Regional Court on an extraordinary measure issued by the Regional Public Health Authority.[84]

As regards the regulation of the Pandemic Act, it can be noted that, in addition to the exceptions for judicial review of extraordinary measures, it also introduced a special obligation for the Ministry of Health and the regional public health authorities to review the extraordinary measures issued under Section 2 of the Pandemic Act at least once every 2 weeks after their issuance. If the reasons for issuing an extraordinary measure no longer exist or have changed, they will revoke or amend them immediately.[85]

Judicial review may also be sought for administrative-legal measures issued under the Public Health Protection Act where, however, it is necessary to distinguish whether the measures are ones under Section 69(1)(b) and (i) of the Act or others. With reference to the above-mentioned legislation on the Pandemic Act, the Supreme Administrative Court is competent to review certain extraordinary measures under Section 69(1)(b) or (i) of the Public Health Protection Act issued in a state of pandemic alert.[86]

Other administrative-legal measures adopted during a pandemic on the basis of the Public Health Protection Act may be challenged in court or in the administrative justice system by filing a motion to annul a measure of a general nature or part thereof. However, in this case, the special rules laid down in the Pandemic Act no longer apply, but the general rules of the Code of Administrative Justice do. A motion for annulment of a measure of a general nature may be lodged within one year from the date on which the measure of a general nature challenged by the motion came into force,[88] and will thus be heard by the competent Regional Court.[89] If it concerns an extraordinary measure issued by the Ministry of Health, then, with respect to the rules of local jurisdiction,[90] the

---

84 Identically, for instance, Hejč, D., Svoboda, T. *Zákon o mimořádných opatřeních při epidemii onemocnění COVID-19. Komentář.* Ed. 1. Praha: C. H. Beck, 2021, p. 178.
85 Section 3(7) of the Pandemic Act.
86 Section 13(1) of the Pandemic Act.
87 The above, however, only applies if such extraordinary measures issued by the Ministry of Health are of nationwide coverage and have been issued in a state of pandemic alert, i.e., after 27 February 2021 (cf., for instance, the resolution of the Supreme Administrative Court of 23 March 2021, Ref. No. 7 Ao 1/2021-32.
88 Section 101(b)(2) of the Code of Administrative Justice.
89 Section 7(1) of the Code of Administrative Justice.
90 Section 7(2) of the Code of Administrative Justice.

Municipal Court in Prague will be the competent one as the seat of the opponent (the Ministry of Health) is in the Capital City of Prague.[91]

Conclusion

The COVID-19 disease and the associated pandemic that has been going on for two years has brought with it a large number of not only new, but mainly problematic issues that have been addressed in both theory and practice and that have had to be dealt with. This has been and still is an even more "sensitive" issue as the measures taken to eradicate or eliminate the coronavirus pandemic have resulted in significant interferences with human rights and freedoms, of which the one which has been and still may be interfered with is the right to property.

One category of such measures is administrative-legal measures, which, both from the theoretical and practical point of view, constitute a rather diverse group. This group can be subdivided according to a whole number of criteria, such as the form in which the measures are adopted, the authority empowered to issue them, or the legal regulation that governs their adoption.

In relation to the legal regulation of administrative-legal measures, it can be stated that the Czech legal order contains a relatively sufficient legal basis for taking administrative-legal measures necessary to eradicate or prevent the occurrence of an epidemic. The adoption of the Pandemic Act, which declared a state of pandemic alert, has undoubtedly contributed to certain improvement. However, the effect of the Act is limited in time,[92] and it naturally only serves to control the COVID-19 epidemic. Should other types of epidemics have to be dealt with in the future, it would be necessary to proceed again under the Crisis Act or the Public Health Protection Act only, or to adopt a special legislation.[93]

In practice, however, even a sufficient legal basis does not prevent measures taken from being subsequently annulled by the courts. The reason for their

---

91 Resolution of the Supreme Administrative Court of 11 June 2021, Ref. No. 2 Ao 4/2021-16.
92 It applies per Section 22(2) of the Pandemic Act that the provisions of Sections 1 to 8 will become null and void after the lapse of 30 November 2022. Cf. also Footnote No. 45.
93 This option, however, does not represent an immediate or the fastest possible solution to the situation, as the preparation and adoption of new (special) legislation can take several months, as was the case of the Pandemic Act, which was adopted as late as in February 2021, i.e., almost one year after the first cases of the COVID-19 disease began to occur in the Czech Republic.

annulment often is not their poor legal arrangement[94] but, in particular, certain inability of the authorities empowered to issue the measures in question to adopt them in a form that meets the requirements of the legislation, in particular the requirement to provide adequate reasoning for such measures. The quality of the justification for pandemic measures must, of course, be assessed in the light of the matter and of the circumstances in which they are issued. However, inadequate justification of pandemic measures was not only a problem in the "early" days of the COVID-19 pandemic; many authorities were even not able to work on better justification of their measures as time went on. As time passes, the demands of the competent courts reviewing these measures naturally increase.[95]

Although it can be stated that during the period of this pandemic a number of problematic issues have already been resolved, especially within the framework of judicial case law, and it could therefore be expected that individual measures will stand up to judicial review, one could observe that the authorities entitled to issue individual measures often do not reflect and deliberately disregard the conclusions of the courts, which causes the subsequent annulment of the contested measures by the courts. However, as long as a measure is not annulled by a court, it is considered valid and effective and should therefore in fact be complied with by individuals, which is apparently what the individual authorities rely on. From a legal point of view, however, such practices by the competent authorities should be considered unacceptable.

References

Hendrych, D. Správní právo. In Hendrych, D. et al. *Správní právo. Obecná část.* Ed 9. Praha: C. H. Beck, 2016.

Sládeček, V. *Obecné správní právo.* Ed. 4 (amended). Praha: Wolters Kluwer ČR, 2019.

---

94 One of the latest decisions through which administrative-legal measures were annulled for not having a support in the Pandemic Act was the judgement of the Supreme Administrative Court of 2 February 2022, Ref. No. 8 Ao 2/2022-53, which annulled the extraordinary measure issued by the Ministry of Health on 29 December 2021, Ref. No. MZDR 14601/2021-34/MIN/KAN, defining conditions for operation of retail trade, provision of certain services, and organization of selected events.

95 Cf., for instance, the judgement of the Supreme Administrative Court of 27.5.2021, Ref. No. 7 Ao 6/2021-112; the judgement of the Supreme Administrative Court of 11.5.2021, Ref. No. 3 Ao 3/2021-27, or the judgement of the Municipal Court in Prague of 31 August 2020, Ref. No. 18 A 22/2020-140.

Staša J. Krizová opatření a kontrola jejich zákonnosti. In: Hlinka, T., Szakácz, A. (eds). *Aktuálne výzvy pre správne súdnictvo*. Zborník príspevkov z medzinárodnej vedeckej konferencie Bratislavské právnické fórum 2021. Bratislava: Comenius University in Bratislava, Faculty of Law, 2021, pp. 91-99.

Staša, J. *Nad významy termínu "opatření" v předpisech správního práva*. Právní rozhledy, 2017, No. 22, pp. 777-786.

Svoboda, T., Hejč, D. *K povaze "krizových opatření", odpovědnosti za škodu a ochraně subjektivních práv (1. část)*. Právní rozhledy, 2021, No. 9, pp. 315-320.

V. Sharp
Ad Hoc Legislation: The Legal Dilemma behind the Customized Approach Towards Crisis Management

1. Introduction

During the times of an unpredictable calamity, when a force majeure brings uncertainty into the matters of a caught-off-guard state and puts the rigidity of the legal system to the trial, the agility in the adoption of remedial measures is often being promoted among the top values of those in charge.[1] It is then that the laws written at a different time and for very different circumstances may seem to stop serving their purpose and the urgent need for an efficient, if one-off, solution prevails over the strict application of the conventional law-making principles. Such events, which can be generally referred to as the "black swans",[2] thereby create an opportunity for the conjunction of the executive and legislative powers, or eventually an intervention of either power into the sphere of another.

Amidst the COVID-19 crisis, the course of unprecedented events gave an impulse for this "extremis malis, extrema remedia"[3] approach to be tested wholescale. It was during these times that a series of single-use *ad hoc* laws and pieces of

---

1   The research presented in the following chapter was carried out as part of the author's Ph.D. studies at the Faculty of Law of Charles University and contains conclusions of a three-year qualitative analysis on the topic of tailor-made laws and their role in the system of public law. The author would like to express his deepest gratitude to prof. Jakub Handrlica, who not only has been supervising the works on the said doctoral thesis, but also introduced the author to the world of academia and encouraged him to unleash his scholarly potential.
2   See TALEB, N. *The Black Swan. The Impact of the Highly Improbable.* 2nd ed. London: Penguin Books, 2010. The contextual meaning of this metaphorical term, as well as its relevance for the administrative law, has been published by the co-authors of this book, see HANDRLICA, Jakub, SHARP (Šarapajev), Vladimír and BLAHOUDKOVÁ, Gabriela. "Black Swans" in Administrative Law. *The Lawyer Quarterly*, No. 3, 2021, pp. 479–492.
3   Latin maxim commonly transposed into English as "desperate times call for desperate measures." See e.g. SPEAKE, Jennifer. *Oxford Dictionary of Proverbs*. Oxford: Oxford University Press, 2015, p. 71.

subsidiary legislation[4] were adopted to minimalize the scope of damages caused by the pandemic. It comes as no surprise that some of these acts were challenged before the court, with some lawsuits making it to the Constitutional Court itself. While every country dealt with the situation in a somehow different way depending upon the specifics of each legal system and chosen crisis resolution tactic, the fundamental pattern is similar enough to be demonstrated on one jurisdiction. In this chapter, the characteristics and controversies of the aforementioned legislative technique will be broken down and analysed predominantly based on the case study of crisis legislation adopted in the Czech Republic and its judiciary review in a broader context of the historically established case law.

2. What Are Tailor-Made Laws?

When talking about *ad hoc* legislation, it is necessary to understand the background of the phenomenon of so-called tailor-made laws and their status in the legal system. Tailor-made laws (also *ad hoc* laws, individual laws or sometimes personalized laws[5]) can be succinctly described as laws "tailored" for a certain person, object, matter, or situation.[6] Being such, tailor-made laws naturally end up lacking (at least to some degree) the element of generality, be it the generality

---

4 This umbrella term will be used throughout the chapter for all general (at least by title) legal acts hierarchically subordinate to laws and other same-level sources of law. In the Czech legal system, that would typically refer to governmental regulations ("*nařízení vlády*") and ministerial decrees ("*vyhláška*").
5 See e.g. BEN-SHAHAR, Omri and PORAT, Ariel. Personalizing Negligence Law. *New York University Law Review*, 2016 Forthcoming: University of Chicago Coase-Sandor Institute for Law & Economics Research Paper No. 731, 2015. Also see PORAT, Ariel and STRAHILEVITZ, Lior J. Personalizing Default Rules and Disclosure with Big Data. *Michigan Law Review*, No. 1417, 2014. As is emphasized by Hans Christoph Grigoleit und Philip Bender, the term "personalization" is used as a synonym of "particularization" or "granularization" rather than to address humanity (see GRIGOLEIT, Hans Christoph, and BENDER, Philip Maximilian. The Law between Generality and Particularity-Potentials and Limits of Personalized Law. *Algorithmic Regulation and Personalized Law: A Handbook* (Christoph Busch & Alberto De Franceschi eds., 2021) (2019): pp. 115–136).
6 The author's definition of tailor-made laws has been introduced in SHARP (Sharapaev), Vladimír. When "Tailor-made laws" are not laws indeed. *The Lawyer Quarterly*, No. 1, 2020, pp. 57–60.

in addressee, or in subject.[7] Although these two defining elements will in most cases be consequent (with particularity logically excluding generality *et vice versa*[8]), the lack of generality should be considered a rather dominant attribute, as some laws can be *de facto* customized while technically remaining general.[9]

In order to distinguish tailor-made laws par excellence from other legislative techniques, we ought to recognize an essential feature of these laws, that is these laws are typically customized quite explicitly. This differentiates unfeigned *ad hoc* legislation from laws disguised as general while clandestinely targeting a particular matter, or conversely, laws that may appear to be tailored but are in fact general when it comes to their classification.[10] The examples of both mentioned categories can be found in many jurisdictions: as for the first one, it is not hard to imagine a general piece of legislation constructed in a way that favors a certain person or a group[11] (or, quite contrary, targets it[12]). Even though lobbying as such often evokes controversies and may be performed in different forms, it is generally accepted in many countries and is even considered a natural part of democratic policymaking.[13] As for the second one, the etymology of law naming

---

7   As the presented definition of tailor-made laws is essentially based on the lack of generality or, some degree of customization, this definition can fit many variations of tailor-made laws, as will be presented further.
8   The logical principles of generality and particularity are quite universal and used in many fields of study. It is therefore possible to compare the understanding of this dichotomy in other disciplines, and also follow the application of these concepts in logical operations such as deduction and induction, which are no less relevant for law as they are for technical sciences. See e.g. SMITH, S. P. The Proclivities of Particularity and Generality. *Journal of Consciousness Exploration & Research*, Vol. 1, Issue 4, 2010, pp. 429–440.
9   This refers to the legislative technique per se rather than to the actual effects of such laws and their applicational impact.
10 See VURMO, Gjergji. *Tailor-made laws in the Western Balkans: state capture in disguise.* Policy contribution No. 2020–12, CEPS Policy Insights, 2020.
11 See e.g. HELPMAN, Elhanan and PERSSON, Torsten. Lobbying and Legislative Bargaining. *Advances in Economic Analysis & Policy*, Vol. 1, No. 1, 2001. See also SEOK, I. The status of legislative lobbying and legislation on lobbyist system. *Dongguk Law Review*, No. 8, 2016, pp. 121–148.
12 E.g. the so-called Lex Babiš. See Martínek, Daniel. Semi-successful Socio-political Transformation in CEE: The Case of the Czech Republic. *Der Donauraum*, Vol. 60, No. 1–2, 2020, pp. 71–86.
13 See e.g. JORDAN, Grant. Lobbying. In FLINDERS, Matthew et al. (eds). *The Oxford Handbook of British Politics*, Oxford Academic, 2010, pp. 365–382.

might depend on historical and political context. For instance, in the times of the Roman Republic and Empire it was customary that the laws be named after the emperor or a sponsoring legislator.[14] This tradition has in some form endured until this day as many laws are (either officially or unofficially) named after their promoters.[15]

If the tailored nature of a law is perceived as a legislatively-technical issue rather than a matter related to its background or the consequences of its adoption (the legislative initiative, drafting process, comment or amendment procedure or the parliamentary procedure), we may find that not only are these concepts theoretically unrelated, but they are also not likely to be applied concurrently.[16] Despite the fact that such misuse of legislative power cannot be completely excluded and should be kept an eye on, especially bearing in mind the dangerous potential of individualized legislation, tailor-made laws, on the other hand, also seem far too overt to pursue goals that ought to be hidden from the general public. Thus, tailor-made laws in the sense derived from the definition above should not be automatically associated with lobbying or further practices aiming to influence the law-making for the sake of promoting interests of a particular third party.

When assessing the attribute of generality in law, it is fitting to emphasize that neither generality nor particularity are categories dealing in absolutes.[17] While the dichotomy of general and particular issues has many implications related not only to policymaking, but also to application of legal rules,[18] it is naturally the latter that is going to interest us in this regard. In basic theory of generally binding legal regulation (i.e. laws),[19] the two key factors that distinguish them

---

14 E.g. Lex Iulia, Lex Publilia, Lex Antonia, Lex Hortensia etc.
15 See WEISSERT, Carol S. Policy entrepreneurs, policy opportunists, and legislative effectiveness. *American Politics Quarterly*, Vol. 19, No. 2, 1991, pp. 262–274.
16 See e.g. SURREY, Stanley S. The Congress and the Tax Lobbyist: How Special Tax Provisions Get Enacted. *Harvard Law Review*, vol. 70, no. 7, 1957, pp. 1145–82.
17 See ENDICOTT, Timothy A. *The generality of Law*. Forthcoming in Luís Duarte d'Almeida, James Edwards and Andrea Dolcetti, eds., Reading HLA Hart's' The Concept of Law' (Hart Publishing 2013), Oxford Legal Studies, Research Paper 41, 2012.
18 See SCHAUER, Frederick. The generality of law. *West Virginia Law Review*, No. 107, 2004, pp. 217–233.
19 The used term is a somewhat flimsy, yet accurate translation of the term "*obecně závazný právní předpis*" existing in Czech legal theory. The author uses this unorthodox and oddly sounding term on purpose in order to express the nature of the law and emphasize the key difference between the generally binding acts (legal regulations), and individually binding acts.

from other forms of regulatory activity, are the generality in subject, and generality in addressee. In the spirit of the archaic legal principle "iura non in singulas personas, sed generaliter constituuntur",[20] this has traditionally been considered the threshold where the authority of the legislative power encountered the authority of the executive power.[21] The relationship between different forms of regulatory acts can be demonstrated on the following table:

	Subject	Addressee
Laws	Generally defined subject	Generally defined addressee
Individual acts	Particular subject	Individually identified addressee
General measures	Particular subject (Generally defined subject)	Generally defined addressee (Individual addressee)

As can be seen from the table above, the only category that *a priori* allows the particularization of either the subject, or the addressee,[22] are the so-called general measures. General measures (in German: *Allgemeinverfügung* or "general decree", in Czech: *Opatření obecné povahy* or "measure of a general nature") have different definitions depending on jurisdiction,[23] but can be jointly described as hybrid acts having features of both legal regulations and individual acts. These measures are neither laws nor individual administrative acts, their issue is governed by a special set of rules and is carried out by an administrative authority

---

20 Latin for "law is not created for individuals, but generally for all". See Digest – Liber Primus, 1.3.8 Ulpianus III ad Sabinum.
21 See BOGUSZAK, J., ČAPEK, J., GERLOCH, A. Teorie práva [Theory of Law]. 2nd revised edition. Prague: ASPI Publilshing, 2004, pp. 47–48.
22 While the particularization of the subject of regulation is typical for general measures, legal theory also suggests that in some cases such measures can also have an individualized addressee. See e.g. HENDRYCH, Dušan (ed.). Správní právo: obecná část [Administrative law: General Part]. 9th issue. Prague: C.H. Beck, Academia iuris, 2016, p. 126.
23 See e.g. Sec. 35 of the German Federal Act on Administrative Procedure (Verwaltungsverfahrensgesetz), or Sec. 171 of the Czech Code of Administrative Procedure (zákon č. 500/2004 Sb., správní řád).

(i.e. a body of the executive branch) instead of a law-making body.[24] As will be made evident further, general measures have played a prominent role during the COVID crisis, as has the contrast between this form of administrative activity and tailor-made laws.

Circling back to the question of generality, despite the fact that legal theory prefers to demonstrate generality and particularity as two quite extreme antipoles, the author believes that it is the degree of generality that determines the nature of a law or another regulatory act. Hence for example when talking about the generality in addressee of a certain regulation, the circle of addressees constitutes a set of persons (either natural or legal) connected by the same defining element. Applying the mathematical set theory,[25] it is possible to rank the circle of addressees from the broadest and thus general, through the narrower circle, to the circle so narrow that it in fact overlaps with a specific person. For instance, the broadest circle of addressees could be offered by hypothetical universally binding laws applying to every individual regardless of territoriality or temporality.[26] Such laws would therefore universally apply:

a) to every natural or legal person regardless of their location, nationality, residence, tax domicile, sex, age, education, criminal record, and further biological, social and bureaucratic factors;
b) at every given moment of time both retroactively and pro futuro.

Should any of the given factors be specified, the circle of addressees will inevitably narrow down, thus making the law less general and more specific. Accordingly, the set of addressees defined via the citizenship of a particular state shall be less general than the set including all persons regardless of their nationality.

---

[24] Provided the nature of these measures and their "philosophical" rapprochement with tailor-made laws, we can also raise a question whether general measures could or should be classified as laws *largo sensu*. For the sake of theoretical clarity, this chapter will strictly differentiate these terms and outline the differences especially in the process of their adoption.

[25] See QUINE, Willard van O. *Set theory and its logic*. Harvard University Press, 2009. See also FRAENKEL, Abraham Adolf, Yehoshua BAR-HILLEL, and Azriel LEVY. *Foundations of set theory*. Elsevier, 1973. On this occasion, the author would like to acknowledge that the use of set theory in the daily practice of law making was introduced to him by Dr. Ondřej Zezulka, an experienced lawyer and brilliant legislator, whom the author hereby sincerely thanks.

[26] Besides the personal scope, the application of law is also determined by jurisdiction and time scope.

The set of addressees defined by two factors (e.g. citizenship of a certain state and age) shall be narrower and thus less general than the set defined by only one factor (citizenship). In other words, according to the theory of sets, every given set is more general than the other if it covers all factors covered by the latter one.[27] By adding further factors and hence gradually narrowing down the circle of addressees of a certain law, we can eventually reach the total particularization where such law would only apply to a single addressee fulfilling the outlined criteria.

The principle of relative generality can be well demonstrated on the analogy with an obstructive practice presumably notorious to all employment lawyers. Civil service, employment, or immigration legislation in a number of cases requires that a vacant position be occupied through an open, independent and transparent selection process.[28] Should an interested party seek to circumvent such regulation and hire a particular person selected prior to engaging in a formal process, one of the possible and most convenient ways to do so is by tailoring the admission criteria to this specific person. Such tailoring can be done in many ways: if the person in question, for instance, has a particular set of skills, the admission criteria can be based on these skills. If such person has some distinctive characteristics, the assessment can be based on these characteristics. Although in most cases it is sufficient to rule out a majority of potential applicants, ad absurdum the outlined criteria could be so strict that they could only be met by a single candidate.[29] The same principle governed by the set theory applies to policymaking.

Having established that the generality of law is not an absolute but rather a relative concept, it is necessary to define the criteria for finding the line separating laws from other regulatory acts, i.e. the point where relative generality turns into particularity. As the generality per se cannot be assessed without context, the

---

27 See De RAEDT, Luc. *Logic of Generality.* In: Sammut, C., Webb, G.I. (eds) Encyclopedia of Machine Learning. Springer, Boston, MA, 2011, pp. 624–631.

28 In case of immigration law, it can also be stipulated that prior to hiring a foreign citizen, the vacant position must be first openly offered to local employment seekers, and can be offered to an alien only provided that no fitting compatriot was found. See e.g. JOUZA, Ladislav. Zaměstnávání cizinců v České republice [Employment of foreign nationals in the Czech Republic]. *Bulletin Advokacie*, 2017.

29 For example, and cum grano salis, if the "desired" applicant was to graduate from a specific university in a specific year with specific classification, while at the same time having command of a unique combination of languages and previous work experience from a specific company.

position of that point may vary in different cases and therefore remains at least partially unclear. It is, however, possible to address this issue based on the criterium of interference with a specific person's rights, namely the intensity of such interference and possibility of defense against it.[30] After all, it is the limited to non-existent defense against legal regulations that evokes a good deal of controversy around tailor-made laws.[31]

When it comes to classification of tailor-made laws, several methods of distinguishment can be used. The first method has already been published by the author[32] and is based on Prof. Timothy Endicott's "modes of generality".[33] The said modes of generality of laws are attributed to the four factors:

a) persons to whom they apply (generality in addressee);
b) conduct which they regulate (generality in subject);
c) time at which they are in effect (generality in temporal scope);
d) place in which they apply (generality in territorial scope).

Bearing in mind that generality is relative with all the mentioned factors, we must acknowledge that, in order for an act to fall under the definition of a tailor-made law, it must indicate a lack of generality of a certain intensity. For instance, it is typical for the laws to be governed by the principle of territoriality meaning that such laws shall have effect only in the territory of a specific state. Similarly, due to the principle of general prohibition of retroactivity, most laws are effective from a certain timepoint further. Although these facts do indicate the decrease in generality and tendency towards particularity, the given factors are still considered general enough to meet the requirements imposed by legal theory.

The second possible classification of tailor-made laws is based on the circumstances under which these laws are adopted and the purpose that they are

---

30 See HANDRLICA, Jakub. Two Faces of Tailor-Mare Laws in Administrative Law. *The Lawyer Quarterly*, No. 1, 2020, pp. 34–47.
31 See also KIRCHHOF, Gregor. *Die Allgemeinheit des Gesetzes. Über einen notwendigen Garanten der Freiheit, der Gleichheit und der Demokratie*. Tübingen: Mohr Siebeck, Jus Publicum 184, 2009. XXI.
32 See HANDRLICA, Jakub, SHARP (Šarapajev), Vladimír and BLAHOUDKOVÁ, Gabriela. "Black Swans" in Administrative Law. *The Lawyer Quarterly*, No. 3, 2021, pp. 479–492.
33 See ENDICOTT, T. *The Generality of Law*. Forthcoming. In: D'Almeida, L. D., Edwards, J., Dolcetti, A. (eds.). Reading HLA Hart's 'The Concept of Law' (Hart Publishing 2013). Oxford: Oxford Legal Studies Research Paper No. 41/2012, University of Oxford, 2013, pp. 3–4.

to serve. In this regard, we can distinguish laws tailored for a certain situation (while potentially remaining general in their subject and addressee) from laws that are less influenced by the circumstances they were created under.

The third classification, which is somewhat similar to the previous one, is based on the German legal theory dividing tailor-made laws into the following categories:[34]

a) *Einzelfallgesetz* ("law for a specific case or event") often used as a synonym of an individual law;
b) *Individualgesetz* ("individual law") governing an individual, explicitly defined case or concerning a specific person;
c) *Maßnahmegesetz* ("law adopted as a measure") being quite self-explanatory;
d) *Anlassgesetz* ("law adopted due to an occasion"), addressing specific situations despite referring to them in general terms.

Apart from the aforementioned categories, it can also be argued that ad hoc legislation can be divided into tailor-made laws *stricto sensu* standing for the unconcealed and openly personalized regulations, and tailor-made laws *largo sensu* including the laws disguised as general in their nature.

3. Crisis Law-Making

The ability of tailor-made laws to target specific problems effectively and agilely did not allow them to stay unnoticed during the recent COVID crisis. Being a naturally and *ex definitionem* fitting tool of crisis management,[35] these laws were in different forms used to create emergency measures attempting to mitigate the undesirable effects of the pandemic. As a matter of example, the German solution included different forms of state regulation, beginning with general measures,[36] through regulations,[37] and ending with

---

34 See SCHNEIDER, H. *Gesetzgebung. Ein Lehr- und Handbuch.* 3rd edition. Heidelberg: C. F. Müller Verlag, 2002, pp. 22–30.
35 See PERFETTI, L. Massnahmeforschriften and emergency powers in contemporary public law. *The Lawyer Quarterly.* 2020, Vol. 10, No. 1, pp. 30–33.
36 See e.g. the recent Allgemeinverfügung zur Bewältigung erheblicher Patientenzahlen in Krankenhäusern Bekanntmachung des Bayerischen Staatsministeriums für Gesundheit und Pflege vom 2. August 2022, Az. G24-K9000-2022/480-1.
37 See e.g. Coronavirus-Einreiseverordnung vom 28. September 2021 (BAnz AT 29.09.2021 V1) or Coronavirus-Testverordnung vom 21. September 2021 (BAnz AT 21.09.2021 V1).

laws.[38] The Czech Republic adopted a similar approach using a variety of legal tools exercising the political will on different levels of legislature hierarchy. Despite the prima facie similarities, there have been some irregularities with the Czech crisis policy making that are worth paying attention to.

First of all, it is necessary to mention that the emergency measures in the Czech Republic were issued in three forms: crisis measured adopted directly by the government, general measures of the Ministry of Health, and laws adopted by the parliament either in emergency or regular hearings. The last category can be classified as a rather paragon example of *Anlassgesetze*, as the laws adopted in connection with the COVID situation were clearly and openly associated with the pandemics, and yet in most cases were still quite general when it comes to their subject or addressees. The association of these laws with this particular situation has even been made obvious by their very names, whereas the examples of such laws include e.g. Act on Extraordinary Measures During the COVID-19 Epidemic[39] or Act on Compensation of Persons Providing Paid Health Services Taking Into Account the Effects of the COVID-19 Epidemic in the year 2021.[40]

The first mentioned law often referred to in the legal community as "Lex Covid,"[41] may be used as an exemplar demonstrating the pattern of crisis legislature. The law stipulates measures for the management of the COVID-19 epidemic (caused by the new coronavirus known as SARS CoV-2) and its impact on the territory of the Czech Republic. On the day this law entered into force, a so-called state of pandemic alert was automatically (*ex lege*) declared.[42] This state of

---

38 See e.g. Entwurf eines Gesetzes zur finanziellen Stabilisierung der gesetzlichen Krankenversicherung (GKV-Finanzstabilisierungsgesetz – GKV-FinStG) or Entwurf eines Gesetzes zur Stärkung des Schutzes der Bevölkerung und insbesondere vulnerabler Personengruppen vor COVID-19 (Drucksache 20/2573).
39 Zákon č. 94/2021 Sb., o mimořádných opatřeních při epidemii onemocnění COVID-19 a o změně některých souvisejících zákonů [Act No. 94/2021 Coll., on Extraordinary Measures During the COVID-19 Epidemic and on the Amendment of Some Related Laws].
40 Zákon č. 160/2021 Sb., o kompenzacích osobám poskytujícím hrazené zdravotní služby zohledňujících dopady epidemie onemocnění COVID-19 v roce 2021 [Act No. 160/2021 Coll., on Compensation of Persons Providing Paid Health Services Taking Into Account the Effects of the COVID-19 Epidemic in the year 2021].
41 Please note that the term "Lex Covid" has been used in the Czech legal environment rather promiscuously and may thus refer to different laws depending on the specific context. There are also modifications of this term such as "Lex Covid Justice", etc.
42 The terminology used by the law suggests that it does' not distinguish between the terms "epidemic" and "pandemic", but uses them interchangeably. Although both terms

pandemic alert may be terminated or reinstated by a resolution of the Chamber of Deputies of the Parliament adopted based on a proposal of the government or one fifth of all deputies. The resolution on the termination of the pandemic alert and its renewal shall be published in the collection of laws.

The law does not directly introduce any particular crisis measures, but instead empowers the Ministry of Health, the regional hygienic stations, and the Hygienic Station of the Capital City of Prague[43] to order emergency measures prescribing certain activities contributing to the fulfilment of the purpose of eliminating the COVID-19 epidemic or the risk of its recurrence said purpose, or prohibiting or restricting certain activities or services, the performance of which could spread the COVID-19 disease, or setting conditions for the performance of such activities or the provision of such services. The Ministry of Health may impose an emergency measure with a full-scope application or with only a multi-region scope. A regional health station may impose an emergency measure within its administrative district.

Despite the fact that the law does not introduce any particular emergency measures, it does typologically, yet quite rigorously define such measures. To provide the reader with an idea of (relative) generality of this definition, the areas of regulation include:[44]

a) restricting public transport or imposing conditions on its operation,
b) restricting the conduct of business or other activities in a business premises, business centers, marketplaces, market stall or other premises used for business or similar activities, or imposing conditions for their conduct, including limiting the hours of operation,
c) restricting the operation of barbers, hairdressers, pedicure, manicure or solarium services, the provision of beauty, massage, regeneration or reconditioning services or the exercise of a trade in which the integrity of the skin is compromised, or imposing conditions for the exercise or provision thereof,

---

have different meanings in medical terminology (see Morens, David M., Gregory K. Folkers, and Anthony S. Fauci. What is a pandemic? *The Journal of infectious diseases*, Vol. 200, No. 7, 2009, pp. 1018–1021.), the two terms will be used as synonyms to maintain consistency with the language used by the law.

43 This particular hygienic station is explicitly mentioned due to the status of the Capital City of Prague technically being both a region and a city, and thus having its own sui generis legal regime.

44 See Sec. 2 paragraph 2 of Act on Extraordinary Measures During the COVID-19 Epidemic.

d) restricting the operation of natural or artificial bathing places or saunas or imposing conditions for their operation,
e) restricting the teaching or other educational activities at universities, higher vocational schools, other schools or educational institution, children's groups, institutions for children in need of immediate assistance, childcare institutions for children under 3 years of age, institutions for the education, teaching and/or out-of-school education of children over 3 years of age or other similar institution, or setting conditions for teaching or other activities therein,
f) restricting the operation of music, dance, gambling or similar social clubs or discos, gambling halls or casinos, including limiting the hours of operation,
g) restrictions on the operation of zoological or botanical gardens, museums, galleries, exhibition spaces, castles, palaces or similar historical or cultural buildings, public libraries, observatories or planetariums, or the establishment of conditions for their operation or use, or
h) restrictions on the holding of musical, theatrical, or cinematographic performances, movement or dance productions, festivals, cultural festivals or shows or other similar events, or the establishment of conditions for their holding.

As can be seen from the cited provision, the degree of generality of different emergency measures is not strictly consistent and varies from almost universal to relatively strictly defined subjects and addressees. The law operates with particularization of all four factors: subject, addressee, as well as time and territoriality. It also explicitly (and quite unorthodoxly) stipulates that "[p]ersons to whom the emergency measure apply are obliged to comply with it", suggesting that the law can only apply to certain addressees.[45] The law also states that the extraordinary measures shall be issued by the Ministry of Health or the regional sanitary stations only to the extent and for the duration strictly necessary, meaning that the particularization of temporary scope is also expected and even promoted.[46] In practice, the principle of temporality of emergency measures can be fulfilled by the use of sunset clauses limiting the temporary scope of such measures.[47]

---

45 See Sec. 2 paragraph 3 of Act on Extraordinary Measures During the COVID-19 Epidemic.
46 See Sec. 3 paragraph 1 of Act on Extraordinary Measures During the COVID-19 Epidemic.
47 See KOUROUTAKIS, A. E. The Constitutional Value of Sunset Clauses. New York: Routledge, 2018, pp. 3–10. See also RANCHORDÁS, S. Sunset Clauses and

While the attributes of COVID laws are rather straightforward, the situation with governmental crisis measures and general measures seems to be more complicated. Crisis measures[48] are issued based on the special empowerment stipulated by the Constitutional Act on the Security of the Czech Republic[49] and Act on Crisis Management.[50] Besides the crisis measures per se, the government also has a sui generis tool related to these measures, that is the power to declare the state of emergency creating the framework for further measures and conditioning their issue.

A crisis measure is defined as an organizational or technical measure designed to address a crisis situation and eliminate its consequences, including measures that interfere with the rights and obligations of persons.[51] Crisis measures are issued by the government acting as a crisis management authority, and their specific form is not in any way specified. Contrary to the emergency measures issued by the Ministry of Health under the Act on the Protection of Public Health applied during the initial epidemic waves,[52] where the law explicitly stipulates that "[m]easures (...) in the field of preventing the emergence and spread of infectious diseases (...) pursuant to Section 80 paragraph 1 point g) (...) shall be issued by the competent public health authority in a form of a general measure",[53] governmental crisis measures must be assessed materially based on their characteristics.[54]

Perceiving crisis measures as tailor-made laws, the main criterium for such assessment would be (apart from the obvious fact that these measures are *ex*

Experimental Regulations: Blessing or Curse for Legal Certainty? Statute Law Review. 2015, No. 1, pp. 28–45.

48 In Czech: *"krizová opatření vlády"* (crisis measure of the government).
49 Ústavní zákon č. 110/1998 Sb., o bezpečnosti České republiky [Constitutional Act No. 110/1998 Coll., on the Security of the Czech Republic].
50 Zákon č. 240/2000 Sb., o krizovém řízení a o změně některých zákonů (krizový zákon) [Act No. 240/2000 Coll., on Crisis Management and on Amendments to Certain Acts (Crisis Act)].
51 See Sec. 2 point c) of Act on Crisis Management.
52 Zákon č. 258/2000 Sb., o ochraně veřejného zdraví a o změně některých souvisejících zákonů [Act No. 258/2000 Coll., on the Protection of Public Health and on Amendments to Certain Related Acts].
53 See Sec. 94a paragraph 2 of the Act on the Protection of Public Health.
54 See HANDRLICA, Jakub, BALOUNOVÁ, Jana, SHARP (Sharapaev), Vladimír. Náhrady a opatření přijatá v době pandemie [Compensations and measures issued during the pandemic]. *Právní rozhledy*, 2020, No. 22, pp. 784–791.

definitionem issued ad hoc for a specific situation) the degree of their generality. Having taken a closer look at those measures and their subject, we can argue that the pattern by which the selection of sets was governed is rather unclear and sometimes even somewhat chaotic. The particularity of their provisions, even though not reaching the degree of full personalization where the addressees could be individually identified, leads to a state where the composition of (relatively narrow) sets creates selective effect and may therefore be discriminatory.[55] For example, one of the first crisis measures issued in spring of 2020[56] prohibited (for a limited period of time[57]) all retail sales and sale of services in the premises, except for the explicitly named businesses such as those dealing with food, computer and telecommunications equipment, audio and video receivers, consumer electronics, appliances and other household products, fuel, hygiene products, cosmetics and other drugstore goods, pharmacies and dispensaries of medical devices, pet food and other animal supplies, eyeglasses, contact lenses and related goods, newspapers and magazines, tobacco products, or laundry and dry cleaning services. While the mentioned sets are still relatively general, if typologically defined, it is still questionable why these specific categories were selected for exception.

The question of a form of governmental crisis measures has been subject to judiciary assessment as these measures were challenged before the Constitutional Court.[58] The somehow controversial resolution accompanied by five dissenting opinions (votum separatum) signed by seven justices out of fifteen[59] concluded that the resolution of the government declaring a state of emergency is primarily an act of application of constitutional law and thus constitutes an *acte gouvernemental*, i.e. a political question which has a normative impact and cannot be subject to review by the Constitutional Court.[60] The court further concluded that

---

55 See WINTR, Jan. K ústavnosti a zákonnosti protiepidemických opatření na jaře 2020 [On constitutionality and legality of anti-epidemic measures in spring of 2020]. *Správní právo*, No. 5–6, 2020, pp. 282–297.
56 Resolution of the Government of the Czech Republic of 14 March 2020, No. 211, on the adoption of the crisis measure prohibiting the retail sales and services.
57 With effect from 6:00 a.m. of 14 March 2020 until 6:00 a.m. of 24 March 2020.
58 Resolution of the Constitutional Court of the Czech Republic of 22nd April 2020, Case No. Pl. ÚS 8/20. The same opinion was reached by the Prague Municipal court in its judgment of 23 April 2020, Case No. 14 A 41/2020.
59 Honourable Justices Jan Filip, Vladimír Sládeček, Radovan Suchánek, Kateřina Šimáčková, Vojtěch Šimíček, David Uhlíř, and Milada Tomková.
60 The court however also stated that the review by the Constitutional Court could not be absolutely excluded in respect of that part of the decision which contained specific

a government resolution on the adoption of crisis measures pursuant to Act of Crisis Management has the nature of a law *sui generis* (generally binding legal regulation), and as such is reviewable in the derogatory procedure. The irony and controversy of this decision lies in the fact that even though the Constitutional Court recognized that governmental crisis measures are general enough to be considered laws, the court has at the same time stated that practically identical extraordinary measures of the Ministry of Health have a form of general measures.[61]

The above conclusion has to do with the so-called formal or formalistic approach towards the perception of general measures.[62] While the material (substantial) form of emergency measures issued by the Ministry of Health under the Act on the Protection of Public Health is at least questionable since these measures are de facto copying those issued by the government in the form of crisis measures, the fact that the formalistic approach has been upheld by the Constitutional Court (whereas the court concluded that the mere designation of the extraordinary measures as general measures is sufficient to determine the form of this act[63]) is at least surprising, as the exact same court was considered a big advocate of the substantial approach as far as general measures had been concerned.[64] The substantial approach towards general measures was also promoted by the Supreme Administrative Court, which had previously stated that "[i]f an act is only formally designated as a general measure, yet from a material point of

---

crisis measures containing generally binding normative rules of conduct, in particular on the basis of a proposal by a political minority.

61 See HEJČ, David. Nezákonnost mimořádných opatření Ministerstva zdravotnictví k onemocnění COVID-19 podle MS v Praze: Když obsah překračuje formu [Illegality of the Ministry of Health's COVID-19 Emergency Measures According to the Municipal Court in Prague: When Content Exceeds Form]. *Soudní rozhledy*, No. 6, 2020, pp. 185–190. Also, see ratio decidendi of the judgment of the Supreme Administrative Court of the Czech Republic of 13 October 2020, Case No. 4 As 258/2020-60 (published in the Collection of Landmark Decisions of the Supreme Administrative Court, Vol. XIX, No. 1/2021).

62 See e.g. KOLMAN, Petr. Transparentnost veřejné správy: Materiální racionalita vs. formální pojetí práva aneb Jde o opatření obecné povahy? [Transparency in Public Administration: Substantive Rationality vs. Formal Conception of Law. What is a Measure of a General Nature?] *Správní právo*, Vol. 46, No. 1, 2013, pp. 38–44.

63 See the resolution of the Constitutional Court of the Czech Republic, Case No. Pl. ÚS 8/20, paragraphs 51 to 54.

64 See the Ruling of the Constitutional Court of the Czech Republic of 19 November 2008, Case No. Pl.ÚS 14/07.

view it does not meet its conceptual features (concreteness of the subject, generality of the addressees), the Supreme Administrative Court will annul it on the objection of the appellant".[65] Despite the fact that the decisions in question are unconventional from the theoretical point of view, formalistic categorization paradoxically happened to have brought some rather positive side effects, as will be shown below. If anything, this decision has proven the line between tailor-made laws and general measures unclear and exposed the practical dimension of a prima facie theoretical problem.

4. Persisting concerns regarding tailored legislation and possible solutions

Despite the fact that the presented evidence shows the exploitation of tailor-made laws growing almost mundane in the past years, as numerous tailor-made laws of some kind were being adopted on a close-to-daily basis as instruments of crisis management, the existence of these laws in the legal system of public law can be still deemed problematic. It is fair to say that tailored legislation has already been held accountable for several attempt to abuse the law in the past, which might have given rise to certain concerns connected to its "potential for evil", if you will.[66] Such metaphorical evil could be found in both direct and indirect products of customized law making depending primarily on the purpose of these laws and the cost that the legislator is willing to pay to reach it. To understand and address the risks of tailor-made legislation based on their undesirable effects, we must identify and categorize these risks. Below the author outlines the key problematic factors having crucial impact on the degree of metaphorical evil a law can achieve, and proposes the possibilities of making at least some amends with customized laws.

First, it must be acknowledged that the concept of generality of laws is of great importance not only to legal theory based on the Ulpianian perception of law, but also for the proper functioning of the state as whole. In the broader context, the gradual blurring of distinctions between laws and further acts creates a

---

65 See the judgment of the Supreme Administrative Court of the Czech Republic of 27 September 2005, Case No. 1 Ao 1/2005-98. This decision has been published in the Collection of Landmark Decisions of the Supreme Administrative Court, Vol. IV, No. 1/2006.
66 This term has been used to describe the development of the main character in Shakespeare's Macbeth. See DEGÜNTHER, Alina. *Good and Evil in Shakespeare's King Lear and Macbeth*. Anchor Academic Publishing, 2014.

dilemma that has to do with the separation of powers.[67] Since one of the building stones of the checks and balances system has been the rather clear distinction of roles of each power,[68] the extension of one (legislative) branch into the sphere of another (executive), although not ipso facto excluded, may be considered a breach of constitutional principal. The question of constitutionality, as well as the relationship between branches of power and the degree of their separation, is country-specific and cannot (nor should) be generalized. It is however safe to claim that tailor-made laws have been unwelcome in many countries. The German *Grundgesetz* even contains an explicit prohibition of tailored legislation stating that a law must apply generally and not only to the individual case.[69] In the Czech Republic, a similar question had been subject to judicial review by the Constitutional Court, which concluded that administrative assessment (being a right attributed to the executive power) cannot be replaced nor bypassed by a law, as such action would interfere with the established division of power.[70]

---

67 See VILE, Maurice John Crawley. *Constitutionalism and the Separation of Powers*. Vol. 92. Oxford: Clarendon Press, 1967. See also CAROLAN, Eoin. *The new separation of powers: a theory for the modern state*. Oxford University Press, 2009.
68 See STAŠA, J. Správní akty [Administrative acts]. In: D. Hendrych (ed.). *Správní právo. Obecná část [Administrative Law. General Part]*. C. H. Beck, 2016, pp. 133–136.
69 See Article 19 paragraph 1 of the Grundgesetz für die Bundesrepublik Deutschland (German Constitution or verbatim "Basic Law for the Federal Republic of Germany"): "*Soweit nach diesem Grundgesetz ein Grundrecht durch Gesetz oder auf Grund eines Gesetzes eingeschränkt werden kann, muß das Gesetz allgemein und nicht nur für den Einzelfall gelten. Außerdem muß das Gesetz das Grundrecht unter Angabe des Artikels nennen.*" [official translation by Prof. Christian Tomuschat, Prof. David P. Currie, Prof. Donald P. Kommers and Raymond Kerr, in cooperation with the Language Service of the German Bundestag: "Insofar as, under this Basic Law, a basic right may be restricted by or pursuant to a law, such law must apply generally and not merely to a single case. In addition, the law must specify the basic right affected and the Article in which it appears."] It should not be left unnoticed that, strictly speaking, the prohibition only applies to those laws restricting basic rights.
70 See the Ruling of the Constitutional Court of the Czech Republic of 28th June 2005, Case No. Pl. ÚS 24/04. This derogatory decision was published in the Collection of Laws as it repealed Section 3a of Act No. 114/1995 Coll., on Inland Navigation, that attempted to declare the public interest in development and modernization of the Elbe waterway in the form of law. Because of the memorable and specific subject, this landmark decision has been known to the legal community under the name of "Weirs of Elbe" (in Czech: "*Jezy na Labi*").

As far as the constitutional dimension of tailor-made laws is concerned, the assessment of this issue is largely dependent upon the political consensus over the model parliamentary system which is or ought to be put in place. As mentioned earlier, it is neither a priori excluded nor unusual that the separation of power is not applied absolutely.[71] Hence, some overlap between the legislative and the executive branch is imaginable, especially in a system where the executive power is directly derived from the composition of the parliament and is in most cases existentially dependent on the parliamentary support.[72] In a system in which the ministers are traditionally appointed from among the Members of the Parliament and the effective and undisturbed functioning of the government is mostly ensured by the parliamentary majority, the strict separation may only remain on paper while the actual disposition shows no balancing whatsoever.[73] In any case, this question must be left open as its political implications exceed the topic of this chapter.

Second, we must assess in what manner are the addressees of such law directly or indirectly impacted by its tailored nature. Should tailor-made laws have no boundaries regarding the degree of their particularity, the legislator could *ex lege* impose duties or govern rights of individual persons.[74] While this situation seems quite extreme and its elimination presents itself as reasonable, solution of this problem is just a mere beginning of the puzzle. Even when the degree of generality is maintained at a relatively decent level, the key problem of tailor-made laws that remains is that these laws can hardly be fought against in the ordinary

---

[71] See ACKERMAN, Bruce. The new separation of powers. *Harvard law review*, 2000, pp. 633–729. See also ABRAMS, Norman. Developments in US anti-terrorism law: Checks and balances undermined. *Journal of International Criminal Justice*, No. 4–5, 2006, pp. 1117–1136.

[72] See COONEY, Barney. The relationship of administrative law to Parliament and ministerial decision making. *Legislative Studies*, Vol. 9, No. 1, 1994, pp. 65–70.

[73] The Czech Republic may serve as an example of such system, as the Parliament can be argued to be dominant in many areas. See WINTR, Jan. *Česká parlamentní kultura [The Czech parliamentary culture]*. Prague: Auditorium, 2010, pp. 336 and 382.

[74] As absurd as this example might sound, this has happened before, and we can find evidence of such laws even in Czech legal history. For instance, Statutory measure No. 39/1968 Coll. of the Bureau of the National Assembly on the loss of office of a Member of the National Assembly provided that a deputy for whom the National Assembly has consented to prosecution and detention and who has evaded prosecution by fleeing abroad shall lose his office. This law, adopted specifically for General Jan Šejna who has escaped to the United States of America, is known as "Lex Šejna".

court of law. Since laws are expected to provide for general rules of conduct, an individual can typically only challenge these laws before the Constitutional Court, and only do so incidentally, i.e. in connection with an infringement of his constitutionally guaranteed rights.[75] In case of crisis legislation, this issue is also closely related to the question of compensation for damages cause by such measures,[76] as laws are generally excluded from state liability.[77]

The outlined issue can be resolved in several ways. If tailor-made laws were to be recognized as an independent sui generis category of laws, one of the possible solutions would be to introduce procedural mechanisms of judicial review of such laws on general, incidental, or semi-incidental basis.[78] The existing framework for the review of general measures can be certainly used as inspiration since it proved to be functional during the review of the extraordinary measures issued by the Ministry of Health of the Czech Republic, as described earlier. Although technically challengeable, the formalistic approach towards these measures enabled their full-scope review and also activated the state liability, thus creating grounds for compensation.

Third and finally, a great deal of concerns about tailored legislation has to do with constitutional (or philosophical, for that matter) limits for legislation. To find a sustainable place for tailor-made laws in legal system, we must ask ourselves a question of whether the legitimacy of our legislators is limitless, and consequently whether laws should be allowed to regulate anything. Where is the line

---

75 See e.g. the Resolution of the Constitutional Court of the Czech Republic of 7 September 2021, Case No. II.ÚS 2185/21.
76 See MELZER, Filip. Poskytování náhrad za újmy vyvolané mimořádnými opatřeními Ministerstva zdravotnictví po jejich zrušení [Compensation for damages caused by emergency measures of the Ministry of Health after their abolition]. *Bulletin advokacie*, 2020, No. 6, pp. 15–23, or ODEHNALOVÁ, Jana. Možnosti náhrady škody vzniklé v důsledku protiepidemiologických opatření [Possibilities of compensation for damages resulting from anti-epidemiological measures]. *Právní rozhledy*, 2021, No. 2, pp. 64–67.
77 See e.g. the judgment of the Supreme Court of the Czech Republic of 26 September 2007, Case No. 25 Cdo 2064/2005, which stated that Ministerial decrees, being a product of the so-called derived legislative activity of a certain ministry, are to be considered normative (generally binding) regulations and not acts issued in an administrative procedure giving rise to the state liability under Act No. 82/1998 Coll. See also the judgment of the Supreme Court of the Czech Republic of 31 January 2007, Case No. 25 Cdo 1124/2005.
78 The difference between incidental and semi-incidental review as used by the author lies in the level of interference required for the active procedural legitimation to be activated.

that legislature cannot cross, presuming there is a line at all? The Constitutional Court of the Czech Republic was presented with a tough task of finding it in a medialized case concerning the shortening of the electoral term of the Chamber of Deputies of the Parliament by a one-off constitutional law[79] In the widely criticized decision,[80] the Constitutional Court, among others, established that laws (or rather acts disguised as laws) cannot be misused and that the mere fact that a certain party or coalition managed to reach a qualified majority[81] sufficient to adopt a constitutional law does not automatically allow such political force to exercise it unlimitedly.[82]

The aforementioned landmark decision can be treated in two ways. We can, as already done by many, analyze it critically, arguing with the reasoning of the Constitutional Court and questioning its legitimacy to interfere into democratic decision making with such intensity. What we can also do is use the arguments formulated by the court to define the conditions under which tailor-made laws can be issued without interfering with the constitutional order and basic principles of a democratic state respecting and promoting the rule of law.

5. Conclusions

During the COVID-19 pandemic, the need for agile crisis management required the engagement of ad hoc legislation intended to target and mitigate the effects of this crisis. Such customized legislation, adopted particularly for this event and only addressing selected subject matters and addressees during a selected time scope, facilitated the study and development of the theory of tailor-made laws. As the afore presented evidence suggests that tailor-made laws exist not only in legal textbooks and archaic case law, but is quite commonly used nowadays thus affecting millions of people, these laws should not be taken lightly and must be thoroughly analyzed. Based on the available data, these laws can be identified,

---

79 Ruling of the Constitutional Court of the Czech Republic of 10. September 2009, Case No. Pl. ÚS 27/09. The case came into general knowledge as the "Melčák Case" (named after the petitioner, MP Miloš Melčák).
80 See KYSELA, Jan, and Jakub STÁDNÍK. Kam Ústavní soud nechodí (a nejen o tom) [Where are the limits of the Constitutional Court (and far beyond)]. *Pravnik*, No. 11, 2021, p. 903.
81 The so-called constitutional majority of three fifths of all elected members of both chambers of the Czech Parliament (i.e. Chamber of Deputies and the Senate).
82 See also WELLMAN, Christopher H. Liberalism, samaritanism, and political legitimacy. *Philosophy & Public Affairs*, Vol. 25, No. 3, 1996, pp. 211–237.

classified, and categorized using different criteria and depending on factors taken into account for such categorization.

As many things in life, the issue of tailor-made laws is not black and white. Customized legislation can be a good servant, but also a terrible master. On the one hand, the legitimacy of an elected body or a body of crisis management provides these body with some authority to exercise the political power through laws – after all, this is what representative democracy is intended for. On the other hand, the concept of individualized legislation bears a great power which, if misused, can mean a great danger not only for individuals directly affected by it, but for democracy itself. Hence, to the dismay of those readers expecting the author to pick sides, we cannot but conclude that tailor-made laws are neither good nor evil. At the end of the day, the question of their existence in any legal system has more to do with the political will than with legal assessment. Nevertheless, should we choose to embrace this form of legislation, it is necessary to create a framework for these laws to be created and enforced, and also introduce mechanisms of their judicial review.

References

Abrams, Norman. Developments in US anti-terrorism law: Checks and balances undermined. *Journal of International Criminal Justice*, No. 4–5, 2006, pp. 1117–1136.

Ackerman, Bruce. The new separation of powers. *Harvard law review*, 2000, pp. 633–729.

Ben-Shahar, Omri and Porat, Ariel. Personalizing Negligence Law. *New York University Law Review*, 2016 Forthcoming: University of Chicago Coase-Sandor Institute for Law & Economics Research Paper No. 731, 2015.

Boguszak, J., Čapek, J., Gerloch, A. Teorie práva [Theory of Law]. 2nd revised edition. Prague: ASPI Publilshing, 2004, pp. 47–48.

Carolan, Eoin. *The new separation of powers: a theory for the modern state*. Oxford University Press, 2009.

Cooney, Barney. The relationship of administrative law to Parliament and ministerial decision making. *Legislative Studies*, Vol. 9, No. 1, 1994, pp. 65–70.

De Raedt, Luc. Logic of Generality. In: Sammut, C., Webb, G.I. (eds) Encyclopedia of Machine Learning. Springer, Boston, MA, 2011, pp. 624–631.

Degünther, Alina. *Good and Evil in Shakespeare's King Lear and Macbeth*. Anchor Academic Publishing, 2014.

Digest – Liber Primus, 1.3.8 Ulpianus III ad Sabinum.

Endicott, Timothy A. *The generality of Law*. Forthcoming in Luís Duarte d'Almeida, James Edwards and Andrea Dolcetti, eds., Reading HLA Hart's' The Concept of Law' (Hart Publishing 2013), Oxford Legal Studies, Research Paper 41, 2012.

Fraenkel, Abraham Adolf, Yehoshua Bar-Hillel, and Azriel Levy. *Foundations of set theory*. Elsevier, 1973.

Grigoleit, Hans Christoph, and Bender, Philip Maximilian. The Law between Generality and Particularity-Potentials and Limits of Personalized Law. *Algorithmic Regulation and Personalized Law: A Handbook* (Christoph Busch & Alberto De Franceschi eds., 2021) (2019): pp. 115–136.

Handrlica, Jakub, Balounová, Jana, Sharp (Sharapaev), Vladimír. Náhrady a opatření přijatá v době pandemie [Compensations and measures issued during the pandemic]. *Právní rozhledy*, 2020, No. 22, pp. 784–791.

Handrlica, Jakub, Sharp (Šarapajev), Vladimír and Blahoudková, Gabriela. "Black Swans" in Administrative Law. *The Lawyer Quarterly*, No. 3, 2021, pp. 479–492.

Handrlica, Jakub, Sharp (Šarapajev), Vladimír and Blahoudková, Gabriela. "Black Swans" in Administrative Law. *The Lawyer Quarterly*, No. 3, 2021, pp. 479–492.

Handrlica, Jakub. Two Faces of Tailor-Mare Laws in Administrative Law. *The Lawyer Quarterly*, No. 1, 2020, pp. 34–47.

Hejč, David. Nezákonnost mimořádných opatření Ministerstva zdravotnictví k onemocnění COVID-19 podle MS v Praze: Když obsah překračuje formu [Illegality of the Ministry of Health's COVID-19 Emergency Measures According to the Municipal Court in Prague: When Content Exceeds Form]. *Soudní rozhledy*, No. 6, 2020, pp. 185–190.

Helpman, Elhanan and Persson, Torsten. Lobbying and Legislative Bargaining. *Advances in Economic Analysis & Policy*, Vol. 1, No. 1, 2001.

Hendrych, Dušan (ed.). Správní právo: obecná část [Administrative law: General Part]. 9th issue. Prague: C.H. Beck, Academia iuris, 2016, p. 126.

Jordan, Grant. Lobbying. In Flinders, Matthew et al. (eds). *The Oxford Handbook of British Politics*, Oxford Academic, 2010, pp. 365–382.

Jouza, Ladislav. Zaměstnávání cizinců v České republice [Employment of foreign nationals in the Czech Republic]. *Bulletin Advokacie*, 2017.

Kirchhof, Gregor. *Die Allgemeinheit des Gesetzes. Über einen notwendigen Garanten der Freiheit, der Gleichheit und der Demokratie*. Tübingen: Mohr Siebeck, Jus Publicum 184, 2009. XXI.

Kolman, Petr. Transparentnost veřejné správy: Materiální racionalita vs. formální pojetí práva aneb Jde o opatření obecné povahy? [Transparency in Public Administration: Substantive Rationality vs. Formal Conception of Law. What is a Measure of a General Nature?] *Správní právo*, Vol. 46, No. 1, 2013, pp. 38–44.

Kouroutakis, A. E. *The Constitutional Value of Sunset Clauses*. New York: Routledge, 2018, pp. 3–10.

Kysela, Jan, and Jakub Stádník. Kam Ústavní soud nechodí (a nejen o tom) [Where are the limits of the Constitutional Court (and far beyond)]. *Pravnik*, No. 11, 2021, p. 903.

Martínek, Daniel. Semi-successful Socio-political Transformation in CEE: The Case of the Czech Republic. *Der Donauraum*, Vol. 60, No. 1–2, 2020, pp. 71–86.

Melzer, Filip. Poskytování náhrad za újmy vyvolané mimořádnými opatřeními Ministerstva zdravotnictví po jejich zrušení [Compensation for damages caused by emergency measures of the Ministry of Health after their abolition]. *Bulletin advokacie*, 2020, No. 6, pp. 15–23.

Morens, David M., Gregory K. Folkers, and Anthony S. Fauci. What is a pandemic? *The Journal of infectious diseases*, Vol. 200, No. 7, 2009, pp. 1018–1021.

Odehnalová, Jana. Možnosti náhrady škody vzniklé v důsledku protiepidemiologických opatření [Possibilities of compensation for damages resulting from anti-epidemiological measures]. *Právní rozhledy*, 2021, No. 2, pp. 64–67.

Perfetti, L. Massnahmeforschriften and emergency powers in contemporary public law. *The Lawyer Quarterly*. 2020, Vol. 10, No. 1, pp. 30–33.

Porat, Ariel and Strahilevitz, Lior J. Personalizing Default Rules and Disclosure with Big Data. *Michigan Law Review*, No. 1417, 2014.

Quine, Willard van O. *Set theory and its logic*. Harvard University Press, 2009.

Ranchordás, S. Sunset Clauses and Experimental Regulations: Blessing or Curse for Legal Certainty? Statute Law Review. 2015, No. 1, pp. 28–45.

Schauer, Frederick. The generality of law. *West Virginia Law Review*, No. 107, 2004, pp. 217–233.

Schneider, H. *Gesetzgebung. Ein Lehr- und Handbuch*. 3rd edition. Heidelberg: C. F. Müller Verlag, 2002, pp. 22–30.

Seok, I. The status of legislative lobbying and legislation on lobbyist system. *Dongguk Law Review*, No. 8, 2016, pp. 121–148.

Sharp (Sharapaev), Vladimír. When "Tailor-made laws" are not laws indeed. *The Lawyer Quarterly*, No. 1, 2020, pp. 57–60.

Smith, S. P. The Proclivities of Particularity and Generality. *Journal of Consciousness Exploration & Research*, Vol. 1, Issue 4, 2010, pp. 429–440.

Speake, Jennifer. *Oxford Dictionary of Proverbs*. Oxford: Oxford University Press, 2015, p. 71.

Staša, J. Správní akty [Administrative acts]. In: D. Hendrych (ed.). *Správní právo. Obecná část [Administrative Law. General Part]*. C. H. Beck, 2016, pp. 133–136.

Surrey, Stanley S. The Congress and the Tax Lobbyist: How Special Tax Provisions Get Enacted. *Harvard Law Review*, vol. 70, no. 7, 1957, pp. 1145–82.

Taleb, N. *The Black Swan. The Impact of the Highly Improbable*. 2nd ed. London: Penguin Books, 2010.

Vile, Maurice John Crawley. *Constitutionalism and the Separation of Powers*. Vol. 92. Oxford: Clarendon Press, 1967.

Vurmo, Gjergji. *Tailor-made laws in the Western Balkans: state capture in disguise*. Policy contribution No. 2020-12, CEPS Policy Insights, 2020.

Weissert, Carol S. Policy entrepreneurs, policy opportunists, and legislative effectiveness. *American Politics Quarterly*, Vol. 19, No. 2, 1991, pp. 262–274.

Wellman, Christopher H. Liberalism, samaritanism, and political legitimacy. *Philosophy & Public Affairs*, Vol. 25, No. 3, 1996, pp. 211–237.

Wintr, Jan. *Česká parlamentní kultura [The Czech parliamentary culture]*. Prague: Auditorium, 2010.

Wintr, Jan. K ústavnosti a zákonnosti protiepidemických opatření na jaře 2020 [On constitutionality and legality of anti-epidemic measures in spring of 2020]. *Správní právo*, No. 5–6, 2020, pp. 282–297.

G. Blahoudková

Compensation for Damage Caused by State Measures Adopted to Combat a Pandemic

Introduction

In times of crisis such as a pandemic, there is more pressure than ever to uphold the rule of law. Under the rule of law principle, the exercise of governmental power is constrained by the law, whereas its existence is a precondition for a democratic society. The rule of law also allows the state under exceptional circumstances to limit some human rights in order to protect other fundamental values. Of course, the interests of individual persons are connected to a network of rights and obligations. Therefore, it is not surprising that the protection of one of these interests can cause harm to others. For example, at the time of the COVID-19 pandemic, the state prioritized health protection in all respects, whereas the price of a slowdown in economic activities was paid. Although the state provided persons with different kinds of state aid in order to support them, they suffered a great loss. As a result, many affected persons still demand to seek compensation for caused damage.

Within the Czech Republic, several statutes provide legal instruments limiting the spread of a contagious disease. The Public health protection act deals with smaller-scale epidemics such as an infective hepatitis outbreak within a single school.[1] If the situation is more serious, i.e., natural disasters, environmental or industrial accidents, accidents or other hazards that threaten life, health or property values or internal order and security to a significant extent, the Czech Government can declare the *state of emergency*.[2] The state of emergency is exceptional as when it is called into action, the public authorities can issue so-called

---

1 Act no. 258/2000 Coll., Public health protection act *[Zákon č. 258/2000 Sb., o ochraně veřejného zdraví a o změně některých souvisejících zákonů* in Czech].
2 The state of emergency is one of four so-called crisis states that can be declared according to the Constitutional Act No. 1/1993 Coll., Czech Constitution *[Ústavní zákon č. 1/1993 Sb., Ústava České republiky* in Czech] and the Act no. 110/1998 Sb., on the Security of the Czech Republic *[Ústavní zákon č. 110/1998 Sb., o bezpečnosti České republiky* in Czech].

crisis measures (*krizová opatření* in Czech) according to the Crisis act,[3] which restrict certain human rights. The possibility of limitation of human rights differentiates the regimes under the Public health protection act and the Crisis act.

So far, the only pandemic experience in the Czech Republic is the COVID-19 pandemic. When it started in 2020, the legal system was not fully prepared to deal with it, and it took some time before the legal practice of combating the pandemic stabilized. During 2020 both listed acts were used to combat the COVID-19 pandemic. These acts differ significantly, especially with respect to the compensation regime for damage caused in connection with them. First, the crisis measures were issued with reference to the Crisis act as it represents the basic legal regulation for dealing with crisis situations of this extent. The crisis measures are the most controversial as the Crisis act establishes a right to compensation for damage caused in connection with crisis measures and for limitation of property rights. Second, the Czech government tried to avoid the risk of paying compensation and further proceeded according to the Public health protection act as it does not oblige the state to compensate for caused damage. However, this Act aims at small-scale epidemics and not a pandemic, and eventually, this procedure was considered illegal by courts.[4]

Finally, as of 2021, the so-called Pandemic Act[5] has entered into effect in the Czech Republic, and it aims specifically at dealing with the COVID-19 pandemic. It is a legal base for the adoption of so-called "emergency measures" (*mimořádné opatření* in Czech) that is a measure of general nature (*opatření obecné povahy* in Czech) regulated by the Act on administrative procedure.[6] The emergency measure can be adopted when the so-called "state of pandemic alert" is declared. Unlike the Crisis act, it establishes right only for compensation for

---

3 Act no. 240/2000 Coll., on Crisis Management (Crisis act) [*Zákon č. 240/2000 Sb., o krizovém řízení a o změně některých zákonů (krizový zákon)* in Czech].
4 The compensation could be potentially claimed with reference to the Act no. 82/1998 Coll., on Act on Liability for Damage Caused in the Exercise of Public Power by Decision or Improper Official Procedure [*Zákon č. 82/1998 Sb., o odpovědnosti za škodu způsobenou při výkonu veřejné moci rozhodnutím nebo nesprávným úředním postupem a o změně zákona České národní rady č. 358/1992 Sb., o notářích a jejich činnosti (notářský řád)* in Czech].
5 Act no. 94/2021 Coll., on emergency measures during a COVID-19 epidemic and amending certain other Acts [*Zákon č. 94/2021 Sb., o mimořádných opatřeních při epidemii onemocnění COVID-19 a o změně některých souvisejících zákonů.* in Czech].
6 Act no 500/2004 Coll., on administrative procedure [*Zákon č. 500/2004 Sb., Správní řád* in Czech].

actual damage caused in connection with the emergency measures and neither lost profit nor limitation of property rights. It can be presumed that in the event of another pandemic, other "tailor-made-law" similar to Pandemic Act would be adopted to combat it. However, if another similar disaster comes in a few years, the Czech government will once again face it empty-handed as no general regulation on pandemics exists.

Despite the Pandemic Act being clear regarding the compensation, the assessment of the compensation regime according to the Crisis act is still of great importance. This is mainly because the Crisis act was used to combat the pandemic until the beginning of 2021 and the general three-year statutory deadline for bringing claims arising from the crisis measures has not yet expired. In the usual course of action, not much attention is paid to the issue of damage caused due to the legal activities of the state. This chapter aims to briefly evaluate this matter with respect to the existing general legal liability regime and current crisis legislation regime.[7] More precisely, it should deal with the issue of compensation for limitation of ownership rights, compensation for damage caused in connection with the emergency measures according to the Pandemic Act, and the damage caused in connection with the crisis measures according to the Crisis act. Today's uncertainty concerns in particular the extent of compensation that should be granted and whether the damage caused by crisis measures of normative nature should be compensated.

Conditions for the existence of legal liability for damage

The "liability for damage" is a special contractual relationship between the pest and the injured party resulting from a previous breach of a legal obligation by the pest, whereas this relationship is based on the pest's obligation to compensate the injured party. The Civil code[8] differentiates between contractual and non-contractual (tort) liability. These two differ in whether the legal obligation is set by contract or statute. Regardless of the source of the legal obligation, the general

---

[7] Under the crisis legislation is understood the Crisis act, Act on the Security of the Czech Republic, Act No. 239/2000 Coll., On the integrated rescue system and on the amendment of some related acts [*Zákon č. 239/2000 Sb., o integrovaném záchranném systému a o změně některých zákonů* in Czech], Act No. 241/2000 Coll., On economic measures for crisis states and on the amendment of some related acts [*Zákon č. 241/2000 Sb., o hospodářských opatřeních pro krizové stavy a o změně některých souvisejících zákonů* in Czech] and others.

[8] Act no 89/2014 Coll., Civil code [*Zákon č. 89/2012 Sb., Občanský zákoník* in Czech].

preconditions for the incurrence of civil liability are (i) an unlawful act or an unlawful situation/state, (ii) pecuniary or non-pecuniary damage to the victim, (iii) a causal link between the unlawful act or unlawful condition and pecuniary damage, and (iv) a fault. The basic premise of this model is the existence of duty as, without duty, there can be no breach of duty, and without breach of duty, there can be no liability.

Despite a fault being a precondition for the existence of general liability for damage, in few cases, the law unburdens the injured party and enshrines the liability for caused damage even if no breach of statute or contract has occurred (so-called liability without fault or strict liability). Strict liability is established in cases expressly provided for by law and is rather exceptional. It is imposed mostly due to the increased risk for other persons.[9] The risk is caused by the probability of damage, its extent and controllability. In connection with pandemic situations, the liability could hardly be based on the state's potentially dangerous activities. Although a special danger can be associated with a pandemic, this danger is not caused by the activities of the state. Thus, if the statute enshrines compensation for the damage caused by state measures, the reason is rather a public interest in this compensation and not the danger imposed by the state.

If the state's action lacks a breach of obligation, such an action is legal. A breach of duty is a precondition for both contractual and statutory liability, and thus a standard feature of liability can be hardly applied to liability for damage caused by lawful acts of the public authority.

Damage caused by such an act can be compensated based on the strict legal liability provided by the statute, but it is rather rare. It constitutes an exceptional hypothesis. The ratio of this compensation is safeguarding an individual interest when the importance of another interest is chosen to be overriding. This gives rise to a special circumstance that the legislator may take into account. With this compensation, the legislator decided to distribute the economic weight of the specific activity. The imputability of liability for legal acts of the state is a controversial theoretical question with widespread application consequences and has not previously received much attention in Czech legal theory. Moreover, despite the term legal liability being used daily regarding this type of damage and possibly compensation, it is not accurate with respect to current Civil law terminology.

---

9 Melzer, F. Občanský zákoník IX. svazek, § 2894–3081 Závazky z deliktů a z jiných právních důvodů [*Civil Code Volume IX, section 2894–3081 Obligations from tort and other legal reasons*]. Nakladatelství Leges, 2019. ISBN 978-80-7502-199-1. Comment on section 2895.

More accurate is to talk about an "obligation to compensate damage" simply because the obligation arises without the state breaking its obligation, and thus no liability arises.

Damage caused by legislation

The Czech division of state powers follows Montesquieu's concept as they are divided into legislative, executive, and judicial powers. The majority within the state elects the legislative body, and thus the emerging legislation is a result of the activities of people's representatives. Within the legislative procedure, the legislator balances competing social and political interests when deciding on the acceptance or non-acceptance of the submitted bill. There is no rule on how a deputy, senator or parliamentary should vote or what the specific result should be.[10] Therefore, the liability for legislation cannot be inferred from the result of the voting on the bill.[11] Moreover, the potentially caused damage can be further justified by the existing public interest or the existence of a social contract as the representatives of the majority choose the interest more vital to them. These decisions belong merely to the legislator, and the law does not generally grant compensation for these kinds of interferences. Similarly, the general courts are not authorized to review these decisions.

Allowing the review of legislative decisions by the general courts would disturb the balance between judicial and legislative powers. The only body authorized to review the legislation is the Constitutional court for compliance with the constitutional order. However, the potential repeal of the statute or its part is not automatically linked to compensation for caused damage as an exercise of the legislative powers must not be hindered by the possibility of claims for damage. Such an option could paralyze the legislative procedure and independent lawmaking process. The legislator bears political responsibility for legislative decisions and if the voters are not satisfied with the performance of his duties, they can express this opinion in next elections. The liability for damage caused by legislation is generally not even accepted in relation to illegal normative acts, neither in the Czech nor European context (with a few exceptions).[12]

---

10 Judgment of the Supreme Court of 13 July 2011, File No. 25 Cdo 1210/2009.
11 Judgment of the Supreme Court of 31 January 2007, File No. 25 Cdo 1124/2005.
12 Oliphant, K. (ed.) The Liability of Public Authorities in Comparative Perspective. Cambridge: Intersentia, 2016.

The European Court of Justice dealt with the matter of damage caused by legal actions in respect to damage caused by the action of the European Economic Community. Advocate general Slynn concluded by virtue of the German concept of "special sacrifice" and the French concept of "unequal discharge of public burdens" that if a person suffered a particularly severe loss as a result of the legal act of the European Economic community administration, then the person could bring an application for compensation for caused damage.[13] However, in this particular case, the court concluded that the alleged damage does not exceed the limits of the economic risks inherent in operating a business and left open the question of whether the compensation would be successfully granted under different circumstances. Slynn's reasoning was followed twenty-four years later by advocate General Maduro in the FIAMM case.[14]

At the beginning of 2000, FIAMM and Giorgio Fedon & Figli seek compensation for damage before the European Court of Justice. The damage was caused by legislative acts of the European Community in relation to the so-called "banana war" between the European Communities and the USA.[15] During the appeal proceedings, the Court of Justice found that the Court of First Instance erred in law when affirming the existence of a regime providing for non-contractual liability of European Communities based on the lawful legislative activities.[16] The Court pointed out that an economic operator cannot claim a right to property in a market share that he held at a given time. Such a market share constitutes only a momentary economic position, exposed to the risk of changing circumstances.[17] Eventually, the Grand Chamber concluded that the legislative measure could lead to liability of European communities if its application leads to restrictions of the right to property or the freedom to pursue a trade or profession where these restrictions impair the very substance of these rights disproportionately and intolerably. Perhaps it could be inferred precisely when no provision for compensation has been adopted to avoid or remedy that impairment.[18] However, in the

---

13 Opinion of Advocate General Slynn, SA Biovilac NV v. Eur. Econ. Cmty., Case 59/83, [1984] E.C.R. 4057, 4091.
14 Opinion of Advocate General Maduro, FIAMM, [2008] E.C.R. I-6513, 62–63
15 Joined Cases C-120/06 P and C-121/06 P FIAMM and Giorgio Fedon & Figli v Council and Commission.
16 The Court of Justice made clear in the FIAMM case that the second paragraph of article 288 of TFEU (current article 340) aims at the damage caused by unlawful acts.
17 See also Case C 280/93 Germany v Council [1994] ECR I 4973, para. 79.
18 Joined Cases C-120/06 P and C-121/06 P *FIAMM and Giorgio Fedon & Figli v Council and Commission.* Para. 184.

FIAMM case the criteria were not fulfilled, and the court left open the question under what circumstances there might be an award of damage with respect to an action that was lawful.

Damage Caused by Acts of Public Administration

A close connection exists between the administration and legislation, as the latter lays down rules for the adoption of administrative acts. Under the rule of law, the state administration is severely limited in its actions, both in private law relations and when exercising its sovereign powers. Public administration is meant a power that authoritatively directly or indirectly decides on rights and obligations of persons that are in an unequal position, whereas the content of the decision of a public body is independent of the will of the person. Public administration can be divided into state administration and self-government, whereas state administration is carried both by state bodies and other bodies to which the exercise of state powers was entrusted by law.[19]

The state administration is to serve all citizens and may be asserted only in cases, within the bounds, and in the manner provided for by a statute.[20] If the public administration acts via means of public law as a superior authority, the administrative body can exercise its powers only for the purposes for which the powers were entrusted and only in cases provided for by statute.[21] With regard to the manner of exercising state power, the public administration body may proceed solely as prescribed by a statute.[22] At the same time, all citizens may do what is not prohibited by statute and nobody may be compelled to do what is not imposed upon them by statute. In this light, the acts of the state administration made in the manner provided by law and within its bounds are made rightly and shall be considered legal (unless exercised in such a manner that it is considered an abuse of rights). However, when performing its activities public administration can naturally cause harm to private persons affected by its actions. This matter concerns all the hypotheses in which the public administration, in order

---

19 Vojtek, P. Odpovědnost za škodu při výkonu veřejné moci [*Liability for damage caused in connection with the exercise of public power* in Czech]. Praha: C.H. Beck, 2012. pp. 7–9. ISBN 978- 80-7400-427-8.
20 Article 2 of the Constitution.
21 Section 2 of the Act No. 500/2004 Coll., on the Administrative Procedure [*Zákon č. 500/2004 Sb., Správní řád* in Czech].
22 By statute are meant relevant procedural rules established by civil, administrative, or criminal law.

to satisfy the interest of the community, causes unjust damage to private citizens, despite having acted through legitimate conduct authorized by law.

On the other hand, if the state does not follow legal limits and illegal action arises from its administration, the state is obliged to remedy the situation. The liability of the state, its bodies or its autonomy bodies arises especially when the powers which they have been given are misused, the powers which they have not been given are used, or the state fails to carry out duties laid upon it. The obligation to compensate is therefore determined based either on the illegality of an act of state administration or on a statutory provision enshrining compensation. With respect to illegal decisions of the state, strict liability is enshrined in the Act on liability for damage caused by the exercise of public power and may arise based on the existence of illegal decision or maladministration. The liability arises if the following conditions are met (i) the occurrence of maladministration or the annulment of an illegal decision giving rise to the damage or injury, (ii) the existence of damage or injury and (iii) a causal link between them. In other words, the occurrence of liability for damage can be established by a breach of a legal (non-contractual) obligation, i.e., a culpable unlawful act.

Still, the matter of state liability for legal acts adopted in accordance with the law was very rarely questioned. And if so, it was connected to very specific areas, just as compensation for damage caused by obligatory vaccination or expropriation. A revival of this issue occurred in 2020 in connection with the pandemic. A different approach is used in France or Germany.

According to the French legal theory of "equality of citizens in bearing public burdens" (*égalité devant les charges publiques* in French), all public activities are assumed to benefit society as a whole. Thus, citizens must bear the resulting burden that usually falls on an individual without compensation. On the other hand, if severe damage is caused to individuals and them alone, the burden shall not fall on them alone, and they should be granted compensation. The latter is known as "unequal discharge of public burdens" (*rupture de l'égalité devant les charges publiques* in French) and is used in extreme cases. This concept aims to restore the inequality that has been caused. Similarly, according to the German concept of "special sacrifice" (*Sonderopfer* in German), individuals who, due to a lawful public act, suffered a special sacrifice, i.e. damage equivalent to an expropriation, must be granted reparation.[23]

---

23 Decisions of the Federal Court of Justice in civil matters volume 6, page 240. (*BGHZ 6, 270 (278/9)*)

However, an analogy of these concepts is neither enshrined in Czech law nor is applied within the Czech legal theory. The damage potentially caused by legal acts of state administration must be solved according to the essential rules of legal liability for damage. The absence of a general legal regime for compensation caused by legal acts of the state does not leave the question unresolved for non-codified cases, but it means that for these cases, the Czech legal regime does not provide compensation as no legal base for liability for damage exists.

Measures Adopted within the Pandemic

According to the World Health Organization, a pandemic is an epidemic occurring worldwide or over a vast area, crossing international boundaries and usually affecting a large number of people. Indeed, when the pandemic hit the globe, usual rules are not sufficient to combat the illness. Prohibition of drinking water from certain sources, restriction of human contact, restriction of transport of persons, and, of course, quarantine have historically been a way of combating the spread of illnesses.[24] These measures have been used in various parts of the world and have proven to remain effective to this day. In a pandemic situation, most of the globe is hit by the same contagious human disease. Thus, very similar measures are applied within federal states, unions, and worldwide. These measures mainly target the same groups of persons – depending on which part of life needs to be limited.

Therefore, it could be hardly argued that adopted measures of widespread nature cause particularly severe loss to individuals as the society as a whole is highly adversely influenced by adopted measures which is a feature of both the German concept of a "special sacrifice" and the French concept of "unequal discharge of public burdens." At the same time, the measures are applied in the course of the anti-pandemic strategy, and ultimate equal treatment would hardly be accomplished to protect health and human lives, especially as there are groups of persons whose activities impose more danger on society than activities of others. Under this presumption, the sacrifice of these groups (i.e. restaurant operators) can hardly be considered *special* under the German or French concept. Also, it cannot be deemed to impair the very substance of property right or freedom to pursue business disproportionately and intolerably under the FIAMM reasoning,

---

24 Richards, E. P. A Historical Review of the State Police Powers and Their Relevance to the COVID-19 Pandemic of 2020, 11 J. NAT'l Sec. L. & POL'y 83, 2020.

especially when the whole new legal framework is adopted to support persons affected by the pandemic situation.

Compensation for Limitation of the Ownership Right

The measures adopted during the pandemic can limit persons in the use of their property. Article 11 of the Charter of fundamental human rights and freedoms stipulates that expropriation or forced limitation of ownership rights is possible only in the public interest, based on statute and for compensation. The Constitutional court had deducted that measure has to be examined via several criteria in order to assess whether it limits the property right. Unless the interference is marked as expropriation or forced limitation of ownership right, the person shall not be entitled to compensation. It has to be examined whether (i) the limitation goes beyond the limitation of the property right of all persons in compliance with the principles of equality, (ii) the intensity of intervention, and (iii) its duration.[25] In the light of these criteria, the compensation shall not cover the cases when the limitation affects all owners equally.[26] The compensation should be granted if the limitation affects the individual owner(s) as he shall be compensated for the distribution of public burdens. For example, a ban on the operation of billboards on motorways and first-class roads or the obligation of the food business operators to provide leftover food to non-profit organizations is not considered limiting the ownership right. Therefore, the expropriation regime has features of a special sacrifice theory.

Moreover, section 11 of the Human right declaration emphasizes the social function of ownership when it stipulates that ownership rights can be limited in favor of the protection of other constitutional interests; for example, its performance must not harm human health. Widespread limitations are usually a reflection of the social function of ownership. In the light of this interpretation, compensation could be granted, for example, for using individual private premises to set up a temporary hospital but not a widespread restriction on the operation of interior sports grounds.

For example, during the COVID-19 pandemic, people were temporarily forbidden to travel between state districts. At that moment, they could not visit their summer houses and temporarily reside there. Entrepreneurs were restricted in renting their rental property for accommodation or use of indoor

---

25 Resolution of the Constitutional court of 7 December 2021, File No. Pl. ÚS 20/21.
26 Ibid.

spaces for seating the customers. However, restrictions were imposed legally and affected almost the entire population. They did not reach the severity of the expropriation, as persons did not lose any component of their property right in the long term. Moreover, the restrictions were only temporary. Suppose we omit any damage caused (as it is different from the limitation of ownership right). In that case, persons are obliged to bear the limitation on the use of property imposed on persons within the pandemic situation. Otherwise, they could also bear the adverse consequences caused by their action contrary to their obligation not to harm human health by performing their property rights.[27]

Additionally, it is important to note that we cannot draw a line between the ownership of consumers and entrepreneurs in the sense that entrepreneurs should be compensated for the inability to use (e.g., rent) their property because as a result of this limitation, they incur a loss of profit. This conclusion arises from the Human declaration, as it stipulates that the ownership of all persons has the same legal content and protection, and thus it cannot be distinguished between entrepreneurs and non-entrepreneurs.

Compensation for Damage Caused in Connection with Crisis Measures under the Crisis Act

The more burning question is whether the compensation for damage caused by crisis measures adopted under the Crisis act will be compensated. The uncertainty arises especially as the Crisis act does not specify the legal nature of the crisis measures and also as the extent of damage which should be compensated is questioned. Section 36 of the Crisis act establishes the right for compensation for damage caused to legal and natural persons in causal connection with crisis measures and exercises carried out under the Crisis act. It states that

> The state is obliged to compensate the damage caused to legal and natural persons in the causal connection with crisis measures and exercises carried out in accordance with this Act. The state can only be released from this liability if it is proven that the injured party caused the damage himself.

It enshrines four preconditions for the compensation to be granted these are (1) adoption of a crisis measure, (2) that causes damage to the affected person, (3) whereas there is a Causal link between the crisis measure and the damage, and (4) the affected person did not cause the damage himself. The section does not

---

27 Article 11 of the Charter of fundamental human rights and freedoms.

cover damage caused by the crisis situation itself due to the absence of the causal link. Enshrined strict liability requires neither the existence of illegality or inaccuracy of the measure nor the culpability. Precisely the opposite, according to this provision, the person is entitled to compensation, assuming that the adopted measure was legal.

The provision was used several times during its existence, always to compensate persons for individual interventions of the state within the crisis state.[28] According to this provision, persons are authorized to obtain compensation when damage to their property is caused due to crisis measures and exercises. By literal interpretation of the provision, it seems it covers compensation for actual damage and lost profits regardless of the nature of the crisis measure, i.e., whether it affects only individuals or society as a whole. The interpretation of this provision was not questioned before 2020.

In 2020 the Czech Government, for the first time, adopted crisis measures of widespread nature. These measures affected a portion of the existing business class – people were forbidden to eat inside restaurants, retail stores and other businesses remained closed – and tremendous damage was caused in the course of their application. Eventually, the affected entrepreneurs objected that according to section 36 (1) of the Crisis act, they are entitled to compensation for caused damage. Despite many lawyers having opportunistically declared that the compensation shall be granted, there is no consensus. The author outlines several aspects that should be taken into consideration when assessing the obligation of the state to compensate damage.

a. Context of the Adoption of Crisis Legislation

The current crisis legislation was adopted in response to devastating floods at the end of the 1990s. At that time, a third of the Czech territory was hit by floods and local authorities lacked appropriate legal instruments to adequately respond to the emerging situation. As a response, the legislator adopted the crisis legislation to allow authorities to effectively respond to large-scale emergencies, such as floods or hurricanes. At the time of adoption of the crisis legislation, the legislator failed to anticipate the consequences of widespread nature measures (just as extensive closure of retail and sports venues or the disruption of cultural events),

---

28 Crisis states are state of danger [*stav nebezpečí* in Czech], state of emergency [*nouzový stav* in Czech], state's threat state [*stav ohrožení státu* in Czech] and state of war [*válečný stav* in Czech].

as these were not an answer to previously experienced emergencies. From the point of view of historical and teleological interpretation, the purpose of section 36 (1) of the Crisis act was probably to compensate for the actual damage caused by actions of the state or other concerned persons, especially members of the integrated rescue system within their operation. Therefore, neither the wording of this provision nor the explanatory memorandum clarifies how to deal with damage caused by measures of widespread nature.

Over the next almost twenty years, section 36 (1) of the Crisis act was applied under different circumstances anticipated by the legislator, just as floods or hurricanes. It was used to compensate a person for removing waterlogged buildings at the bank of the Vltava River in Prague,[29] destruction of the crawler loader,[30] or damage caused by creating a trough for drainage.[31] In the listed examples, there were active and immediate interventions of the state authorities to the persons' property. The interventions were performed via the crisis measures, and the persons' properties were destroyed. Moreover, in these cases, the state's action did not consist of restrictions on business activities. It consisted of the use, modification, or destruction of specific property, whereas it was necessary to immediately proceed with the action to avoid further damage or injury. Section 36 (1) of the Crisis act was a legal base for compensation for the value of the destroyed property and the provision of funds to restore the original state. From the circumstances of its adoption and subsequent use, it seems sure that section 36 (1) of the Crisis act should not aim at compensation for damage caused by measures of widespread nature which would cause damage to many entrepreneurs in services and their suppliers.[32] However, the Crisis act was proven to be effective during the pandemic, and the Court or other authorities did not question its application. Therefore, the argumentation that the obligation to compensate affected persons should be exempt because the legislator did not expect the Crisis act to be applied to combat pandemics seems to be insufficient.

---

29 Decision of Czech Supreme Court of 17 June 2009, File No. 25 Cdo 1649/2007.
30 Decision of Czech Supreme Court of 10 January 2019, File No. 25 Cdo 1480/2018 and Resolution of Czech Constitutional Court of 14 May, 2019, File No. III. ÚS 1141/19.
31 Decision of Czech Supreme Court of 23 August 2016, File No. 25 Cdo 700/2016.
32 For example, according to a study published by the *Centre for Economic and Market Analysis* carried out for the *Czech Association of Breweries and Malthouses*, brewery sales fell by more than 1,104 million Czech crowns from March to May of 2020.

b. Legal Nature of Crisis Measures

The Crisis act does not determine the legal nature of crisis measures. After the crisis measures of widespread nature were adopted in 2020 as a response to the pandemic, the question of their true legal nature has arisen. Their assessment had to reflect the circumstances of crisis legislation adoption and its future usage. The Crisis act contains a list of measures that may be adopted when the crisis state is declared, and these measures vary significantly in their scope depending on the situation. For example, prohibition of entry, residence, and movement of persons in defined places or territories would be assessed differently if the entry is prohibited to a narrow local territory, such as a lakebed or part of a forest and differently if it is a ban on travelling abroad (i.e., basically a ban on entering the territory of a foreign country). Thus, depending on the specific situation, a crisis measure may be of a different legal nature.[33] In some cases, these can be considered individual decisions, e.g., when it concerns a specific building or land, a measure of general nature issued as an act of public administration or legal regulation *sui generis* when generally applicable to all persons present in the territory of the Czech Republic, e.g., prohibition of depositing funds in accounts abroad.

The legal nature of crisis measures issued during the COVID-19 pandemic was assessed by the Czech Constitutional court, which acknowledged that these measures were, in fact, of general nature and should be considered law regulation *sui generis*.[34] The Constitutional court pointed out that crisis measures were applied to the entire territory of the Czech Republic and the unlimited number of persons[35] According to the Czech legal theory, measure with such attributes fulfil the characteristics of legal regulation, especially as they have a generally defined range of addressees and contain generally binding rules of conduct.[36] Moreover, according to the Charter of fundamental human rights and freedoms, human rights can be limited only by a statute. As crisis measures do limit human rights significantly, they shall be thus considered as a legal regulation *sui generis* as formally they are closer to statutes than secondary legislation even though the Czech Government is not authorized to issue these. The latter is also supported by the fact that the crisis measures were published in the Statute Book, among

---

33 Resolution of Czech Constitutional court of 16 June 2020, File No. Pl. ÚS 20/20.
34 Law regulation is understood as generally applicable law. See Resolution of Czech Constitutional of 16 June 2020 File No. Pl. ÚS 20/20, point 13.
35 Resolution of Czech Constitutional court of 5 May 2020, File No. Pl. ÚS 10/20.
36 See Boguszak, J., Čapek, J., Gerloch, A. Teorie práva [*Legal Foundations* in English]. 2. vyd. Praha: ASPI, 2004, pp 39 et seq.

other statutes. This assessment must be considered when assessing the compensation for damage caused by them.

It was not yet judicially decided whether the state should compensate individuals for damage caused by crisis measures of normative nature. However, the question of compensation for legislative acts was previously dealt with regarding the Act on Liability for Damage Caused due to the Exercise of Public Power. According to this Act, a person can claim compensation for damage caused by illegal decisions or maladministration. The higher courts have dealt with the question of whether the unlawful normative act can be considered maladministration, and eventually, they concluded that they cannot. Therefore, even if the statute is issued in some way wrongly, the person cannot claim compensation for caused damage.[37]

This concept reflects a view that liability for damage can be connected only with the act by which the legislation is applied, but not with the legislation itself. This conclusion was also confirmed by the Constitutional court, which has expressed an opinion that even if the action or non-action of the Parliament as a legislator is found contrary to constitutional rules, the Parliament cannot be considered a public authority according to article 36 of the Charter of fundamental human rights and freedoms which enshrines a right for compensation for damage caused by an illegal decision of public administration.[38]

Similarly, the Czech Supreme court deducted that the Government's issuance of a normative legal act is not an "official procedure" under the Act on State Liability for Damage Caused due to the Exercise of Public Power. If no breach of European law is alleged, state liability for damage caused by Government's normative legal act shall not be inferred.[39] Therefore, the above conclusion shall be applied both to normative acts adopted by the legislator and the public administration.[40]

---

37 Potentially person could claim the compensation based on provisions included directly in the Constitution as it happened in case of regulated rents, when the Constitutional court deducted the existence of a special compensatory claim based on the illegal limitation of the right to property. See Resolution of Czech Constitutional court of 28 April 2009, File No. Pl. ÚS-st. 27/09.
38 Resolution of Czech Constitutional court of 8 July 2010, File No. Pl. ÚS 36/08.
39 Judgment of the Supreme Court of 13 July 2011, File No. 25 Cdo 1210/2009.
40 Svoboda, T., Smutná, V. K odpovědnosti za újmu způsobenou podzákonnou normotvorbou [Liability for damage caused by secondary legislation in English]. Právník, 2016, No. 10, pp. 914–915.

Therefore, if the compensation for damage caused in connection with crisis measures of normative nature is granted, it would be exceptional as it would mean that the legislator chose one specific type of normative act for compensation.[41] Moreover, a particular type of legally and rightly issued normative act. With respect to systematic interpretation, if the compensation is not granted for the damage caused by the illegal normative acts, even more, it should not be granted for the damage caused by legal acts of state. Especially as neither limitation regarding the number of entitled persons nor the extent of compensated damage exists.

This conclusion is also supported by the fact that the Constitution assumes compensation neither for legal nor illegal normative acts. It is neither a manifestation of liability for damage caused by the defective exercise of public power,[42] right to property,[43] nor the right to freedom of movement and residence.[44] The right for such compensation does not arise from constitutional rights nor international human law treaties (thus, the existence of this provision is relatively rare). Constitutional Court even previously assessed the existing regime of compulsory vaccination and did not find the absence of a compensatory regime violating the human rights principles included in the Charter of fundamental human rights and freedoms.

This is different compared to the damage caused by the state administration, whereas the Charter of fundamental human rights and freedoms stipulates that "[e]verybody is entitled to compensation for damage caused him by an unlawful decision of a court, other State bodies, or public administrative authorities, or as the result of an incorrect official procedure". The Act on Liability for Damage Caused due to the Exercise of Public Power implements the obligation of the state to provide compensation contained in the Constitution. Therefore, enshrining the liability for the crisis measures of normative nature seems rather non-conceptual. Instead, these remarks tend to be to the detriment of the compensation regime for the damage caused by normative legal acts.

---

41 See Handrlica, J., Balounová, J., Sharapaev, V. Náhrady a opatření přijatá v době pandemie (*Compensation and measures adopted during a pandemic* in English). Právní rozhledy, 2020, č. 22, pp. 784–791.
42 Article 36 of the Charter of fundamental human rights and freedoms.
43 Article 10 of the Charter of fundamental human rights and freedoms.
44 Article 14 of the Charter of fundamental human rights and freedoms.

c. The Extent of Compensated Damage

The Czech Ministry of Interior and former Minister of Finance expressed an opinion that lost profit due to crisis measures during the COVID-19 pandemic shall not be compensated and the provided state aid is sufficient.[45] However, the interpretation of the Crisis act does not support this conclusion.[46] Section 36 (1) of the Crisis act expressly states that "the damage should be compensated". According to the Civil code, the damage consists of "actual damage" (*damnum emergens*) and "lost profit" (*lucrum cessans*). Therefore, when the Crisis act grants compensation for "damage," it should cover both actual damage and lost profit. Other public law statutes follow this distinction as the term "actual damage"[47] is used when only actual damage should be compensated. For example, compensation for actual damage is enshrined by Act on nature and Landscape Protection[48] or Act on hunting.[49] In other cases, the legislator used both terms "actual damage" and "lost profit" in order to distinguish between these two.[50] However, the Crisis act uses the general term *damage* without narrowing it in any way.

On the other hand, the law must not lead to an absurd or wholly impracticable conclusion or a worse result than the original issue. As the state only redistributes funds, it would have to collect financial resources from those who gained

---

45 Interview with the Ministery of Finance for the Czech state television. Available at https://ct24.ceskatelevize.cz/domaci/3067696-schillerova-nechce-odskodne-za-uslyzisk-pro-firmy-podle-stanjury-mela-rezignovat (accessed: 15 March 2022)
46 Simiarly in Melzer, F. Poskytování náhrad za újmy vyvolané mimořádnými opatřeními Ministerstva zdravotnictví po jejich zrušení [*Compensation for damages caused by measures of the Ministry of Health after their repeal* in English] in Bulletin advokacie, č. 6/2020.
47 Actual damage means the decrease in value of the damaged property compared to the situation as it was before the damage was caused, i.e., it represents what had to be spent to restore the original property of the injured party. Korecká, V. Skutečná škoda [*Actual damage* in English]. In: Hendrych, D. a kol. Právnický slovník. 3. vydání. Praha: C. H. Beck, 2009.
48 Act No. 114/1992 Coll., Czech National Council on Nature and Landscape Protection, section 81b.
49 Act No. 449/2001 Coll., On hunting, section 16.
50 I.e. according to the section 75 of the Act No. 527/1990 Coll., on Inventions, Industrial Designs and Improvement Proposals [*Zákon č. 527/1990 Sb., o vynálezech, průmyslových vzorech a zlepšovacích návrzích* in Czech], the injured party has the right to compensation if his intellectual property rights are infringed, whereas he is entitled to have replaced what the property of the injured party diminished (actual damage) and what would have been achieved if the loss event had not occurred (lost profit).

profit and distribute them to those who have not. Widespread compensation for lost profit during a pandemic seems absurd and could actually cause more considerable economic damage than was the one originally caused by the pandemic. If a high percentage of entrepreneurs would claim compensation for lost profit, the aim of provision 36 (1) of the Crisis act disappears. In such a case it would be almost that everyone would pay compensation to everyone. Another significant obstacle to claiming a lost profit is the burden of proof. The affected person would very hardly prove the amount of potential profit. Lastly, the chosen solution must also be rational. Considering this interpretation, the chances of getting compensation for lost profits seem negligible, although the wording indicates the opposite.

Also, the amount of state aid support would have to be considered when deciding on the amount of lost profit that should be granted. The amount of state aid decreases the amount of lost profit, and courts would have to take this into account. Moreover, under the specific circumstances of a pandemic, it is more than probable that courts would not be convinced that individuals would be able to make more profit than the state contributed to them through state aid. Of course, some businesses were forced to close altogether during the pandemic and others were allowed to operate under tightened rules. Both ways, when calculating the lost profit, the entrepreneurs would have to take into account the changed customers' behavior which (i) cannot be realistically calculated when the state measures are in action, and (ii) cannot be blamed on the state when the state measures are waived (e.g., tourist are allowed to travel to other states but do not do so due to the fear of infection).

d. Concept of Special Sacrifice

Neither the statute nor the Explanatory memorandum expresses the intention behind section 36 (1) of the Crisis act. The author tends to believe that this provision may be considered a demonstration of the principle of *special sacrifice*. Simply said, the Crisis act provides legal instruments for the protection of public interest in crisis situations, whereas as a result, damage can be caused to individuals. If the individual's interest is harmed, while others benefit from this loss, the possible damage of the individual shall be compensated from public sources. However, during a pandemic, people worldwide are adversely affected by the situation and anti-pandemic measures. Human contact is kept to a minimum to eliminate the risk of the spread of contagious human disease. Therefore, within the individual states, these are not only individuals who are negatively affected but the whole community. Moreover, the fact that sacrifice is paid by many around the globe is a basic precondition for the existence of a pandemic. As a result, the concept of special sacrifice could hardly be applied when the essential precondition of the only individual(s) being harmed is not fulfilled.

Further, at this point of our political development, persons adversely affected by Crisis measures are not left without help. Precisely the opposite, countries and communities are adapting and allowing flexible creation of new state aid rules. For example, during the COVID-19 pandemic, the European Union adopted a "Temporary Framework for State Aid Measures" to ensure liquidity for vulnerable companies to prevent a severe economic downturn.[51] These rules allowed EU member states to provide entrepreneurs with exceptional state aid support, whereas they had the character of compensation for objective costs at the Czech level. The sacrifice paid for the protection of public health is thus reduced by the provided support from the state, which is basically paid by everyone economically active via their taxes. Moreover, economic remnants of this state aid will remain in the treasury to be paid by further generations. This form of state support should already at least partly compensate the loss incurred by individuals for the benefit of society.

Third, it must be taken into account that the state is obliged to protect its citizens, and individuals are obliged to act in such a way as not to cause unjustified damage to the life or health of another. The fact that some are limited in their businesses and use of their property is also a manifestation of their preventive duty. Otherwise, if they carry out their activities and endanger persons' health and lives, they could bear the consequences. In this light, it is not a special sacrifice of persons while protecting the public interest, but their general duty.

Similarly, the Regional Court in Berlin has refused the application of the concept of special sacrifice in connection with damage caused to innkeepers by lockdown during the COVID-19 pandemic. The plaintiff claimed compensation against the State of Berlin for the loss caused by measures ordered due to the spread of the disease and the associated closure of restaurants. The court has argued that the impairments suffered should be compensated if they are considered an "unreasonable special sacrifice." However, in this case, the loss was not regarded as an unreasonable special sacrifice but rather as a loss within the range of an acceptable general life and entrepreneurial risk.[52] Similarly, the district court of Heilbronn refused to grant compensation to a self-employed hairdresser

---

51 Temporary Framework for State Aid Measures to support the economy in the current COVID-19 outbreak (2020/C 91 I/01).
52 Decision of District Court in Berlin of 13 October 2020, File No. 2 O 247/20.

based on section 56 of the Infection Protection Act.[53] The court stated that a requirement for entitlement for compensation is the adoption of a measure under Section 56 (1) of the Infection Protection Act, whereas the provision does not cover the measure on general closings of businesses.[54]

e. The economic capability of the state

The Czech Republic should dispose of its property efficiently and economically and its property shall not be unreasonably reduced in its scope or value.[55] The state earns most of its funds through taxes from persons within the Czech Republic. These financial funds are further used to fulfil the state's essential functions, just as ensuring the operation of the state's offices and securing the elderly or sick. If the colossal item of compensation for entrepreneurs is added to the state budget, it might not be in the power of taxpayers to hand over to the state enough money to allow it to compensate affected persons and perform state-entrusted functions simultaneously. As a result, the compensations could lead to a limitation of the performance of state activities and cause more serious damage than the crisis measures themselves.

This disproportionate interference with the state's property and possibly also with individuals' social rights should be a reason for the constitutional limitation of the state's liability for damage.[56] Also the Constitutional Court has previously pointed out that the right to compensation for damage caused by the exercise of public power is not absolute and unlimited. It acknowledged that the possibility of disproportionate obligation to pay compensation could lead to the so-called chilling effect. This could be reflected by a defensive approach when exercising the public powers (e.g., prudent decision-making) or resignation to exercise them at all.[57]

---

53 Act on the Prevention and Control of Infectious Diseases in Humans [*Gesetz zur Verhütung und Bekämpfung von Infektionskrankheiten beim Menschen (Infektionsschutzgesetz – IfSG)*]. Federal Law Gazette I page 473 [BGBl. I S. 473]. Issued on 20 July 2020.
54 Decision of District Court in Heilbronn of 29 April, 2020, File No. I 4 O 82/20.
55 Section 14 of the Act No 219/2000 Coll., on the property of the Czech Republic [*Zákon č. 219/2000 Sb., o majetku České republiky a jejím vystupování v právních vztazích*].
56 See Svoboda, T. K povaze "krizových opatření", odpovědnosti za škodu a ochraně subjektivních práv (2. část) [*The legal nature of 'crisis measures', liability for damage and the protection of subjective rights (Part 2)*]. Právní rozhledy, 2021, No. 10, pp. 348–357.
57 Resolution of the Constitutional court of 8 October 2019, File No. IV. ÚS 2287/18.

Above that, general acceptance of compensation for damage caused by crisis measures would be unsustainable for the state and could lead to state bankruptcy.[58] If the compensation is after all granted, it would have to be reduced by the number of subsidies, repayable financial assistance, and other support provided to mitigate the pandemic. Otherwise, the reasonability of state aid would be questioned. The legislator *pro futuro* resolved this matter for the COVID-19 disease as the Pandemic Act already contains a provision on offsetting these.

Eventually, it has been argued that not so many legal claims have been raised against the state, and thus the amount of compensation would not be enormous if granted. However, many persons may wait for the first judicial decision to be made in order to decide whether to bring their claim to court. If the previous claims are denied, they do not bring their claim and save high costs of legal proceedings. On the other hand, if the compensation is once granted, the number of submitted applications could increase fivefold.

f. Length of Court Proceedings

When applying for compensation, the affected person should first claim their damage with the office that issued the measure. For example, according to the Ministry of the Interior, as of the beginning of March of 2021, the Ministry received 418 claims for damage caused by state measures in connection with the COVID-19 pandemic. In the Czech legal system, if the administrative body decides not to compensate or does not express an opinion within six months, it is only possible to file a lawsuit and bring the claim to the competent court. To claim damage toward the Ministry of the Interior, the person should turn to District Court for Prague 7, whereas the average length of civil proceedings at this court is 513 days.[59] Therefore, it may be expected that the first Judicial decision on this matter will be issued at the end of 2022. Whatever the findings of the District Court will be, the unsuccessful parties will probably appeal against them.

---

58 A little less shutdown: Companies can now demand compensation [*Ein bisschen weniger Shutdown: Können Betriebe jetzt Entschädigung verlangen?* In German]. In: Legal Tribune Online, 16.04.2020, available at https://www.lto.de/persistent/a_id/41322/ (accessed: 09 January 2022).

59 Statistics issued by the Ministry of Justice, available at https://www.justice.cz/web/msp/statisticke-udaje-z-oblasti-justice (accessed: 12 March 2022).

Consequently, the proceedings will be transferred to the Municipal Court in Prague, where the average length of appeal proceedings is 76 days,[60] and the follow-up decision could be issued in the first quarter of 2023. As this matter is not tight by many previous decisions and seems somewhat controversial, follow-up proceedings will likely follow at the Supreme and Constitutional Court level. These courts would issue their decisions no sooner than in 2024. So far, no final judicial decision has been made in this respect, and thus we can only presume the outcome. Anyway, the courts will have to take into account that a broad interpretation of the Crisis act would be revolutionary in terms of comparative law.

The final interpretation will have to be made by the relevant courts within the judicial proceedings. When deciding, the courts will have to keep in mind the potential consequences of their decision, as granting widespread compensation could lead to state bankruptcy. So far, the Constitutional court has had the chance to assess one case of a low-value dispute on whether the fact that the claimant was not granted compensation for the cost of the RT-PCR test violates the Constitutional rules enshrined by the Charter of fundamental human rights and freedoms. The general court has confirmed that Section 36 (1) of the Crisis act does not establish a right to compensation for the adoption of crisis measures having the nature of a normative act. Also, the state is generally not responsible for legislation and, according to section § 36 (1) of the Crisis act, is only liable for damage caused by its activities in the implementation of specific crisis measures, which are individual in nature and are directed against specific natural or legal persons.[61] It concluded that it does not, and it is matter for ordinary courts to assess the legislator's intention, the systematic context of the adopted regulation, and interpret the law in a rational manner with regard to its wording. However, as the decided matter was a low-value dispute, an appeal to a higher ordinary court was not allowed. The decision showed that not granting compensation is not against constitutional rules, but it can be still granted based on the interpretation of the Crisis act. Therefore, we will have to wait for the final decision until it gets to the higher courts, taking several years.

---

60 České soudnictví 2020: Výroční statistická zpráva (*Czech Justice 2020: Annual Statistical Report*). Available at https://www.justice.cz/documents/12681/719244/Ceske_soudnict vi_2020.pdf/43b3020e-fc02-44a4-bb2c-a124ce85f57b (accessed: 15 February 2022).
61 Decision of District court for Praha 7 of 26 May 2021, File No. 4 C 50/2021-69.

g. Foreign Judicial Experiences

A hint of a judicial position can be seen in the judicial decision made by the Austrian Constitutional Court which concluded that the state aid substituted the compensation for caused damage.[62] A COVID-19 regulation[63] was issued on 15 March 2020, and a legal basis for its adoption was the COVID-19 Measures Act.[64] It introduced, among other things, a ban on the entry of customers into the business premises with certain exceptions.[65] This regulation, of course, led to a temporary closure of businesses in an effort to stop the spread of the disease, which interfered with the fundamental right to the property provided in Section 5 of the Basic state Law.[66]

Section 13 (2) of the COVID-19 Measures Act states that provisions of the Epidemics Act[67] on the closure of business establishments are not applicable where a measure under § 1 of the COVID-19 Measures Act has been issued. This provision excludes the application of section 32 of the Epidemics Act that provides compensation for lost profit incurred due to the measures adopted under this Act. Obviously, the COVID-19 Measures Act itself does not provide for compensation caused as a result of the adopted measures. Consequently, several companies filed a constitutional complaint with the Austrian Constitutional Court and declared that their right to property according to section 5 of the Basic Law and Article 1 of Protocol 1 to the European Convention on Human Rights was violated. Claimants also claimed that the principle of equality laid down in section 7 of the Federal Constitutional Act[67] and section 2 of the Basic state law were violated.

---

62 Decision of the Austrian Constitutional court of 14 July 2020, File No. G 202/2020-20.
63 Regulation: Preliminary Measures to Prevent the Spread of COVID-19 [*Verordnung: Vorläufige Maßnahmen zur Verhinderung der Verbreitung von COVID-19* in German]. Federal Law Gazette II No. 96/2020 [BGBl. II Nr. 96/2020]. Issued on 15 March 2020.
64 Federal Act on Interim Measures to Prevent the Spread of COVID-19 (COVID-19 Measures Act – COVID-19-MG [*Bundesgesetz betreffend vorläufige Maßnahmen zur Verhinderung der Verbreitung von COVID-19 (COVID-19-Maßnahmengesetz – COVID-19-MG)* in German]. Federal Law Gazette No. 12/2020 [RGBl. I Nr. 12/2020].
65 Exceptions to the ban are specified in the section 2 of the COVID-19 regulation.
66 The basic state law on the general rights of citizens in English). RGBl. Nr. 142/1867 (Federal Law Gazette No. 142/1867 [Das Staatsgrundgesetz über die allgemeinen Rechte der Staatsbürger]. Issued on 21 December 1867.
67 Epidemic Act [*Epidemiegesetz* in German]. Federal Law Gazette 186/1950, as amended by Federal Law Gazette I 114/2006 [BGBl. 186/1950, idF BGBl. I 114/2006].

Notably, the Austrian Constitutional Court acknowledged that the ban on entry to business premises has the same effect as a ban on the operation of a business and thus constitutes a significant interference with claimants' right to property. On the other hand, the court held that many state aid measures were adopted to support businesses forced to stop operating. These measures aimed to cushion the ban's impact on entry into business premises and substitute the compensation according to the Epidemics Act as affected companies are entitled to financial support. Due to the provided financial aid, the ban on entry does not constitute a disproportionate interference with the fundamental property right. Thus, the right to compensation cannot be derived from the right to property. The court also emphasized that property restrictions were deemed necessary to avoid the spread of COVID-19. As a result, the constitutional court held that the lack of right to compensation does violate neither the fundamental right to property nor the principle of equality.

Regarding the principle of equality, the Austrian Constitutional Court came to a significant conclusion concerning the right to compensation under the Epidemics Act. As mentioned, the Epidemics Act provides a legal base for compensation for lost profit in the event of the closure of businesses, while the COVID-19 Measures Act does not. The Court concluded that these two Acts could not be compared as the Epidemics Act aims at local epidemics, e.g. only closing certain businesses that present specific risks. Still, it does not cover measures of widespread nature that affect a large portion of entrepreneurs and the economy in general. The court also acknowledged that the legislator enjoys a margin of appreciation when it comes to the COVID-19 pandemic. The state aid package to support the economy pursues the same objective as the Epidemics Act 1950. Thus, the decision not to apply the compensation regime under the Epidemics Act is not contrary to the principle of equality.

Compensation for Damage Caused in Connection with Emergency Measures under the Pandemic Act

The Pandemic Act enshrines an obligation of the state to compensate persons for actual damage caused when the "state of pandemic alert" is declared. The obligation arises when (i) the actual damage (ii) is caused in casual connection with (iii) existing emergency measures according to the Pandemic Act or the Act on the protection of Public Health aimed at combating the COVID-19 pandemic (iv) during the state of pandemic alert. Moreover, the Pandemic Act directly addresses the matter of compensation for lost profit when it limits the compensation only to actual damage. The provision on compensation was added to the Act by amendment proposal, whereas the amendment proposal was not supplemented with a sufficient explanatory memorandum.[68] Moreover, as the Act was adopted within a state of legislative emergency without proper parliamentary debate to be carried out, there are no explaining comments on how the provision should be interpreted. The enshrined compensation raises questions, especially concerning the compensation for damage caused by acts of normative nature and the extent of damage that should be compensated.

The Pandemic Act was adopted after one year of experience with the COVID-19 pandemic. At the time, the public bodies had a quite clear image of what measures had to be available to effectively combat the pandemic and what legal issues had been raised in the past year. That is probably why the Pandemic Act expressly states that emergency measures adopted according to this Act are measures of general nature. Measures of general nature stand between legislative acts and individual decisions, i.e. act issued by the public administration that regulates the status of an unlimited number of addresses on a specific matter. However, materially the measures adopted within the COVID-19 pandemic according to the Pandemic Act are still measures of normative nature as their content is not much different from the previously adopted measures according to the Crisis act. In contrast, these were considered by the Constitutional Court legal regulation *sui generis*. Therefore, the question may arise whether this nature of the emergency measures could affect the compensation for damage.

The Constitutional court has previously sided with the material approach to the measures of general nature. However, it does not mean that when the emergency measure itself is of normative nature, whereas the statute labels it as a measure of general nature, it shall not be considered a measure of general nature. Just the opposite, the legal provisions on measures of general nature shall be applied even though, from a material point of view, it would not be a measure of a general nature. According to the case law of the Czech Supreme Court, if the legislator anticipates a specific activity of an administrative body and sets a particular form for this activity, it cannot be deduced from the content of the issued act that it is an act of other forms than that expressly provided by the statute.[69] Moreover, if public law norms can be interpreted in several ways, it is necessary to prefer the one that interferes with fundamental rights or freedom as little as

---

68 Document of the Chamber of Deputies of the Parliament of the Czech Republic of 18 February 2021, No. 7543 "Amendments and other proposals for the document No. 1158".
69 Resolution of the Czech Supreme Court of 6 August 2010, File No. 2 Ao 3/2010-55.

possible.[70] This presumption is based on the constitutional principle *in dubio pro libertate*.[71] Assessing the emergency measures as an act of normative nature would be detrimental to individuals as compensation for crisis measures as regulation *sui generis* would probably not be granted. Therefore, the author tends to believe that persons should be granted compensation despite the normative nature of emergency measures. Moreover, the legislator had to be aware that these fulfil the characteristic of the act of normative nature and expressly enshrined the obligation to compensate for damage anyway.

A related issue is the extent of damage that should be compensated, as the outlined approach seems to bear high compensation costs. The Pandemic Act strictly narrows the compensation when it (i) limits the compensation only to actual damage (not lost profit) and (ii) reduces the amount of compensation by the amount of subsidies and other state aid support provided to mitigate the effects of the COVID-19 pandemic and the effects of emergency measures.

When claiming the compensation, the actual damage and its amount still have to be proven by the affected person. Consequently, the damage is reimbursed to the extent that the affected person proves that the damage could not have been prevented. On the other hand, the Constitutional Court previously dealt with this matter, and it concluded that if a person cannot accurately determine and prove the amount of damage caused by an illegal decision or maladministration but proves and justifies that such damage has occurred, general courts should determine the amount of damage at the discretion of the individual circumstances.[72] When claiming compensation, the affected person will have to assess the impacts of the pandemic situation if the emergency measures were not adopted. If the government is again forced to limit the performance of business activities, it is hardly imaginable that the state authorities would assess the damage caused to individual persons individually as it would be an incredible administrative burden. In this respect, it seems much more likely that the state would again grant a state aid widely and the compensation provided according to the Pandemic Act would further supplement the granted state aid compensation.

---

70 Judgment of the Constitutional court of 19 November 2008, File No. Pl. ÚS 14/07.
71 Article 1 (1) and article 2 (4) of the Constitution. Article 2 (3) and article 4 of the Charter of fundamental human rights and freedoms.
72 Judgment of the Constitutional court of 24 July 2014, File No. II. ÚS 1430/13-2.

Conclusion

The author is of the opinion that liability for damage caused by the crisis measures should generally not be excluded under the Crisis act and persons should not be left without help. However, the responsibility of the state for the economic situation of persons shall not be limitless. The obligation to financially support the affected person should be interpreted in the light of individual circumstances and the financial possibilities of the state. The state should choose such a form of assistance which seems rational at the moment of crisis and is not absurd or wholly impracticable.

The state chose to support the affected persons in form of state aid support. Under the extraordinary circumstances, it may not even be in the power of the state to compensate all the damage incurred as such an approach would be unsustainable. Just in 2020, the total amount paid to affected persons in a form of a compensation bonus exceed 50 billion Czech crowns and in total the Czech state spent more than 240 billion Czech crowns on measures combating the pandemic in 2020.[73] No matter how the courts approach this issue, they could not dispense with these purely economic criteria.

When deciding on the obligation to compensate persons according to section 36 of the Crisis act, courts will have to take into account several aspects apart from the literal wording of the provision. First of all, courts will have to assess the context of the adoption of the Crisis act and, if appropriate, assess whether the relevant provision of the Act could be interpreted contrary to its original purpose. This includes the assessment of the fact that the crisis measures are of normative nature (whereas the state does not usually compensate persons for damage caused by normative acts) and whether lost profit belongs to the extent that should be compensated. Regardless of the outcome of this interpretation, courts cannot ignore the economic consequences of widespread compensation as these could lead to the state bankruptcy when the state could become unable to fulfil its basic social tasks. This conclusion is also indicated by the outlined experience from abroad. The main aim of the court ruling should be to find fair solution for persons who did not obtain sufficient assistance.

The author considers the compensation regime according to the Pandemic Act to be a step in the right direction. The Pandemic Act reduces the compensation

---

73 Press release on the implementation of the state budget published by the Ministry of Finance. Available at https://www.mfcr.cz/cs/aktualne/tiskove-zpravy/2020/pokladni-plneni-sr-40094 (accessed: 1 April 2022).

by the amount of subsidies and other state aid support. If the pandemic hits the Czech Republic again and the state aid is granted, affected persons will be mainly supported by state aid which should suffice in most cases. However, persons highly affected by the emergency measures can turn to the Ministry of Finance and claim compensation according to the Pandemic Act for damage not covered by the state aid support. This could pro future solve the situation of persons who previously claimed that they were neglected by the state aid support regime. Thus, it could provide support to these persons who bear extraordinary burdens to protect public interests. Despite the fact that it was not expressly stipulated, this form of support could be considered a manifestation of the special sacrifice theory.

References

Boguszak, J., Čapek, J., Gerloch, A. Teorie práva [*Legal Foundations* in English]. 2. vyd. Praha: ASPI, 2004.

Handrlica, J., Balounová, J., Sharapaev, V. Náhrady a opatření přijatá v době pandemie (*Compensation and measures adopted during a pandemic* in English). Právní rozhledy, 2020, č. 22, pp. 784–791.

Korecká, V. Skutečná škoda [*Actual damage* in English]. In: Hendrych, D. a kol. Právnický slovník. 3. vydání. Praha: C. H. Beck, 2009.

Melzer, F. Občanský zákoník IX. svazek, § 2894–3081 Závazky z deliktů a z jiných právních důvodů [*Civil Code Volume IX, section 2894–3081 Obligations from tort and other legal reasons*]. Nakladatelství Leges, 2019. ISBN 978-80-7502-199-1. Comment on section 2895.

Melzer, F. Poskytování náhrad za újmy vyvolané mimořádnými opatřeními Ministerstva zdravotnictví po jejich zrušení [*Compensation for damages caused by measures of the Ministry of Health after their repeal* in English] in Bulletin advokacie, č. 6/2020.

Oliphant, K. (ed.) The Liability of Public Authorities in Comparative Perspective. Cambridge: Intersentia, 2016.

Richards, E. P. A Historical Review of the State Police Powers and Their Relevance to the COVID-19 Pandemic of 2020, 11 J. NAT'l Sec. L. & POL'y 83, 2020.

Svoboda, T., Smutná, V. K odpovědnosti za újmu způsobenou podzákonnou normotvorbou [*Liability for damage caused by secondary legislation* in English]. Právník, 2016, No. 10, pp. 914–923.

Svoboda, T. K povaze "krizových opatření", odpovědnosti za škodu a ochraně subjektivních práv (2. část) [*The legal nature of 'crisis measures', liability for damage and the protection of subjective rights (Part 2)]*. Právní rozhledy, 2021, No. 10, pp. 348–357.

Vojtek, P. Odpovědnost za škodu při výkonu veřejné moci [*Liability for damage caused in connection with the exercise of public power* in Czech]. Praha: C.H. Beck, 2012. pp.7–9. ISBN 978-80-7400-427-8.

Ius, Lex et Res Publica
Studies in Law, Philosophy and Political Cultures

Edited by
Anna Jaroń

Vol. 1   Anna Jaroń: Socio-Economic Constitutional Rights in Democratisation Processes. An Account of the Constitutional Dialogue Theory. 2012.

Vol. 2   Stanisław Filipowicz: Democracy – The Power of Illusion. 2013.

Vol. 3   Teresa Dukiet-Nagórska (ed.): The Postulates of Restorative Justice and the Continental Model of Criminal Law. As Illustrated by Polish Criminal Law 2014.

Vol. 4   Agnieszka Kupzok: Enforcement of Patents on Geographically Divisible Inventions. An Inquiry into the Standard of Substantive Patent Law Infringement in Cross-Border Constellations. 2015.

Vol. 5   Alicja Jagielska-Burduk / Wojciech Szafrański: Legal Issues in Cultural Heritage Management. A Polish Perspective. 2016.

Vol. 6   Maciej Mataczyński (ed.): The Takeover of Public Companies as a Mode of Exercising EU Treaty Freedoms. 2017.

Vol. 7   Maciej Barczewski (ed.): Value of Information. Intellectual Property, Privacy and Big Data. 2018.

Vol. 8   Pawel Smoleń, Marcin Burzec: Introduction to Polish Tax Law. 2018.

Vol. 9   Łukasz Pohl, Konrad Burdziak: Judicial Interpretation of the 1997 Criminal Code Provisions on Self-Defence. 2019.

Vol. 10 Adam Szot: Judicial Review of Administrative Discretion. The Influence of Court Decisions on Administrative Actions. 2019.

Vol. 11 Michał Peno / Konrad Burdziak (eds.): The Concept of Modern Law. Polish and Central European Tradition. 2019.

Vol. 12 Leszek Leszczyński / Bartosz Liżewski / Adam Szot (eds.): Potential of Precedent in the Statutory Legal Order. 2019.

Vol. 13 Łukasz Bolesta: In Search of a Model for the Legal Protection of a Whistleblower in the Workplace in Poland. A legal and comparative study. 2020.

Vol. 14 Paweł Chmielnicki / Adam Sulikowski (eds.): New Perspectives on Legislation. A Comparative Approach. 2020.

Vol. 15 Marcin Burzec / Beata Kucia-Guściora / Paweł Smoleń: Agricultural Activity in Poland: A Fiscal and Legal Study. 2020.

Vol. 16 Magdalena Półtorak / Ilona Topa (eds.): Women, Children and (Other) Vulnerable Groups. Standards of Protection and Challenges for International Law. 2021.

Vol. 17 Josef Albert Fox: Die polnische Verfassung vom 3. Mai 1791. Hintergründe der Entstehung und der Außerkraftsetzung. Stellung Polens im Zeitalter der Aufklärung. 2021.

Vol. 18 Barbara Janusz-Pohl (ed.): Juvenile Justice Systems: Poland-Brazil-Portugal. 2021.

Vol. 19 Leszek Leszczyński: General Reference Clauses in the Judicial Process. Context of Legislative Intentions Interpretative Discretion. 2021.

Vol. 20 Francisco J. Campos Zamora: Das Problem der Begründung richterlicher Entscheidungen. Eine Analyse auf der Grundlage der Theorie der juristischen Argumentation. 2021.

Ius, Lex et Res Publica
Studies in Law, Philosophy and Political Cultures

Edited by
Barbara Janusz-Pohl and Anna Jaroń

Vol. 21 Aneta Skorupa-Wulczyńska: Language Rights of the Citizen of the European Union. 2022.

Vol. 22 Mateusz Osiecki: International Legal Aspects of Aerial Terrorism. Methods of Law Enforcement in Avia-tion. 2022.

Vol. 23 Vladimír Sharp / Gabriela Blahoudková / Jakub Handrlica (eds.): Law, Pandemics and Ownership Restrictions. 2022.

www.peterlang.com

Lightning Source UK Ltd.
Milton Keynes UK
UKHW021058170123
415494UK00016B/979

9 783631 882023